Democratization of Intelligence

This comparative analysis of the sometimes fraught process of achieving democratic governance of security intelligence agencies presents material from countries other than those normally featured in the Intelligence Studies literature of North America and Europe. Some of the countries examined are former Communist countries and several in Latin America are former military regimes. Others have been democratic for a long time but still experience widespread political violence. Through a mix of single-country and comparative studies, major aspects of intelligence are considered, including the legacy of and transition from authoritarianism; the difficulties of achieving genuine reform; and the apparent inevitability of periodic scandals. Authors consider a range of methodological approaches to the study of intelligence and the challenges of analysing the secret world. Finally, consideration is given to the success – or otherwise – of intelligence reform, and the effectiveness of democratic institutions of control and oversight. This book was originally published as a special issue of *Intelligence and National Security*.

Peter Gill is Honorary Senior Research Fellow at the University of Liverpool, UK. He was previously Research Professor in Intelligence Studies at the University of Salford, UK. He was awarded a Leverhulme Emeritus Fellowship in 2010 and is preparing *Intelligence Governance and Democratisation: a comparative analysis of the limits of reform*, to be published by Routledge in 2016.

Michael M. Andregg is an adjunct professor in the Justice and Peace Studies Department at the University of St Thomas in St Paul, Minnesota, USA. He has also taught at the University of Minnesota, USA, where he now designs new graduate courses, such as 'Searching for Wisdom'.

Democratization of Intelligence

Edited by
Peter Gill and Michael M. Andregg

LONDON AND NEW YORK

First published 2015 by Routledge

2 Park Square, Milton Park, Abingdon, Oxon OX14 4RN
711 Third Avenue, New York, NY 10017, USA

Routledge is an imprint of the Taylor & Francis Group, an informa business

First issued in paperback 2017

Copyright © 2015 Taylor & Francis

All rights reserved. No part of this book may be reprinted or reproduced or utilised in any form or by any electronic, mechanical, or other means, now known or hereafter invented, including photocopying and recording, or in any information storage or retrieval system, without permission in writing from the publishers.

Notice:
Product or corporate names may be trademarks or registered trademarks, and are used only for identification and explanation without intent to infringe.

British Library Cataloguing in Publication Data
A catalogue record for this book is available from the British Library

ISBN 13: 978-1-138-85531-1 (hbk)
ISBN 13: 978-1-138-05909-2 (pbk)

Typeset in Sabon
by RefineCatch Limited, Bungay, Suffolk

Publisher's Note
The publisher accepts responsibility for any inconsistencies that may have arisen during the conversion of this book from journal articles to book chapters, namely the possible inclusion of journal terminology.

Disclaimer
Every effort has been made to contact copyright holders for their permission to reprint material in this book. The publishers would be grateful to hear from any copyright holder who is not here acknowledged and will undertake to rectify any errors or omissions in future editions of this book.

Contents

Citation Information	vii
Notes on Contributors	ix

1. Comparing the Democratization of Intelligence
   Michael M. Andregg and Peter Gill — 1

2. Comparing the Democratization of Intelligence Governance in East Central Europe and the Balkans
   Marina Caparini — 11

3. Intelligence, Crisis, and Democracy: Institutional Punctuations in Brazil, Colombia, South Africa, and India
   Marco Cepik and Christiano Ambros — 36

4. Comparing Intelligence Democratization in Latin America: Argentina, Peru, and Ecuador Cases
   Eduardo E. Estévez — 65

5. The Spies Who Came from the Tropics: Intelligence Services and Democracy in Brazil
   Joanisval Brito Gonçalves — 94

6. Democratic Oversight in Fragile States: The Case of Intelligence Reform in Bosnia and Herzegovina
   Helge Lurås — 113

7. Balancing Democratic Civilian Control with Effectiveness of Intelligence in Romania: Lessons Learned and Best/Worst Practices Before and After NATO and EU Integration
   Florina Cristiana (Cris) Matei — 131

Index — 149

Citation Information

The chapters in this book were originally published in *Intelligence and National Security*, volume 29, issue 4 (August 2014). When citing this material, please use the original page numbering for each article, as follows:

Chapter 1
Comparing the Democratization of Intelligence
Michael M. Andregg and Peter Gill
Intelligence and National Security, volume 29, issue 4 (August 2014)
pp. 487–497

Chapter 2
Comparing the Democratization of Intelligence Governance in East Central Europe and the Balkans
Marina Caparini
Intelligence and National Security, volume 29, issue 4 (August 2014)
pp. 498–522

Chapter 3
Intelligence, Crisis, and Democracy: Institutional Punctuations in Brazil, Colombia, South Africa, and India
Marco Cepik and Christiano Ambros
Intelligence and National Security, volume 29, issue 4 (August 2014)
pp. 523–551

Chapter 4
Comparing Intelligence Democratization in Latin America: Argentina, Peru, and Ecuador Cases
Eduardo E. Estévez
Intelligence and National Security, volume 29, issue 4 (August 2014)
pp. 552–580

Chapter 5
The Spies Who Came from the Tropics: Intelligence Services and Democracy in Brazil
Joanisval Brito Gonçalves
Intelligence and National Security, volume 29, issue 4 (August 2014) pp. 581–599

CITATION INFORMATION

Chapter 6
Democratic Oversight in Fragile States: The Case of Intelligence Reform in Bosnia and Herzegovina
Helge Lurås
Intelligence and National Security, volume 29, issue 4 (August 2014)
pp. 600–618

Chapter 7
Balancing Democratic Civilian Control with Effectiveness of Intelligence in Romania: Lessons Learned and Best/Worst Practices Before and After NATO and EU Integration
Florina Cristiana (Cris) Matei
Intelligence and National Security, volume 29, issue 4 (August 2014)
pp. 619–637

Please direct any queries you may have about the citations to
clsuk.permissions@cengage.com

Notes on Contributors

Christiano Ambros is a PhD candidate in Political Science at the Federal University of Rio Grande do Sul, Porto Alegre, Brazil, and Analyst at the State Investment and Development Agency.

Michael M. Andregg is an adjunct professor in the Justice and Peace Studies Department at the University of St Thomas, St Paul, Minnesota, USA. He has also taught at the University of Minnesota, USA, where he now designs new graduate courses, such as 'Searching for Wisdom'. His PhD in Genetics is from the University of California, Davis, USA (1977), but early on he turned his attention to the causes of war, writing a book about these causes which won a National Peace Writing Award in 1999. He has been arranging panels at intelligence conferences since 1989.

Marina Caparini conducts applied research on security and justice governance, particularly in post-conflict and post-authoritarian settings. She is currently Senior Research Associate at the Institute for Security Studies in Pretoria, South Africa, for which she is conducting field-based research on the police component of African peace support operations. From 2010–2014 she was Senior Research Fellow at the Norwegian Institute of International Affairs working on peacekeeping and local peacebuilding. She previously held positions as Deputy Director of the Security System Reform Program at the International Center for Transitional Justice, and Senior Fellow at the Geneva Centre for the Democratic Control of Armed Forces. She received her PhD in War Studies from King's College London; her dissertation compared internal security reforms in several East Central European states undergoing democratization.

Marco Cepik is Professor of Comparative Politics and Strategic Studies at the Federal University of Rio Grande do Sul, Porto Alegre, Brazil, and Director of the Centre for International Studies on Government.

Eduardo E. Estévez is an independent consultant who specializes in intelligence and security, including police reforms and citizen security, and a member of the Fundación de Estudios Económicos y Políticas Públicas in Argentina. He has contributed chapters to *Who's Watching the Spies? Establishing Intelligence Service Accountability* (2005); and *Intelligence Elsewhere: Spies and Espionage*

NOTES ON CONTRIBUTORS

outside the Anglosphere (2013). He is a contributor to *World Police Encyclopedia* (2006); and *Diccionario Inteligencia y Seguridad* (2013).

Peter Gill is Honorary Senior Research Fellow at the University of Liverpool, UK. He was previously Research Professor in Intelligence Studies at the University of Salford, UK. He is the author of *Policing Politics* (1994) and *Rounding Up the Usual Suspects?* (2000), as well as co-author of *Intelligence in an Insecure World* (2012). He is co-editor of the *PSI Handbook of Global Security and Intelligence: National Approaches* (2008) and *Intelligence Theory: Key Questions and Debates* (2009). His current research focuses on the democratization of intelligence in former authoritarian regimes, research for which he was awarded a Leverhulme Emeritus Fellowship in 2010.

Joanisval Brito Gonçalves is a Senior Consultant on Foreign Affairs and Defence at the Senate of Brazil, and the only technical advisor on intelligence for the Brazilian Joint Committee on Intelligence Oversight at the Brazilian Parliament. He holds a PhD in International Relations from the University of Brasilia, Brazil. Before serving in the Legislative branch, he was an intelligence officer at the Brazilian Intelligence Agency (ABIN). He also teaches International Relations, International Law and Strategic Studies in various Brazilian universities.

Helge Lurås is the founder and director of the Centre for International and Strategic Analysis, Norway. He has experience from the Norwegian Institute of International Affairs, Norwegian Armed Forces, NATO, the UN and from private sector consultancy. He holds an MSc degree in Business Studies, as well as a bachelor degree in Sociology, Social Anthropology and the History of Ideas.

Florina Cristiana (Cris) Matei is a Lecturer for the Centre for Civil-Military Relations at the United States Naval Postgraduate School, Monterey, California, USA. She has researched, published and lectured on a wide range of issues concerning civil-military relations, democratization, Security Sector Reform, intelligence and counter-terrorism. She earned an MA in International Security Affairs from the Naval Postgraduate School, and a BSc in Physics from the University of Bucharest, Romania. She is now a PhD candidate in the Department of War Studies of King's College London, UK.

Comparing the Democratization of Intelligence

MICHAEL M. ANDREGG AND PETER GILL

ABSTRACT This introductory article discusses some of the main themes that are contained within this collection originally delivered as papers to two conferences. There is brief consideration of some issues of method and major themes relating to the legacy of authoritarian regimes, the process of change and the current state of 'democracy' are identified. Continuing controversies and uncertainties around intelligence have important implications for democratic governance in many countries which must encourage more comparative work in this key area of intelligence studies.

Introduction

This collection of articles originated as papers delivered to two conference panels in February and March 2011. The first was under the auspices of the International Political Science Association and European Consortium of Political Research in São Paulo, Brazil, and the second as part of the Intelligence Studies section at the International Studies Association in Montreal, Canada. The organization of the two panels was somewhat different in that the specific intent at São Paulo was to present papers that were themselves comparative as between a number of national intelligence structures while the Montreal panel presented a number of more detailed country studies. However, it was agreed that the richness of the papers merited joint publication and hence this Special Issue. The object of this introductory essay is to pick out some of the main themes that are contained within the papers with the ambition of encouraging more comparative work in this key area of intelligence studies.

The single-country studies here (Joanisval Gonçalves, Helge Lurås and Cris Matei) add to or, in some cases, update the published work on intelligence democratization in, for example, Bruneau and Boraz[1]

---

[1]Thomas Bruneau and Steven Boraz, *Reforming Intelligence: Obstacles to Democratic Control and Effectiveness* (Austin, TX: University of Texas Press 2007).

and Farson et al.[2] There are a number of articles that have in recent years sought to further the cause of comparative study of intelligence[3] and the papers here by Marina Caparini, Marco Cepik and Chris Ambros, and Eduardo Estévez might be seen as some implicit response to the argument that scholars need now to add comparative analysis to the increasingly rich array of single-country studies of democratization. As a basis, of course, we do have an extensive comparative politics literature on democratization but key questions remain as to how this might be applied to the distinctive field of intelligence as a government activity. What is clear from the pre-existing literature and the articles here is that intelligence is, in some sense, the last frontier for attempts to democratize previously authoritarian governmental structures and processes.

Some Definitions and Questions of Method

The countries discussed here represent a rich variety in terms of democratic experience. India has been described as the 'largest democracy in the world' since it achieved independence from Britain in 1947 and South Africa shifted rapidly from an authoritarian, racist state to being formally democratic in the early 1990s. Of the Latin American countries, only one, Colombia, has met democratic criteria in terms of regular, competitive elections for most of the last 60 years though the extensive violence it has suffered must question the adequacy of such formal definitions. The other cases are European and share some common experience in having communist governments until the collapse of the Soviet Union and Warsaw Pact during 1989–91. The articles concentrate on the issue of civilian internal security intelligence; in Latin America, of course, a key element in democratization was removing military agencies from internal security and policing and confining them to defence issues but, with one or two exceptions, we do not deal with the issue of military intelligence *per se*.

For us as editors – one US, one Brit – a final recommendation for the collection is that it discusses intelligence in countries outside the Anglo-American sphere which so dominates intelligence studies to date: in the collections by Praeger (*Strategic Intelligence*, 2007, 5 volumes), Routledge (*Handbook of Intelligence Studies*, 2009) and Oxford University Press (*Oxford Handbook of National Security Intelligence*, 2010) of the 134 authors, 70 per cent were US and 15 per cent UK. A quick survey of the contents of 124 articles suggests 64 per cent concerned *only* the US. Such

---

[2]Stuart Farson et al. (eds.) *PSI Handbook of Global Security Intelligence: National Approaches*, 2 vols. (Westport, CT: Praeger Security International 2008).
[3]Glen Hastedt, 'Towards the Comparative Study of Intelligence' *Conflict Quarterly* 11/3 (1991) pp.55–72; Kevin O'Connell, 'Thinking About Intelligence Comparatively', *Brown Journal of World Affairs* 21/1 (1991) pp.189–99; Peter Gill, '"Knowing the Self, Knowing the Other": The Comparative Analysis of Security Intelligence' in Loch K. Johnson, *Handbook of Intelligence Studies* (London: Routledge 2007) pp. 82–90.

myopia can be dangerous as well as parochial, since all of the world's current hottest conflict zones speak languages far removed from English.[4]

Most though not all countries discussed here have recent experience of authoritarian governments but what is it that they aspire to become? In authoritarian regimes the primary if not sole objective of security and intelligence agencies is the preservation of the regime and suppression of opposition. As such, agencies may be controlled by the ruling party, be part of a military command structure or function as an autonomous 'state within a state' but what they all enjoy is the absence of any independent oversight. In democracy the functions of security intelligence are defined in line with a more inclusive definition of national security threats; although monitoring 'enemies of the state' remains, it should be the case that they pose a genuine threat to public security rather than simply political opposition. Further, democracy requires that security and intelligence activities are subject to control and oversight in the interests of effectiveness, efficiency, legality, propriety and respect for rights. At least, that is the goal but we must examine to what extent intelligence governance actually achieves real change rather than merely providing a cloak of legitimacy that hides the continuation of older intelligence activities.

The ability of intelligence agencies to subvert formal oversight mechanisms can hardly be overstated. The veil of secrecy combined with the lack of expertise common to political overseers, and the press of other work to which they must attend, enables all kinds of deceptions. In the USA the requirement that all involved sign non-disclosure agreements neuters most effective exposure should wrongdoing be detected. A US Congressman told one of us bluntly that the House and Senate oversight committees were intended and designed to 'overlook' more than to oversee. And the sitting Chair of the Senate intelligence committee once confided privately that one must be 'very careful because when these guys get mad, there are real consequences'.[5] This comment was in a context of exposing an illegal domestic intelligence operation, something that occurs far more frequently than most suppose. Many American politicians have found that covert skills at manipulating elections abroad are transferrable to troublesome congressmen at home. Even where information is provided, overseers must inspect it closely, for example, although the Congress has sought to ensure that it receives advance notice of intended CIA covert actions, this has not prevented major rows. The CIA briefed senior congressional members in 2002 about the use of 'enhanced interrogation' techniques but once the controversy about torture erupted years later, the precise nature of these briefings was hotly disputed.[6] The publication of 'leaked' internal

---

[4]Philip Davies and Kristian Gustafson, *Intelligence Elsewhere: Spies and Espionage outside the Anglosphere* (Washington, DC: Georgetown University Press 2013) examines a number of important countries.
[5]Private communications.
[6]For example, Massimo Calabresi, 'Pelosi Faces Off with Obama on CIA Oversight', *Time*, 25 June 2010.

National Security Agency (NSA) documents since June 2013 has detailed governments' attempts to achieve total surveillance of the Internet and other communications.[7] We cannot consider here the many issues raised but they include elements of all the 'usual suspects' accounting for inadequate democratic control of intelligence: outdated or otherwise inadequate legal frameworks, insufficiently informed or curious overseers and a propensity for agencies to be 'economical with the truth', if not actually providing misleading information. If these problems persist in the well-resourced US oversight structure, the potential for the relatively impoverished structures of all other countries to be misled by the agencies is even greater.

Questions of method are considered explicitly in some of these articles and implicitly in others. Caparini argues that both detailed case studies and comparison are required in order to generate general findings that might inform reform efforts. Most of the studies here rely on traditional historical and institutionalist approaches that have dominated the study of intelligence democratization to date. This is hardly surprising since, as noted by Bruneau and Boraz,[8] intelligence centres on state power and democratization (as well as de-democratization) are clearly historical processes. Cepik and Ambros and Estévez make use of concepts developed in evolutionary biology and political science to frame their analyses in terms of the debate between 'path dependency' and 'punctuated equilibrium' and focus on the specific impact of crises in order to understand how systems adapt, or not. Where comparison is conducted the question of case selection arises and two approaches are manifest here: Caparini and Estévez look at 'sub-regions' where there are important historical and cultural similarities in order to explicate further similarities or significant differences. Cepik and Ambros choose their countries on the basis that they are at roughly equal levels of economic and social development. Comparisons may also be made between time periods; here, for example, Matei examines the differences in Romania between pre- and post- EU/NATO accession.

We do not want to conduct a lengthy analysis of comparative method here but draw on some of the major literature in the field to provide a framework for this discussion.[9] Without suggesting some required sequence for democracy to come about, it seems to us useful to distinguish three periods: the legacy, the change and where the country is now.

---

[7]The documents and associated discussion can be viewed at <http://www.theguardian.com/world/the-nsa-files?INTCMP=SRCH> (accessed 28 August 2013).
[8]Bruneau and Boraz, *Reforming Intelligence*, p.2.
[9]Jean Grugel, *Democratization: A Critical Introduction* (Basingstoke: Palgrave 2002); Juan Linz and Alfred Stepan, *Problems of Democratic Transition and Consolidation: Southern Europe, South America and Post-Communist Europe* (Baltimore, MD: John Hopkins University Press 1996); Georg Sørensen, *Democracy and Democratization: Processes and Prospects in a Changing World* (Boulder, CO: Westview Press 2008).

The Legacy

Most of the literature to date has concentrated on authoritarianism as the legacy for democratizing countries. This has had two main manifestations: in Europe, Soviet-style communism or 'state socialism'; and in Latin America, military dictatorships. Of course, these broad classifications concealed differences that are examined in the articles below, for example, the security and intelligence services of the Warsaw Pact were not just modelled on the Soviet KGB but were actually subservient to it in what amounted to a denial of national sovereignty. Other East European states, notably, Romania (see Matei) and Yugoslavia (see Caparini, Lurås) retained greater national independence even if their security services could be just as unpleasant. There were also differences between Latin American military regimes: Estévez distinguishes the relatively 'progressive' militaries of Peru and Ecuador from the 'neo-liberal' Argentina. However, what these countries shared was an effective merging of internal and external security in a single doctrine of regime protection by means of widespread surveillance of society and the repression of dissent by 'political police'. However, authoritarianism was not the only legacy – in some countries there will have been a previous period of colonial rule or even a short period of democracy. These earlier legacies may be very significant; for example, as shown by Caparini and Lurås, it is impossible to understand developments in the Western Balkans without taking into account the historical relationships of its several national and ethnic groups prior to the period of Communist rule instituted at the end of the Second World War. Thus, as Estévez notes, there is no starting afresh for countries.

The Change

The term 'transition' is used by several authors; indeed, Caparini refers to the 'triple transition' in Eastern Europe of securing national autonomy, democratization and marketization. However, we have avoided the use of the term here because it can imply a particular, pre-ordained destination of democratic intelligence architecture. Rather, we prefer to retain the idea that democratization is a process rather than an event and that, as such, it may stop or go into reverse.[10] However defined, change may well take a 'long and winding road' in a field of state activity where pervasive secrecy facilitates resistance to what officials may perceive as threats to their organizations and budgets. In these articles we see a variety of approaches to analysing the change that takes place (or seeking to explain why it does not.) For example, periods of relative stability characterize security and intelligence systems (as with government more generally) but periods of rapid change may be experienced at certain critical 'junctures' (Estévez) or 'moments' (Cepik and Ambros). Gonçalves and Lurås both identify quite long periods after the formal demise of the *ancien regime* when change seems

---

[10]See Charles Tilly, *Democracy* (Cambridge: CUP 2007) on 'de-democratization'.

to simmer slowly through a series of false starts or apparent stasis. The key question raised is therefore the extent to which periodic crises produce real change or whether agencies successfully resist, perhaps with some minimal adaptation. It is not always easy, especially at the time, to assess correctly just how significant change is – Estévez suggests that critical junctures are those at which some pre-existing possibilities are closed off; if this is the case with democratic changes then it implies that de-democratization itself is closed off and that the editors' more general argument does not stand. We are content for now to leave this issue up for debate and empirical analysis.

Generally in the social sciences it is customary to examine change through the prisms of agency and structure. Using the former term when discussing intelligence can be confusing since we are concerned with intelligence 'agencies' so we use the term 'actors' to describe those who can be significant in an area of state policy that, under authoritarian regimes, is so clearly linked to the fate of specific rulers. Caparini notes that ministers in fledgling democracies continued to view agencies as a key instrument for the surveillance of opposition politicians in the context of competitive elections that were a new experience for all concerned. Of course, 'actors' may be institutions as well as individuals and, from a different perspective, Estévez compares the respective roles of executives and legislatures in stimulating a shift towards democracy in Latin America. But even if actors make their strategic and tactical choices, as a well-known nineteenth-century German philosopher observed, they do not do so in circumstances of their own choosing. There are structures of culture, rules and institutions providing the context within which choices as to what is desirable and/or feasible are made. The most distinctive context for intelligence governance is the ubiquity of secrecy. This constrains debate in many ways; insiders can manipulate it to reduce the numbers of people involved in debates and to set the parameters of what is possible. Consequently, as Cepik and Ambros note, the closed nature of intelligence systems can minimize the impact even of scandals. *Some* degree of secrecy is necessary for effective intelligence but, bearing in mind Lord Acton's observation that 'Everything secret degenerates, even the administration of justice; nothing is safe that does not show how it can bear discussion and publicity',[11] the problem is how to square the secrecy circle. The challenge is to install structures of control and oversight that minimize the potential for intelligence to degenerate.

A complementary path to control of intelligence excess or corruption is development of a professional ethos among practitioners.[12] In medicine and law this process took about a century. So patience is recommended, and results in those fields are far more visible to polite society. Many attempts to create codes of ethics for spies have faced stiff opposition from powerful individuals and from bureaucracies that actually fear ethical constraints on

---

[11]Lord Acton, letter, 23 January 1861 (published in Lord Acton and his Circle, Letter 74, ed. by Abbot Gasquet, 1906) <http://www.positiveatheism.org/hist/quotes/quote-a.htm>

[12]Jan Goldman, *Ethics of Spying: A Reader for the Intelligence Professional*, 2nd ed. (Lanham, MD: Scarecrow Press 2010).

their sacred 'methods'. The codes that are publicly visible are shockingly rudimentary, as if written by children instead of mature, moral adults. The excuse of 'worst case scenarios' and 'national security emergencies' is ever handy to apologists of torture, murder and corruption of other people's governments. But ethics is at root the fundamental difference between intelligence that protects people and core values like freedom, and malignant political police who parasitize their peoples in service to evil employers. So with patience, much work remains to be done on social controls like oversight mechanisms that actually work, and on internal controls that help practitioners become servants of social ideals even when faced with horrific exigencies and hostile bureaucracies.

One specific aspect of structure that provides an interesting contrast in these articles is the international context within which national intelligence architectures develop. Potential entry to NATO and the EU has provided a distinctive set of sticks and carrots for former communist countries in central and south-eastern Europe, though once accession is achieved the pressure for greater democratic transparency reduces. For example, Matei notes how the reform emphasis shifted after EU accession was achieved in Romania and Caparini discusses the somewhat ambiguous impact of these international pressures. There are no real Latin American equivalents to these multi- and supra-national organizations in relation to democratization but there has been a clear change in the position of the regional hegemon. For the duration of the Cold War, the United States' main priority was that governments in its Central and South American 'backyard' be anti-communist and this was a significant factor in the installation and/or maintenance of military regimes. During the last 20 years, however, the US has found it easier to embrace democratizing tendencies in the region, even if these have been rather narrowly defined in terms of free market liberalism and Gonçalves notes the relevance of North American models of intelligence and its governance to developments in Brazil.

Where are Regimes Now?

Before we get down to considering where states are, there is an earlier question that needs to be asked in comparative analysis: is there a 'state'? Our cursory review of the intelligence studies literature demonstrated the dominance of studies of modern, affluent, bureaucratic, Westphalian states, primarily in the Anglo-American world. This is understandable and has been highly productive in generating more general ideas of how intelligence and its governance 'works' or, ideally, 'should work'. But we must beware that these ideas cannot be simply transplanted worldwide and more recent and current developments suggest strongly that we may be reaching the limits of what can be learned from ever more detailed studies of *state* intelligence architectures. There are clearly-recognizable states in all but one of the countries included in this collection, but we must note the implications of debates about ethnicity or nationality, sometimes connected with border issues. In Bosnia and Herzegovina, as shown by Lurås, and Kosovo, these amount to serious contestation of the 'state'.

Where there is a state, the democratization literature encourages us to ask whether reforms have been 'consolidated' such that democracy is 'the only game in town',[13] whether change has ground to a halt in a condition of 'feckless pluralism'[14] or 'pseudodemocracy'[15] or may actually have regressed such as is generally recognized to have occurred in Russia since 2000.[16] We have already made clear our preference for viewing democratization as a process which might be reversed and so any evaluations of individual countries on this score may only be temporary but there are other important questions to be examined. For example, Estévez makes the important point that the restoration of democracy is, by itself, not a sufficient condition to trigger intelligence reform; this reminds us that intelligence is a distinctive state activity. Given secrecy and the proximity of intelligence to governments anxious to reassure publics that they can provide security in turbulent times, security and intelligence officials are well-placed to remain as an 'authoritarian enclave'.[17] This will be more likely the longer public fear and suspicion of intelligence persists and, if elected politicians are reluctant to risk being 'tainted' by association with intelligence, then, as Lurås notes in Bosnia, it may be easier for professionals to control reform and maintain the autonomy of agencies. This is not healthy, especially when we remember, as Cepik and Ambros observe, that the tension between security and democracy guarantees the inevitability of periodic crises.

Another factor to be taken into account is the capacity of the state, depending on a range of factors including its fiscal base, levels of education and training and so on. In parallel with the ambiguous contribution of international bodies noted in the previous section, the impact of richer Western nations on intelligence democratization in poorer European countries has been significant, though driven as much by the desire to make operational alliances as to encourage democratization *per se*. So we need to ask the question whether changes in intelligence governance have been successful in increasing the sovereign autonomy of new democracies or, rather, based on offers of training, equipment and other resources in return for local support, have cemented their somewhat liberalized structures into a broad Western-led intelligence coalition. This would be dangerous if the focus of local intelligence were directed more towards the priority targets of donors than a careful evaluation of local security threats. The US and UK have premised much of their assistance of the last decade on their perception of a global jihadist threat which, if it exists at all in many countries, is insignificant by comparison with, say, threats from corruption

---

[13]Linz and Stepan, *Problems of Democratic Transition and Consolidation*, p.15.
[14]Thomas Carothers, 'The End of the Transition Paradigm', *Journal of Democracy* 13/1 (2002) pp.5–21.
[15]Larry Diamond, *Developing Democracy: Towards Consolidation* (Baltimore: John Hopkins University Press 1999) p.15.
[16]Andrei Soldatov, 'Russia', in Farson et al. (eds.) *PSI Handbook of Global Security and Intelligence: National Approaches*, vol. 2, pp.479–97.
[17]Diamond, *Developing Democracy*, pp.133–4.

and organized trafficking. For example, the four countries compared by Cepik and Ambros are all democracies and all suffer from extensive criminal and political violence, but only in India does some part of this derive from jihadism.

Other current developments reinforce the recognition that 'democracy' and 'intelligence' do not sit comfortably together, for example, the growing significance of the corporate security and intelligence sectors and their relationships with state agencies.[18] These constitute networks of security provision and raise profound questions about the quality of intelligence governance because they are largely beyond the reach of democratic governments. Cash-strapped governments and/or those imbued with enthusiasm for privatization may well find it convenient, if not actually necessary, to implement their security goals through private corporations, and democratic control of such 'corporatist' arrangements is hardly on the agenda.[19]

Conclusion

These articles have great relevance as we contemplate the significance of current events for intelligence governance. Cepik and Ambros note that crises and scandals, which are endemic within intelligence, may be benign and creative in enabling systems to react to overdue changes. Whether they do so in a productive manner depends on the lessons learned, if any. Caparini notes that policymakers, reformists and practitioners can all learn from the study of change in intelligence organizations while Estévez reminds us that some problems persist in ways suggesting that lessons often are not learned or, once learned, are then forgotten. For example, do lustration and vetting for new agencies achieve the goal of more professional intelligence agencies and, if not, why not? If unreconstructed ideologues and human rights abusers are kept out of the new agencies, where do they go? Do they have adequate pensions or are they left to their own devices to make a living by hiring out their skills and old contacts to new corporate employers or, even worse, criminal organizations? Finally, how effective are the new control and oversight institutions of democracy in, if not preventing crises then, at least ameliorating them and turning them to productive use in terms of increasing the effectiveness and propriety of intelligence? As can be seen in a number of contributions here, the danger is that the formal establishment of oversight can give a false sense of security and permit continuing inefficiencies and corruption to exist for a long time until, almost certainly, a major legitimacy crisis erupts.

Differences between healthy democracies and police-states may be the most significant distinctions in political theory. As so many authors have noted, there are intrinsic and serious contradictions between ideal democracy

---

[18]For example, Patrick E. Kennon, *The Twilight of Democracy* (NY: Doubleday 1994).
[19]See Tim Shorrock, *Spies for Hire: The Secret World of Intelligence Outsourcing* (NY: Simon & Schuster 2008).

and security institutions that rely on secrecy for their power. Power corrupts, absolute power corrupts absolutely, and everything secret degenerates; these principles have been shown to be true repeatedly in human history. Therefore the process of democratization from police-state antecedents which our authors explore is of great importance to democracies that wish to endure. The difficult tasks of promoting ethical identity among intelligence practitioners and effective oversight by institutions removed from the corruptive processes that afflict central governments are critical if democracy is to survive the corrosive effects of intelligence agencies turning on the peoples who create and empower them.

It must be abundantly clear that, as this is written, these are very far from purely academic questions. There are continuing intelligence controversies with important implications for democratic governance in many Latin American countries and, perhaps even more so, in the new democracies of south-east Europe that struggle to sustain themselves in the face of continuing nationalist questions and war-ravaged political economies that bred corrupt networks of government, crime and business. Beyond the scope of this collection: the Arab Awakening in the Middle East has seen the overthrow of dictators in Tunisia and Libya but there is ongoing repression in Bahrain, Egypt, Syria and Yemen and general uncertainty as to the longer-term outcomes. Even where dictators have left the stage, the extent to which security, intelligence and military organizations remain embedded in those societies present a profound challenge to those who would bring about democratic change. Clearly, it cannot be assumed that these nations will simply adopt some liberal-democratic model for the control and oversight of state intelligence agencies, especially where significant decentralization results in networks of multiple security actors in corporate and civil society sectors.[20] We hope that this collection will provide a basis and inspiration for further comparative analysis of this crucial topic.

Acknowledgements

Peter Gill thanks the Leverhulme Trust for their award of an Emeritus Fellowship that has supported the research, including attendance at relevant conferences, on which this paper is based.

---

[20]Peter Gill and Lee Wilson, 'Intelligence and Security Sector Reform in Indonesia', in Davies and Gustafson, *Intelligence Elsewhere*, pp.157–80.

Comparing the Democratization of Intelligence Governance in East Central Europe and the Balkans

MARINA CAPARINI

ABSTRACT This article discusses the reform of intelligence governance in two sub-regional groupings of former communist states: East Central Europe and the Balkans. These two sub-regions are delineated according to the pace and nature of transformations that they have undergone since the collapse of communist rule and their relations with respect to the European Union, the key political and economic organization in Europe. A number of lessons are drawn from comparing experiences in the two sub-regions relating to democratic reform of the security apparatus, and in particular the intelligence sector. Significant factors in the consolidation of democratic governance of intelligence include the nature of precursor communist-era regimes and the legacies they created, whether armed conflict has occurred during the transition, the extent and character of external (especially EU) assistance, and the strength of media and civil society. These factors appear to have influenced how transitional regimes have sought to introduce institutional reforms to constrain the powers of those services and their susceptibility to arbitrary use. They also have influenced measures taken to redress abuses by intelligence services under the preceding communist regime and the legitimation of the post-authoritarian state.

Introduction: The Importance of Comparison

The intelligence sector is an essential component of the security apparatus of the state, empowered to gather information and produce intelligence to advise government policymakers on current and future threats to national security. Yet due to its collection of and control over sensitive information, it may be misused to protect those in power and advance special interests. Governing elites in authoritarian states have typically employed the state intelligence and security services as instruments of surveillance, control and repression as they seek to discredit or control anyone perceived to be questioning key claims or the basis of legitimacy of the governing regime.[1] Intelligence agencies also have been used as instruments of surveillance and control vis-à-vis other security institutions and the wider state apparatus, as seen both under communist rule in Eastern Europe and in various authoritarian regimes of the Middle East and North Africa.[2] More recently, intelligence agencies in 'defective democracies' such as Turkey have been analyzed as components of the 'deep state', that is, as instruments facilitating control by autonomous military and security institutions and undemocratic informal institutions over weak civilian political and administrative authorities.[3]

Consequently the development of an effective, professional, democratically controlled and accountable intelligence sector constitutes an integral element of the democratic state, and is a key political and policy issue confronting states in transition from authoritarian rule. Yet despite the emergence over the past two decades of a rich academic literature on democratization and the more recent policy literature on the transformation of security sector institutions in diverse post-authoritarian and post-conflict contexts, reform and governance of the intelligence sector in transitional contexts remains under-examined in both academic and policy literature. Although a modest number of academic analyses of intelligence reform in democratizing contexts are now available, there continues to be a particular lack of comparative perspectives and insights from experiences beyond English-speaking western democratic states.[4]

---

[1] Eva Bellin, 'Coercive Institutions and Coercive Leaders' in Pripstein Propusney and Penner Angist (eds.) *Authoritarianism in the Middle East* (Boulder, CO: Lynne Rienner Publishers 2005); Thomas Plate and Andrea Darvi, *Secret Police: The Inside Story of a Network of Terror* (Garden City, NY: Doubleday & Co. 1981).

[2] On the role of secret police in communist systems, see Jonathan Adelman (ed.) *Terror and Communist Politics: The Role of the Secret Police in Communist States* (Boulder, CO and London: Westview Press 1984) and Krysztof Persak and Lukasz Kaminski, *A Handbook of the Communist Security Apparatus in East Central Europe, 1944–1989* (Warsaw: Institute of National Remembrance 2005). On security and intelligence agencies in Middle Eastern security sectors, see Basma Kodmani and May Chartouni-Dubarry, 'The Security Sector in Arab Countries: Can it be Reformed?', *Institute of Development Studies Bulletin* 40/2 (2009) pp.96–104.

[3] Mehtap Söyler, 'Informal Institutions, Forms of State and Democracy: The Turkish Deep State', *Democratization* 20/2 (2013) pp.310–44.

[4] The small but gradually growing literature on comparative intelligence governance includes Chris Ferguson and Jeffrey O. Isima (eds.) *Providing Security for People: Enhancing Security through Police, Justice and Intelligence Reform in Africa* (Shrivenham: Global Facilitation Network for Security Sector Reform 2004); Sandy Africa and Johnny Kwadjo (eds.) *Changing Intelligence Dynamics in Africa* (Birmingham: GFN-SSR and African Security Sector Reform Network 2009); Greg Hannah, Kevin O'Brien and Andrew Rathmell, *Intelligence and Security Legislation for Security Sector Reform*, RAND Europe Technical Report TR-288-SSDAT (Cambridge: RAND Europe 2005); Stuart Farson, Peter Gill, Mark Phythian and Shlomo Shpiro, *PSI Handbook of Global Security and Intelligence, Volumes I and II* (Westport, CT and London: Praeger Security International 2008); Hans Born and Marina Caparini (eds.) *Democratic Control of Intelligence Services* (Aldershot and Burlington, VT: Ashgate 2007); Hans Born, Loch Johnson and Ian Leigh, *Who's Watching the Spies:*

DEMOCRATIZATION OF INTELLIGENCE

One of the more surprising lacunas is the lack of comparative perspectives of intelligence reform in the former communist states of Eastern Europe, where the internal security apparatus had for so long functioned as the primary instrument of the communist party's monopoly of the state and its use of surveillance, intimidation and coercion to enforce compliance on its own citizens. By the end of the Cold War, all of the former satellite states of the Soviet Union shared fundamentally similar institutional structures for internal security. Intelligence agencies in these state socialist regimes had functioned as the party's political and ideological police, using their capacities to monitor and collect sensitive information about the private lives of citizens with the aim of reinforcing party domination as well as furthering the agency's corporate interests.[5] In the early communist state, internal security institutions had been directly responsible for consolidating party rule, enforcing compliance of its citizens with communist ideology, and defending the communist party-state from its internal enemies and political opposition. It did so through its use of coercive powers of arrest and detention, surveillance, extensive informant networks, indoctrination and other forms of control over political, economic and social life. The most repressive rule was experienced during the consolidation of the young communist state under Stalinist-era leaders, with gradual easing of repression in the post-Stalinist era. Nevertheless, the degree of control and intensity of repression varied over time and across the states comprising the 'Eastern bloc', and certain countries (the German Democratic Republic, post-1968 Czechoslovakia, Albania, Romania) retained strong authoritarian rule up to the collapse of the party-state in late 1989, reflected in the pervasive presence and influence of their state security services. In short, the intelligence services played a central role in consolidating the former communist regimes, and remained a feared feature across the diversity of regime sub-types that had evolved across the region by the fall of the Berlin Wall. Yet despite functioning as the underpinning of the communist regime, as Robert Jervis notes, most analyses of democratic transitions 'say very little, if anything, about how these services are to be pushed, harnessed, and/or won over to the new governing arrangements'.[6]

Establishing Intelligence Service Accountability (Dulles, VA: Potomac Books 2005); Larry Watts, 'Intelligence Reform in Europe's Emerging Democracies', *Studies in Intelligence* 48/1 (2001); Florina Cristiana Matei and Thomas Bruneau, 'Intelligence Reform in New Democracies: Factors Supporting or Arresting Progress', *Democratization* 18/3 (2011); Kieran Williams and Dennis Deletant, *Security Intelligence Services in New Democracies: The Czech Republic, Slovakia and Romania*, Studies in Russia and East Europe Series (London: Palgrave 2001).
[5]Miroslav Hadjic, 'Intelligence Governance in the Western Balkans: A Comparative Perspective', DCAF Project on Strengthening Intelligence Governance in the Western Balkans, Geneva, DCAF (2013) p.8.
[6]Robert Jervis, 'Intelligence, Civil-Intelligence Relations, and Democracy' in Thomas C. Bruneau and Steven C. Boraz (eds.) *Reforming Intelligence* (Austin, TX: University of Texas Press 2007) p.xix.

More than 20 years after the collapse of communism across much of Eastern Europe, the former satellite states of the Soviet Union, hitherto constituting the 'Eastern bloc', today represent a wide diversity in regime types, from the continuing authoritarianism of Moldova, Belarus and Uzbekistan to the new members of the European Union – pluralistic, democratic states of Poland, the Czech Republic, Hungary (although some backsliding has occurred among former front-runners of democratization).[7] Because of the now considerable diversity of the former communist group of states, comparative analysis would usefully focus more narrowly on similar sub-groups of post-socialist states. Identifying and comparing patterns in the experiences of two similar sets of cases can help to deepen understanding of democratization and of the intelligence sector's place within that broader process.

This article describes the main findings of comparative research into reforms aimed at establishing more democratically controlled and accountable intelligence sectors in two sub-regional groupings among the former communist states in East Central Europe and the Balkans. The two former communist groups of states examined here can be delineated according to their current international political standings in the Euro-Atlantic integration process (that is, progress towards membership of the two core regional political and security organizations, NATO and especially the European Union). Although not a precise barometer of democratic consolidation, and certainly offering few if any explicit benchmarks in terms of the democratic governance of intelligence services, EU accession in particular suggests a minimum threshold of rule of law, respect for human rights, pluralistic political systems, and democratic governance, including of the security sector.

Eight countries of East Central Europe (ECE) – Poland, Hungary, the Czech Republic, and Slovakia, but also including Slovenia and the Baltic states of Latvia, Lithuania and Estonia sharing similar post-communist pathways – have widely been acknowledged to have developed pluralist political systems and democratic systems of governance. The East Central European states underwent wide-ranging political and economic transitions after the fall of the communist regimes in 1989, gaining membership in the European Union on 1 May 2004. The accession process facilitated democratic and economic transformation through targeted support and assistance underpinning the candidate states' obligation to comply with conditions for accession – namely implementing the 31 chapters of the *acquis communautaire* that defined the legal and institutional framework to be achieved. The transitions were often internally tumultuous and at certain periods stalled (for example, under Vladimír Mečiar in Slovakia, and more recently Viktor Orbán's Hungary has regressed through the re-centralization of power), and in some cases are marked by continuing problems with human rights (for instance, minority rights protections for groups like

---

[7] In particular, Hungary has experienced significant rollbacks in democratic governance since the 2010 election that installed Prime Minister Viktor Orbán.

the Roma).[8] Nevertheless, this group of countries is widely considered to have successfully democratized and transformed their polities sufficiently to be considered consolidated democracies. Their democratic transformation has included the reform of formerly repressive state security apparatuses to more democratically controlled and more accountable institutions responsible for providing the public good of national and public security.

In contrast, the eastern Balkan countries of Bulgaria and Romania, and those currently designated by the European Union as 'Western Balkan' states – Albania and the former Yugoslav states of Serbia, Croatia, Bosnia-Herzegovina, the Former Yugoslav Republic of Macedonia, and Montenegro[9] – have undergone more problematic and in some cases violent transitions. Although Bulgaria and Romania gained EU membership in 2007, continuing problems of embedded corruption and organized crime networks challenge their development pathways, including governance of intelligence services, and suggest they can be grouped with the other Balkan countries for the purposes of this article. One characteristic that distinguishes the ECE group of states from the Balkans is whether former ruling communist elites were successfully challenged by opposition forces in the first democratic elections after 1989. Successful cases of transition to democratic governance in Poland, Hungary, then Czechoslovakia, Slovenia and the Baltic countries saw opposition parties overcoming the former communist elites in the first democratic elections after 1989. By contrast, the initial wave of Balkan political elites elected to government in 1989–91 neither embraced fundamental reform, nor sought to develop closer cooperation with the EU. Comparative research has linked this 'bridging with the communist past' with a delay in the onset of serious democratic transition.[10]

Armed conflict, the dissolution of Yugoslavia, and political instability resulting from unresolved issues of contested statehood all inhibited democratic consolidation in the Balkans. The breakdown of communist control in the Yugoslav federation of ethnically-defined constituent republics released centrifugal pressures. Where ethnic groups were not contained by the boundaries of the new successor states, the legitimacy of the state was challenged and inter-ethnic armed conflict resulted, delaying reform and

---

[8] Brad K. Blitz, 'Evaluating Transitions: Human Rights and Qualitative Democracy in Central and Eastern Europe', *Europe-Asia Studies* 63/9 (2011); Marina Caparini, 'State Protection of the Czech Roma and the Canadian Refugee System' in Didier Bigo, Sergio Carrera and Elspeth Guild (eds) *Foreigners, Refugees or Minorities?* (Farnham: Ashgate 2013) pp.131–150; Judit Tóth, 'Czech and Hungarian Roma Exodus to Canada: How to Distinguish Between Unbearable Destitution and Unbearable Persecution' in Bigo, Carrera and Guild, *Foreigners, Refugees or Minorities?*, pp.39–54.

[9] Slovenia, part of the former Yugoslavia, is typically categorized as an East Central European state due to its rapid democratization and early accession to NATO and the EU.

[10] Ana Stojanova, 'Defective Democracies: Challenges to Democratic Consolidation in the Western Balkans' in Claire Gordon, Marko Kmezic and Jasmina Opardija (eds.) *Stagnation and Drift in the Western Balkans: The Challenges of Political, Economic and Social Change* (Bern: Peter Lang 2013) p.52. See also Valerie Bunce, *Subversive Institutions* (Cambridge: Cambridge University Press 2000).

development. Prolonged nationalist and authoritarian rule by Franjo Tudjman in Croatia and Slobodan Milošević in Serbia, and the introduction of international trusteeship over Bosnia posed particular challenges. Whereas East Central European states focused primarily on political (democratization) and economic challenges, with some state-building elements, several of the Balkan states faced more profound challenges in the economic backwardness of Romania and Albania, in addition to the post-war challenges of comprehensive state-building while forging national unity and consolidating national identity.[11] The movement of Balkans countries towards EU membership was consequently delayed. Bulgaria and Romania underwent a problematic accession, missing the 2004 wave of enlargement, but, despite severe deficiencies in quality of governance and rule of law, were permitted to join in 2007.[12] Only in mid-2013 did the first Western Balkan country, Croatia, gain EU membership. Several Western Balkan countries are currently official candidate countries for EU membership, including Serbia, Macedonia and Montenegro, but likely face a long wait until they attain membership. Membership prospects for Bosnia and Herzegovina (BiH), Kosovo and Albania remain dim for the foreseeable future due to continuing internal challenges.

What relevance, if any, have these differences between ECE and the Balkans had on the reform of intelligence governance? What were the key similarities, and how did processes of intelligence governance democratization differ between these sub-regions? And what does a sub-regional comparison tell us about reforming intelligence sectors within democratic transitions in post-authoritarian and post-conflict contexts? To begin answering these questions it is necessary to understand the impact of contextual factors on intelligence reform in order to target and shape future intelligence reform assistance. It is important not only to understand specific changes (in legislative frameworks, organizational structures, personnel, procedures and oversight bodies and their capacities) but also why reform unfolded in the way that it did – that is, the factors and dynamics that impeded, or facilitated, areas of reform. Identifying the lessons learned from intelligence reform processes in these two post-socialist sub-regions might also offer insights for intelligence reform processes in other regions.

Communist Legacies

Intelligence agencies in the 'state socialist' satellite regimes of the Warsaw Pact were patterned on the Soviet model, sharing broadly similar organizational structures and characteristics and the common functions of defending the party-state from internal enemies and political opposition. The state security agencies or secret police, with the 'militia' (police) in a subordinate and supporting role, were responsible for protecting the socialist

---

[11]Taras Kuzio, 'Transition in Post-Communist States: Triple or Quadruple?', *Politics* 21/3 (2001) p.174.
[12]Gergana Noutcheva and Dimitar Bechev, 'The Successful Laggards: Bulgaria and Romania's Accession to the EU', *East European Politics and Societies* 22/1 (2008) p.116.

regime from internal threats by suppressing potential sources of political criticism, opposition and instability, ensuring compliance and control of the population through pervasive surveillance and informant networks, and policing popular compliance with the regime's ideology.[13] Until the collapse of the state socialist regimes, the security apparatus functioned as the 'sword and shield' of the ruling communist parties, protecting them from their enemies through varying degrees of surveillance and suppression of resistance.

During the Stalinist era across Eastern Europe, the secret police protected the position of the ruling party and inculcated fear within society through pervasive monitoring, surveillance and repression. However, the post-Stalinist era saw growing diversity across East Central Europe in the degree to which secret police penetrated state and society and functioned as repressive instruments, with high levels of coercion, surveillance and repression by the secret police continuing in some cases – Romania, GDR, Bulgaria and Albania – while Hungary was the most liberal case, evolving into a more benign role as the regime sought to build their domestic legitimacy. In post-1968 Czechoslovakia the secret police reasserted repressive control over state and society.

The repudiation of Stalinist policies by his successor Nikita Krushchev and the passing of Stalinist-era leaders throughout the satellite states of Eastern Europe also ended widespread terror of citizens and purges. East European communist countries began to take divergent developmental paths: Poland and Hungary developed 'soft' authoritarianism, while Bulgaria, Czechoslovakia (post-1968) and the German Democratic Republic remained hard-line authoritarian states, and Romania developed a clan-based neo-Stalinist regime under Ceausescu. Informant networks permeated the public and private lives of citizens to varying degrees. In countries that retained repressive internal security apparatuses until the collapse of the communist regime, such as former East Germany, Czechoslovakia and Ceausescu's Romania, these pervasive informant networks were despised and feared. In the soft authoritarian regimes, such as János Kádár's Hungary (the 'happiest barracks in the camp'), the internal security organs had a far less pronounced role. Yet even in liberal Hungary they were still perceived by the public as latent threats. The desire to avoid a return to the type of overt coercion and harsh social control of the Stalinist era under Mátyás Rákosi and the crushed 1956 revolution, as well as the desire to retain improved access to consumer goods, reinforced self-policing on the part of the population.[14] Similarly, Yugoslavia's State Security Service, both at federal and republic levels, was characterized by more restraint than in several East European countries during the Cold War era. Yet the Yugoslav security service contained a large proportion of Serbs, even at the level of the

---

[13]On the role of secret police in communist systems, see Adelman (ed.) *Terror and Communist Politics* and Persak and Kaminski, *A Handbook of the Communist Security Apparatus in East Central Europe*.

[14]Istvan Lovas and Ken Anderson, 'State Terrorism in Hungary: The Case of Friendly Repression', *Telos* 54/Winter (1982–83) pp.77–85.

constituent republics, and the federal level service was responsible for identifying and 'neutralizing' nationalist groups both within Yugoslavia as well as externally through assassination of émigré Yugoslavs, and remained a feared instrument of the regime.[15]

Further, as the key instruments of surveillance and control of the state and society, the secret police in most satellite states of East Central Europe were characterized by a fundamental duality in that they served not only the national party-state leadership, but also Moscow. Secret police of satellite states were accordingly subject to a combination of institutional penetration, indoctrination, surveillance, co-option and material rewards in order to secure their compliance.[16] Only communist Romania, Albania and Yugoslavia had managed to extricate themselves from Soviet domination of their state security. And while Yugoslavia's state security agencies became more benign in the late communist period, Nicolae Ceausescu's Romania and Enver Hoxha's Albania maintained highly intrusive and repressive secret police in the service of the national communist party. Albania began easing outright repression, pervasive surveillance and arbitrary arrests by the *Drejtoria e Sigurimit të Shtetit (Sigurimi)* only after Hoxha's death in 1985, while Ceausescu's repressive *Departamentul Securității Statului (Securitate)* sustained the personality cult around the dictator by policing dissent and opposition, and inculcating fear through extensive surveillance and informant networks until his violent overthrow and death in the palace coup and bloody events surrounding the Romanian 'revolution' of 1989.[17]

The Triple Transition

All former communist states in Europe thus encountered the challenge of undergoing a 'triple transition'. First, those countries which had been satellite states of the Soviet Union – integrated members of the Warsaw Pact, hosting Soviet advisers or secret police who penetrated the state bureaucracy including the armed forces and militia to uphold the party-state – faced essential state-building challenges with the acquisition of de facto sovereignty. They had to develop one of the most critical areas of statehood: their capacities to independently formulate and implement their internal and external security policies. The second concurrent challenge faced by post-communist states was to transform single party-states into pluralistic and democratic political systems. The third challenge was the transition from centrally planned socialist towards free market economies.

---

[15] John Hatzadony, *Intelligence-State Relations in Democratization: The Croation Intelligence Community 1989–1999*, PhD dissertation (Case Western Reserve University 2002) pp.53–4.
[16] Adelman (ed.) *Terror and Communist Politics*.
[17] On Albania see US Library of Congress, 'Domestic Repression Under Hoxha and Alia', Albania Country Study, 1992. On Romania see Dennis Deletant, 'The *Securitate* and the Police State in Romania, 1964–89', *Intelligence and National Security* 9/1 (1994) pp.22–49 and Dennis Deletant, 'Romania' in Persak and Lukasz (eds.) *A Handbook of the Communist Security Apparatus in East Central Europe*, p.285.

This triple transition had implications for the reform and activities of intelligence agencies. The state-building challenge included the development of an effective, professional and apolitical national intelligence system, one that served nationally-identified priorities and interests. The implications of democratic transformation for the security sector and intelligence agencies included the requirements that security institutions were bound by and operated within the law, and were subject to civilian democratic control and oversight. It also required the learning of democratic habits, such as norms of non-politicization of intelligence and intelligence agencies among political elites.

Beginning in the early 1990s, neo-liberal reforms and economic restructuring swelled the ranks of unemployed, and in countries where secret police had been extensive, spurred the development of organized crime at the lower levels. In Bulgaria, the dislocation created by economic reforms and public funding cuts to social clubs, in particular wrestling and other sports clubs, was directly linked to the growth of organized criminal groups. Originally engaged in protection rackets, these groups progressed to gambling, car theft and smuggling, before morphing into legal insurance companies.[18] The loosening of state controls on markets created alternative employment opportunities especially for intelligence personnel, since in the communist-era state security personnel typically controlled foreign trade. The extensive communist secret police apparatuses that were dismantled or transformed in the post-communist period resulted in a flow of former personnel to the criminal economy.[19] In numerous countries, former state security personnel were directly implicated in the development of organized crime.[20] All post-communist states experienced increased rates of crime and corruption in the immediate aftermath of the fall of the communist regime. As overt state controls over society through the coercive institutions of state security and militia (police) and the criminal justice system were scaled back or dismantled, organized crime encountered ideal conditions for growth, further spurred by severe economic and social dislocation.

The number and diversity of countries in East Central Europe and the Balkans creates challenges for comparative analysis of intelligence governance reforms in the confines of a journal article. To illustrate the types of challenges faced by countries within the former communist states of the two sub-regions, examples from several countries have been selected. Among the countries that did not experience armed conflict, Hungary, Czechoslovakia, Romania and Albania in 1989 covered a spectrum of sorts in terms of internal repression: at one end, Hungary was a relatively liberalized society and economy. At the other end, Ceausescu's Romania was the only remaining neo-totalitarian

---

[18]Katerina Gachevska, 'Fighting Organized Crime as a Security Threat: Lessons Learned from Bulgaria', *Journal of Regional Security* 7/1 (2012) p.4.

[19]Philip Gounev and Tihomir Bezlov, *Examining the Links between Organized Crime and Corruption* (Sofia, Bulgaria: Centre for the Study of Democracy for the European Commission 2010) p.64.

[20]Maria Los and Andrzej Zybertowicz, *Privatizing the Police State: The Case of Poland* (London: Palgrave 2000).

regime in the Eastern bloc, with Albania just beginning to emerge from the shadow of the Hoxha regime's repression following his death in 1985. And somewhere in the middle, with an orthodox communist ruling party and strong suppression of dissent, was Czechoslovakia.[21] Today, Hungary, the Czech Republic and Romania are members of the EU, and seen as more or less consolidated democracies although Romania remained ruled by former communist party official Ion Iliescu from 1989–96, a period in which little substantive democratic reform was achieved despite surface changes in legislation and institutional structures, and since then has experienced a long, problematic transition. Examples are also drawn from the Balkan states that experienced armed conflict in the dissolution of former Yugoslavia, namely Bosnia and Herzegovina, Serbia and Croatia, of which only Croatia is considered to have undergone sufficient democratic consolidation to be admitted to the European Union.

The Politicization of Intelligence Agencies, Actors and Products

Even when intelligence agencies were established explicitly to function as politically neutral state bodies, in each of the three ECE countries these agencies were frequently used as political resources by members of the executive in their struggles with other members of the executive, sometimes with coalition partners, and certainly with regard to the political opposition, media and civil society.

For example, although the Hungarian authorities sought to explicitly prevent the politicization of the intelligence sector that occurred under the former state socialist regime, the legal framework submitted the services to strong executive control, and in practice those individuals who fulfil senior government functions are closely linked to the ruling political party/parties.[22] Commonly throughout the post-communist region even today, the civil service remains politicized in practice, as suggested by the replacement of mid- to senior-level state officials with the advent of each new government.[23] According to some observers, contrary to the assumption that EU accession process and conditionality successfully de-politicized the civil services of new member states, civil services of post-communist states remained politicized or, as in Hungary, became re-politicized.[24]

---

[21]This section is drawn from Marina Caparini, *Internal Security Reform in Post-Communist Europe: A Study of Democratisation in the Czech Republic, Hungary and Romania*, PhD dissertation (King's College, University of London 2010).
[22]Global Integrity, 'Global Integrity Report: Hungary', 2008, p.45.
[23]Tony Verheijen and Aleksandra Rabrenovic, 'The Evolution of Politico-Administrative Relations in Post-Communist States: Main Directions' in T. Verheijen (ed.) *Politico-Administrative Relations: Who Rules?* (Bratislava: Network of Institutes and Schools of Public Administration in Central and Eastern Europe NISPAcee 2001) pp.410–26.
[24]Jan-Hinrik Meyer-Sahling, 'The Changing Colours of the Post-Communist State: The Politicization of the Senior Civil Service in Hungary', *European Journal of Political Research* 47 (2008) pp.1–33.

From late 1989, scandals repeatedly erupted in East Central European countries around allegations or evidence of secret service surveillance of members of opposition political parties, parliamentarians, members of the media, and activists, suggesting that the security services were vulnerable to politicization. This occurs when security-intelligence activity is 'a point of conflict between organized political groups', when it 'meddles into public political elections and power relations', or 'when security data and assessments are influenced by the established political positions'.[25] Tim Edmunds similarly identifies the phenomenon of 'partification': while concurring that complete depoliticization of security sector actors is neither feasible nor realistic, politicization becomes negative insofar as it involves 'the rapaciously partisan cooption of security sector actors to a particular political party or personality'.[26]

Politicization of intelligence services across post-communist East Central Europe was most evidently of the first two types, as suggested by regular leaks of sensitive information that compromised specific individuals holding important positions in the political, economic or social spheres. The frequency with which scandals involving the alleged political misuse of the intelligence services occurred in Hungary through the 1990s and 2000s, sometimes acting as an impetus for the introduction of further measures, has been described with some justification as revealing a predilection for 'control by scandal' rather than 'control by law'.[27]

Despite formal measures to insulate the agencies from political dynamics, politicization has been a persistent problem with regard to the Czech Republic's civilian counter-intelligence service, as reflected in frequent shifts in the locus of executive control over the Security Information Service (*Bezpečnostní informační služba* – BIS) as well as frequent allegations of political surveillance and other inappropriate or unlawful behaviour.[28] The role of the Interior Ministry vis-à-vis the BIS continued to be viewed with suspicion in Czech society. Direct control over the BIS shifted within the executive from the president to a minister without portfolio, to prime minister and back to a minister without portfolio. Parliamentary oversight of the intelligence services has remained limited, with efforts to increase oversight resisted by the BIS. Thus, while the Czech Republic established formal democratic control of domestic intelligence according to changes in legal and constitutional frameworks, the internal security sector remained problematic through

---

[25] Harry Howe Ransom, 'The Politicization of Intelligence' in Stephen J. Cimbala (ed.) *Intelligence and Intelligence Policy in a Democratic Society* (Dobbs Ferry, NY: Transnational 1987) p.26.
[26] Timothy Edmunds, 'Intelligence Agencies and Democratisation: Continuity and Change in Serbia after Milosevic', *Europe-Asia Studies* 60/1 (2008) note 2, 26.
[27] Bela Revesz, 'How to Consolidate Secret Services in East-Europe after Transition', *Regio – Minorities, Politics, Society* 1 (2007) p.106.
[28] Kieran Williams, 'Czechoslovakia 1990–2' and 'The Czech Republic since 1993' in Williams and Deletant, *Security Intelligence Services in New Democracies*.

the 1990s and 2000s due to inadequate accountability mechanisms and politicization.

Intelligence services in the Balkans and successor states of Yugoslavia were similarly instrumentalized by political actors. Overt examples of politicization of intelligence actors in Balkans states were seen, for example from 1992–7 in Albania under Sali Berisha.[29] Croatia's intelligence services were highly politicized under Franjo Tudjman's nationalist and authoritarian presidency from 1990 until his death in 1999 and were used to harass political opponents and critical individuals in the media and civil society, while the multiple services were themselves riven by inter-agency rivalries.[30] Intelligence reform in Serbia encountered some of the greatest challenges in the region because of the way that intelligence services had been employed during the authoritarian regime of Slobodan Milošević to protect it from internal dissent, and through its links with organized crime to sustain the war effort among ethnic Serb nationalists in Bosnia and Croatia. The lingering effects of politicization were seen following Milošević's ouster with the evolving territorial-political issues of Serbia's relations with Albanian insurgents in the south, Montenegro, and Kosovo. Despite the implementation of various legislative and institutional reforms and some evidence of effective democratic control over intelligence services today in Serbia, the Serbian public continues to perceive the services as politicized instruments of a small group of political elites.[31]

Varying Impact of Intelligence Scandals

In countries where the initial post-communist elections created a break with the past and where democratic opposition and civil society were mobilized, revelations and scandals early in the transition period resulting from unreconstructed intelligence agencies tended to exert an important impact on subsequent reforms and on political dynamics. A key example of this was Dunagate, Hungary's 'Watergate' scandal in 1990, which led to important changes in oversight of intelligence and swung electoral support away from the socialists and towards the democratic opposition parties. The scandal was a result of evidence of continuing state security surveillance of Opposition politicians despite the new legality of the opposition parties, a new constitution guaranteeing freedom of association, and promises by the state socialist caretaker government to ban covert surveillance. Surveillance reports on the opposition went to the highest levels of the government and senior socialist party members. The scandal resulted in the rapid dismantling of Directorate III/3, replacement of the State Security Agency and important

---

[29]Dyrmishi, 'Intelligence Governance in Albania'.
[30]Stephane Lefebvre, 'Croatia and the Development of a Democratic Intelligence System (1990–2010)', *Democracy and Security* 8/2 (2012) pp.115–17.
[31]Edmunds, 'Intelligence Agencies and Democratisation'; Denis Coragic, 'Are Security and Intelligence Services in Serbia Politicized?', *Western Balkans Security Observer* 5/18 (2010) pp.29–40.

changes to the control and oversight of intelligence agencies.[32] The scandal also helped to swing public opinion away from the former communists and towards democratic parties in the lead-up to the 1990 elections.[33]

Another example is provided by Czech experience in late 1989, when Czechoslovakia was ruled by a caretaker coalition government. The democratic forces were reluctant to engage with defence or intelligence, and left these to the communist party to run in the period leading up to the first elections. In 1990 it was discovered that the communist-era State Security (*Státní bezpečnost* – Stb) was secretly burning and shredding its files. Estimates of destroyed files include one-third of files on active operations and over 75 per cent of personnel files.[34] The scandal led to the dismantling of those parts of the Stb considered to have been most active in political activities against internal enemies.

In Romania, however, where the revolution merged with a palace coup and the 1989 fall of Ceausescu did not represent a real break with the past, the neo-communist Ion Iliescu succeeded Ceausescu as president and governed with authoritarian tendencies until the *ruptura* of the 1996 elections. Misuse and scandals of the intelligence agencies had little impact on reform: while the *Securitate* was ostensibly disbanded in early 1990, continuity in state security personnel and methods was evident. For example, the new state security agency was implicated in coordinating the transportation of Jiu Valley miners to Bucharest in response to Iliescu's call to help defend the new 'democratic regime', and their subsequent attacks against the democratic opposition parties, students, and anti-communist public demonstrators in 1990 and several times thereafter.[35]

Lustration and Trust

How transitional regimes deal with tainted individuals linked to formerly abusive intelligence agencies and other key positions within the previous regime is a highly sensitive political issue that influences citizen perceptions of trust and legitimation in the post-authoritarian state. Lustration and vetting have proven to be lasting, contentious issues in the domestic politics of transition states. Most post-communist countries have implemented some

---

[32]Istvan Szikinger, 'National Security in Hungary' in Jean-Paul Brodeur, Peter Gill and Dennis Töllborg (eds.) *Democracy, Law and Security: Internal Security Services in Contemporary Europe* (Aldershot and Burlington, VT: Ashgate 2003); and 'Hongrie: Le gouvernement prend le contrôle des services secrets', *Le Monde*, 23 January 1990.

[33]Miklós Sükösd, 'Democratic Transformation and the Mass Media in Hungary: From Stalinism to Democratic Consolidation' in Richard Gunther and Anthony Mughan (eds.) *Democracy and the Media: A Comparative Perspective* (Cambridge: Cambridge University Press 2000) p.147.

[34]Pavel Zacek, 'Secret Services in Murky Times', *New Presence: The Prague Journal of Central European Affairs* Spring (2004) p.20.

[35]Tom Gallagher, 'Romanian Tyranny Seen from Above and Below', *European History Quarterly* 35 (2005) p.565; John Gledhill, 'Three Days in Bucharest: Making Sense of Romania's Transitional Violence, 20 Years On', *Europe-Asia Studies* 63/9 (2011).

sort of lustration or vetting process by which individuals linked to abusive former state security agencies or the highest levels of the communist party were prohibited from working in, or removed from, positions of public trust such as key posts in state administration.[36] But lustration has frequently been a partial, flawed process, sometimes motivated by considerations of gaining tactical political advantage and engineered accordingly (for example, introduced before an election and having the strategic impact of discrediting members of the opposition).[37] Moreover, different forms of lustration impart different effects. Recent research has established that dismissal of compromised officials has been linked to increased trust in state institutions in the Czech Republic. Albania, Bulgaria, and Germany also implemented systems of dismissing individuals tainted by their past activities. Countries that introduced alternative forms of lustration, such as those based on giving officials a 'second chance' based on their confession of past associations, had more mixed results.[38] Early in the transition period, regular scandals resulted from revelations that a significant number of intelligence officials or high-ranking government officials had been agents or collaborators of communist-era state security. The allegations and political (mis)use of information about an individual's involvement with former regime's state security (intelligence) services continues to this day to be a factor in political competition and to haunt contemporary politics in many former communist countries.

The Value of Multiple Oversight and Accountability Mechanisms

Achieving accountability and democratic control of intelligence agencies is more likely when there is a plurality of actors with some sort of oversight role. The establishment of parliamentary committees overseeing the intelligence agencies in states transitioning away from authoritarian rule is not necessarily a guarantee of effective public oversight.[39] Such committees have often been under resourced, lacking in expertise or critical oversight capacities, sometimes lacking the will or interest to exercise critical oversight of the intelligence sector or have functioned essentially as a rubber stamp.

---

[36]Lustration is the term used for a transitional justice mechanism adopted in almost every post-communist East European country that involves a law-based process of screening of individuals to determine their involvement in the former regime and their suitability for higher public positions. Individuals who are found to have been communist officials or to have worked or informed for the state security agency are typically excluded or removed from these positions. In some lustration approaches, individuals have the opportunity to hold or retain a position if they confess their prior association. See Cynthia M. Horne, 'Assessing the Impact of Lustration on Trust in Public Institutions and National Government in Central and Eastern Europe', *Comparative Political Studies* 45/4 (2012) p.413.

[37]Helga Walsh, 'Dealing with the Communist Past: Central and East European Experiences After 1990', *Europe-Asia Studies* 48/3 (1996) pp.413–28.

[38]Susanne Y.P. Choi and Roman David, 'Lustration Systems and Trust: Evidence from Survey Experiments in the Czech Republic, Hungary and Poland', *American Journal of Sociology* 117/4 (2012) pp.1172–201.

[39]Watts, 'Intelligence Reform in Europe's Emerging Democracies'.

Additionally, countervailing institutions in systems of checks and balances may be weakened in their oversight role by corruption or politicization. The Serbian Committee for Defence and Security (CDS), although vested with significant legal powers to investigate and conduct oversight of the security services, has performed in a weak and superficial manner. The lack of interest of its members in exercising robust oversight of the security services, despite numerous training sessions, is credited to strong party discipline and a mechanism which until 2011 enabled political parties to force the resignation of members of parliament who did not toe the party line. The CDS further has an extremely broad mandate with responsibility over the entire security sector, yet its members tend to lack expert knowledge and tend to hold several committee appointments simultaneously, while receiving little support from the overburdened small staff working for the CDS.[40]

In Hungary an important role has been played by several institutions, including the Constitutional Court, judiciary, parliamentary commissioners for human rights, data protection, protection of minorities and, on occasion, by civil society and the media. The impact of the different institutions on intelligence oversight may shift over time in transitional states as the political and legal systems evolve and consolidate. For example, Hungary's activist Constitutional Court exercised important influence on intelligence oversight under László Sólyom's presidency of the Court from 1989–98 and ruled on several key pieces of legislation concerning internal security, for example, striking down parliament's effort to punish former communist officials for violating the rights of their political opponents by claiming law should be applied retroactively.[41] It also struck down the parliament's effort to pass a lustration act that would require background checks to identify those who had carried out activities for the state security organs, obtained information and collaborated with the secret police, or had been members of the fascist World War II-era Arrow Cross Party. The proposed legislation was both severe in substance and extensive in scope, potentially affecting 12,000 people in government and state administration, the media, as well as legal and academic circles. The Court's ruling resulted in the revision of the lustration legislation and ultimately in a considerably milder and more circumscribed lustration mechanism. During this period the Court provided an interpretation of the rule of law that set the tone for subsequent legislation and constitutional interpretation.[42] However, over time, with the politicization of the appointment process and the replacement of its president and

---

[40]Predrag Petrovic, 'Intelligence Governance in Serbia', for the project Strengthening Intelligence Governance in the Western Balkans, Geneva Centre for the Democratic Control of Armed Forces, 2011, pp.17–19.

[41]On Retroactive Criminal Legislation, Decision 11/1992: 5 March 1992, Hungarian Constitutional Court. Translated and reprinted in Laszlo Solyom and Georg Brunner (eds.) *Constitutional Judiciary in a New Democracy: The Hungarian Constitutional Court* (Ann Arbor, MI: The University of Michigan Press 2000) pp.214–28.

[42]Csilla Kiss, 'Constitutionalizing the Revolution', paper prepared for the 2003 Annual Meeting of the American Political Science Association, 28–31 August 2003, p.15.

members, the Court lost its catalyzing role and its influence diminished.[43] Over time, then, the effectiveness and relevance of both direct and indirect intelligence oversight mechanisms may wax and wane, based on wider dynamics within the system of governance.

Media and Civil Society Organizations

The media and civil society groups, particularly human rights groups, play a potentially important role in public oversight and in facilitating accountability by uncovering and investigating misconduct, and mobilizing public opinion that may result in corrective measures by government. In general, journalists who report on state and public security institutions encounter the challenging task of securing access and developing good relations with official sources, whilst maintaining journalistic objectivity and the professional scepticism that enables critical analysis.[44] Media in some former communist states have taken an active, in some cases extremely active, interest in intelligence agencies, particularly in countries where intelligence agencies had been deeply implicated in abuses under the previous regime and where political struggles over the intelligence agencies or their products are ongoing. Media reports in the 1990s in post-communist states of East Central Europe frequently focused on intelligence agencies. Yet media coverage of the intelligence sector is also vulnerable to sensationalism or may be the subject of deliberate manipulation through the release of falsified or misleading information, which is a particular danger when political actors vie for control over intelligence or when the sensitive information is used to wage party political battles.

Highly punitive criminal laws against defamation, libel or insult of public officials were common to a number of East Central European states and Balkan states emerging from communism, and these were used by certain post-communist governments to protect powerful individuals, the government, or the state from critical media news reporting.[45] During the first presidency of Ion Iliescu from 1990–6, journalists who investigated and reported on issues surrounding the Romanian intelligence services, including Iliescu's past alleged connections to the KGB, were subject to

---

[43]Kim Lane Scheppele, 'Democracy by Judiciary (or Why Courts Can Sometimes be More Democratic than Parliaments)', paper prepared for the conference on Constitutional Courts, Washington University, 1–3 November 2001.

[44]Marina Caparini, 'Security Sector Reform and the News Media' in Marina Caparini (ed.) *News Media and the Security Sector: Journalists on Telling the Story* (Zurich and Berlin: LIT 2010) pp.15–17.

[45]Elena Yanchukova, 'Criminal Defamation and Insult Laws: An Infringement on the Freedom of Expression in European and Post-Communist Jurisdictions', *Columbia Journal of Transnational Law* 41 (2003); Ana Karlsreiter and Hannah Vuoko (eds.) *Ending the Chilling Effect: Working to Repeal Criminal Libel and Insult Laws* (Vienna: OSCE Office of the Representative of Freedom of the Media 2004). See also Council of Europe, 'Defamation and Freedom of Expression: Selected Documents', H/ATCM (2003) 1 (Strasbourg: Council of Europe 2003), especially the speeches by Peter Noorlander and Vesna Alaburic, pp.25–33.

surveillance and intimidation.[46] In the last three years of President Sali Berisha's presidency between 1994 and 1997, attempted muzzling of media reporting on abuses and corruption within the Albanian intelligence services and other government bodies occurred through the prosecution and conviction of several journalists for dissemination of state secrets, or by invoking laws against defamation of public officials. Journalists and publishers were also arbitrarily detained and subject to violent attacks for critical news reports.[47]

In the contemporary, highly connected world of telecommunications, leaks, whistleblower accounts, media and civil society investigations cross borders. In 2012 Polish Prime Minister Donald Tusk complained that Poland was a 'political victim' of leaks by former US intelligence and administration officials several years back which had revealed the involvement of Poland and other foreign governments including Lithuania and Romania in hosting secret prisons where terrorism suspects have been interrogated by CIA personnel.[48] As demonstrated by the apathetic response by the Polish press to the external revelations of Poland's involvement in the CIA rendition programme and several years delay before any real journalistic investigation of the allegations was undertaken, a relatively free press will not necessarily provide robust public oversight of intelligence and security scandals when these are perceived to serve strongly held state interests, such as the value placed on very close relations between Poland and the US.[49] In the face of outright denial by the governments of the 54 countries that have now been implicated, and as in the Polish example of media complacency, investigations by international non-governmental organizations such as Human Rights Watch, Open Society Foundation, Amnesty International, Helsinki Committee, and the human rights bodies attached to the UN and Council of Europe have progressively documented complicity with the US programme of extraordinary rendition and torture ('enhanced interrogation' – see further below).[50]

External Actors and Assistance

International influence and assistance in the intelligence domain has been problematic from the perspective of democratic governance. Intelligence

---

[46] V.G. Baleanu, 'A Clear and Present Danger to Democracy: The New Romanian Security Services are Still Watching', Conflict Studies Research Centre, Royal Military Academy Sandhurst, 1996.

[47] Human Rights Watch, 'The Cost of Speech: Violations of Media Freedom in Albania' 14/5 (2002) p.10; and Arjan Dyrmishi, 'Intelligence Governance in Albania', Geneva, DCAF, 2012, pp.6, 22.

[48] Monika Scislowska, 'PM: Poland is "Victim" of US Leaks on CIA Prison', *Salon*, 29 March 2012.

[49] Adam Bodnar, 'CIA Secret Detention Places in Poland – Current Legal Developments', *Interights Bulletin* 16/1 (2010) p.38.

[50] For example see Open Society Justice Initiative, *Globalizing Torture: CIA Secret Detention and Extraordinary Rendition* (NY: Open Society Foundation 2013).

reform remains relatively neglected as a component in the supposedly holistic and 'joined-up' area of security sector reform (SSR); development agencies are reluctant to engage in this area, and the development of effective and accountable intelligence agencies is still not adequately reflected either in the body of SSR literature or as major components of donor SSR programmes. Rather, intelligence reform is usually the subject of bilateral assistance and mentoring by Western agencies, usually of major powers, with responsibility for engagement left to the agency itself.[51] In an area where the good governance-centred principles of SSR are far less emphasized than in other components of security systems, it is more likely that the interests of particular donors who provide bilateral assistance, typically in the interests of facilitating information sharing and cooperation, will tend to be prioritized over the needs of the beneficiary agency and society more broadly. Typical Western interests in cultivating close ties with transitional state intelligence sectors include securing local intelligence and optimizing intelligence sharing and cooperation, developing reliable contacts, and advancing their own national policy agenda, for example, US government objectives linked to the 'war on terror'.

Further, the role of multilateral organizations in post-1989 East Central European intelligence governance reform was not encouraging: although NATO openly set out criteria for democratic control of the armed forces and civil–military relations, it had no comparable requirements regarding intelligence agencies. Rather, the predominant concern that affected the ECE intelligence sector was to ensure that the new partner states had systems in place for the adequate protection of sensitive information they might receive from NATO and its member states. Consequently, the imperative of passing new state secrecy laws in order to meet NATO requirements for protection of classified information tended to roll back advances in governmental transparency that had been made in post-communist countries through freedom of information legislation.[52]

Nor was the European Union much engaged with intelligence governance reform. For example, only once did it raise concern over the extensive powers wielded by Romania's intelligence services and the necessity to subject them to democratic control. In its first assessment report (the 1997 Opinion or *avis*) once the accession process formally got underway, the Commission observed that: 'The secret services continue to wield extensive powers regarding the classification of official documents, phone tapping and searches. This state of affairs is largely attributable to the ambiguity of the legislation governing their activities'.[53] It then noted the Romanian government's intention to strengthen parliamentary oversight by creating a parliamentary committee to

---

[51] Alex Martin, 'The Lessons of Eastern Europe for Modern Intelligence Reform', *Conflict, Security & Development* 7/4 (2007) p.552.
[52] Alasdair Roberts, 'Entangling Alliances: NATO's Security of Information Policy and the Entrenchment of State Secrecy', *Cornell International Law Journal* 36 (2003).
[53] European Commission, 'Agenda 2000 – Commission Opinion on Romania's Application for Membership of the European Union', Doc/97/18, Brussels, 15 July 1997, p.14.

oversee foreign intelligence services. Thereafter, the intelligence domain was largely ignored insofar as the political elements of the Copenhagen criteria were concerned (that is, the rule of law, democracy, respect for human rights, rights of minorities). This stood in contrast to the EU's monitoring of the Romanian police, which were much more the subject of criticism. The EU also criticized corruption, which permeated the entire public sector. To the extent that the intelligence sector of candidate states has been addressed in the context of EU enlargement, it has largely related to the collection and sharing of intelligence relevant to border management, efforts to counter organized crime, drug trafficking, money laundering and corruption, and terrorism, particularly in terms of facilitating cross-border cooperation between police, customs and judiciaries of candidate and member state agencies on a technical basis under the Justice and Home Affairs (JHA) chapter of the *acquis*.

The failure of the EU to exercise influence over candidate states' process of intelligence governance reform has constituted a missed opportunity with wider implications with respect to democratic governance. For example, EU leverage on the early post-communist regime of Ion Iliescu was especially weak, as evidenced by the regime's repeated use, despite warnings from the EU, of the collective violence by miners from the Jiu Valley, organized with the collaboration of state security officials to launch several violent attacks on student demonstrators and political opposition in Bucharest, as mentioned above.[54]

A rare instance of explicit and public EU pressure on the subject of intelligence reform occurred in reaction to the attempt to establish a separate, militarized intelligence agency, the General Directorate for Protection and Anti-Corruption (GDPAC), under order of the Romanian minister of justice. GDPAC was headed by a former *Securitate* colonel who had been implicated in the violence against demonstrators in late 1989.[55] The European Commission had first criticized the GDPAC in its 2004 report, and it was this, underpinned by repeated scandals and problems of human rights abuses in prisons, financial improprieties, attempts to influence members of the judiciary, and illegal surveillance of political figures, that contributed to the eventual disbanding of the intelligence agency.[56]

Gaps in the legislative and oversight framework of transitional states concerning intelligence governance have been exploited by international and domestic actors

At least three former communist countries – Poland, Lithuania and Romania – have been identified as having actively participated in the CIA's

---

[54]Ion Bogdan Vasi, 'The Fist of the Working Class: The Social Movements of Jiu Valley Miners in Post-Socialist Romania', *East European Politics and Societies* 18/1 (2004).

[55]Craig Smith, 'Eastern Europe Struggles to Purge Security Services', *New York Times*, 12 December 2006.

[56]Valentin Fernand Filip, *The Intelligence Phenomenon in a New Democratic Milieu: Romania – A Case Study*, Master's thesis (Naval Post-Graduate School, Monterrey, CA, 2006) pp.18–19.

programme of 'extraordinary rendition' through the secret detention on their territory from 2003–5 of 'high value detainees' suspected of involvement in terrorism. This participation was based on the NATO invocation of Article 5 of collective defence in early October 2001 and subsequent bilateral agreements with the US government. Dick Marty, Rapporteur for the Parliamentary Assembly of the Council of Europe, reported that the agreements secured extremely broad permissions from those governments and their intelligence services for the US government to launch the CIA covert action via personnel, aircraft and vehicles within their territory, paired with protections against interference and oversight – that is, guarantees of the physical security of US government personnel involved, commitment to high level of secrecy and security of information, and exclusion of those activities from parliamentary oversight.[57]

According to a Council of Europe report, Romania's participation in the rendition program was enabled by a combination of patchy Romanian oversight of intelligence (parliamentary oversight existed over the main civilian domestic agency, but not over military intelligence), facilitated by lax EU scrutiny over intelligence accountability and oversight, and NATO's self-interested policy requirements, resulting in tightened controls over the security of confidential information and an ability to withhold relevant information from various actors in the executive and legislative domains. In short, a small group of internal actors circumvented existing Romanian safeguards by involving the military intelligence agency, over which there was no parliamentary oversight, with the US CIA programme on extraordinary rendition. Deliberate withholding of information about Romanian participation in the programme, specifically from other members of the executive and the parliament, subverted democratic control and accountability.[58] Romanian participation in the CIA's extraordinary rendition programme still has not been officially acknowledged by Bucharest, despite investigations conducted by the European Parliament, Council of Europe, various human rights NGOs, and documents filed in a US court case in 2011, which all confirm CIA flights to Bucharest and implicate Romanian involvement.[59] The situation is little better in the case of East Central European countries that participated in the rendition programme. While Polish prosecutors in 2012

---

[57]Parliamentary Assembly of the Council of Europe, 'Secret Detentions and Illegal Transfers of Detainees Involving Council of Europe Member States: Second Report', Committee on Legal Affairs and Human Rights, Rapporteur Mr Dick Marty, 7 June 2007, especially paras 72–90.
[58]Parliamentary Assembly, Council of Europe (PACE), 'Secret Detention and Illegal Transfers of Detainees Involving Council of Europe Member States: Second Report', Rapporteur Dick Marty, 7 June 2007; European Parliament, 'Report on the Alleged use of European Countries by the CIA for the Transportation and Illegal Detention of Prisoners', Temporary Committee on the alleged use of European countries by the CIA for the transportation and illegal detention of prisoners, Rapporteur Giovanni Claudio Fava, Final, 30 January 2007, A6-0020/2007.
[59]'US Court Case Confirms CIA Rendition Flights to Bucharest', Nine O'Clock.ro, 1 September 2011; 'Romania Denies Hosting Secret CIA Prisons', CNN.com, 7 September 2011.

charged the former intelligence chief Zbigniew Siemiątkowski for his role in allowing the CIA to run such a secret detention centre and violating international law, charges were dropped the following year amid speculation of political interference with the investigating prosecutors.[60]

The Lingering Effects of Armed Conflict: Delayed Democratic Consolidation

In addition to the challenges of the triple transition, mentioned above, several states of former Yugoslavia encountered a fourth transition from armed conflict to peace. With lingering material and psychological legacies of warfare and ethnic cleansing and ongoing processes of reconciliation, several of these states have been subject to the sustained presence or intervention of the international community. The three transition challenges above were all made more complex by the legacies of war and ethnic conflict: building a normalized peacetime state was delayed, and in the case of Bosnia this had to take place in the context of a society deeply fractured by the territorial and political results of ethnic cleansing. Borders within the region are also still being stabilized, as shown by Kosovo's declaration of independence from Serbia in 2008, and the start of normalization of relations from late 2012 between Pristina and Belgrade over the northern Kosovo-Serbia border.

The ethnic conflict and wars delayed the onset of democratizing reforms. The reform process began at different times among the Western Balkan states: only for Slovenia did 1989 signal the onset of reform. For the rest, reforms were delayed by the onset of conflict and, in some cases, more authoritarian wartime and post-war regimes. In Serbia and Croatia especially, the war-time regimes of Milošević and Tudjman introduced authoritarian measures that delayed movement towards democratization. The experience of war also affected public perceptions of the legitimacy of the security apparatus. While victors in war (Croatia) saw the prestige and power of the military strengthened, even the losers (Serbia) saw their security apparatus accumulate power and influence.[61] The greatly strengthened powers and autonomy of security services and other security institutions under Milošević buttressed institutional resistance within the security forces to reforms in the years after Milošević was removed from power and democratization began. For Serbia, there is some debate over whether reform began in October 2000 (the date of the removal of Milošević) or 2006 (the date Montenegro left the State Union of Serbia and Montenegro, and a new constitution was adopted in Serbia); in contrast, Croatian reform began after the departure of Franjo Tudjman in 2000. And while the 1995 Dayton Agreement marked the date

---

[60]'What Happened in Stare Kiejkuty?', *The Economist*, 9 July 2013; 'Polish Prosecutors to Drop Charges in CIA Jail Inquiry – Report', *Reuters*, 19 February 2013; Joanna Berendt and Nicholas Kulish, 'Polish Ex-Official Charged with Aiding CIA', *New York Times*, 27 March 2012.

[61]Miroslav Hadzic, 'Measuring the Extent of Security Sector Reform in Serbia – Framing the Problem', *Western Balkans Security Observer*, No. 7–8, October 2007–March 2008, p.25.

for fundamental change in Bosnia, intelligence reform did not begin in earnest until 2004.

The Problem of Organized Crime

The Balkan countries occupy a strategic position in the corridor that has historically linked Europe, the Middle East and Central Asia. Under the post-World War II communist regimes that ruled throughout the Balkans, extensive black-market activity developed with the complicity of party officials. With the fall of communism, state security officials were well positioned to take advantage of the privatization of state-owned industries. The outbreak of war, and the implementation of the UN sanctions regime against Yugoslavia (Serbia and Montenegro) beginning in 1992, provided ideal conditions for these officials, who had cultivated criminal elements as informants and operatives during the communist regime as well as the paramilitary groups that emerged during the conflict, to make money on the black market. The war in Yugoslavia facilitated the growth of organized crime throughout the Balkans. Today the 'Balkan route' constitutes the primary trafficking corridor for heroin from Afghanistan to markets in Western Europe. Communist-era state security police throughout the region had controlled arms exports as well as illicit trafficking of weapons and drugs, and these agents (in particular those who lost their positions in the mass sacking of communist-era personnel by some post-communist governments) were among those best positioned on the collapse of communism to embark on entrepreneurial capitalist ventures that developed existing networks for the smuggling of contraband, namely cigarettes, drugs and stolen cars.[62] The links between Serbian intelligence and security forces with organized criminal groups involved in trafficking oil and cigarettes were used to smuggle weapons and other resources to ethnic nationalist groups in neighbouring areas in the 1990s; the lingering impact of the links between the intelligence sector and organize crime groups on post-Milosevic politics in Serbia was also visible in the March 2003 assassination of Serbian Prime Minister Zoran Đinđić.[63]

Conditionality: A More Complicated Carrot and Stick of Potential EU Membership

The Western Balkans generally have experienced the intervention or influence of other institutional/multilateral actors on the reform processes to a far greater extent than the East Central European states. These states saw more active and sustained involvement by multilateral institutions in conflict management, state-building and peacebuilding. The European Union, World Bank, United Nations Development Programme (UNDP), International

---

[62]Misha Glenny, 'Balkan Organised Crime' in Judy Batt (ed.) *Is There an Albanian Question? Chaillot Paper no. 107* (Paris: Institute for Security Studies 2008) p.90.
[63]Nemanja Mladenovic, 'The Failed Divorce of Serbia's Government and Organized Crime', *Journal of International Affairs* 66/1 (2012) pp.195–209.

Monetary Fund (IMF) and the Organization for Security and Cooperation in Europe (OSCE) have had a long presence and have decisively influenced the focus of reform efforts, as have the two long-running EU post-conflict operations in Bosnia and Kosovo. International intervention continues to influence transition processes in certain states – Bosnia, Serbia and Kosovo – including in the reform of their security and intelligence sectors. Although intelligence reform in Bosnia appears to have experienced a measured degree of success, the international community's direct and prolonged interventions in Bosnia and Kosovo have also arguably created a culture of dependency and perpetuated state weakness.

Like their counterparts before them in East Central Europe, most political elites of Western Balkan countries share the goal of eventually achieving EU membership. The progression from potential to actual candidates and ultimately member states would entail a transformation of the state and economic sectors and incorporation of the EU *acquis*. However both the context and the process of EU accession are now more complex for the Western Balkan states than they were in the previous rounds of enlargement. In the context of the ongoing economic difficulties in Europe, there is little appetite among EU member states for further widening of membership. Accession for Croatia in July 2013 benefited from public opinion that has been strongly in favour of both NATO and EU membership, which allowed governing elites to justify reform to the security sector in terms of meeting 'Euro-Atlantic standards', thus removing it as a subject of potentially contentious politics.[64] Consequently there are now two categories of states in the Western Balkans vis-à-vis the EU: first, there are those that have candidate status, including FYROM, Montenegro and Serbia (public opinion in Serbia has long favoured EU membership but not NATO membership). The other category is of 'potential members' – Bosnia and Herzegovina, Kosovo, and Albania – states whose prospects for membership in the foreseeable future remain dim.

The European Union has progressed in making the Copenhagen criteria more defined and in developing enforcement mechanisms to ensure new member states adhere to the normative compact undertaken through membership. The European Union has in particular sought to influence internal security reform, primarily law enforcement and the justice system, but also increasingly the substantive focus of intelligence agencies. One of the key ways it has done so is through the shift it has stewarded in the view of organized crime, from essentially a social issue concerning the roots of organized crime, to the portrayal of organized crime as a fundamental threat to national security. The anti-organized crime agenda has grown, reflected in the Justice and Home Affairs agenda, the accession conditionality of the Stabilization and Association Process (SAP) and the policy conditionality of the promise of visa-free travel through the EU in return for improvements to the border management capacities of the candidate and potential candidate states of the region, especially with regard to the control of irregular migration.

---

[64]Hadzic, 'Measuring the Extent of Security Sector Reform in Serbia', p.25.

Conclusions

The intelligence sector, and especially its potential to be instrumentalized by political actors, has been underappreciated in the study of democratic transitions. The challenges posed by secret activities to effective oversight and accountability risks undermining people's trust and belief in the legitimacy of the functions and mandates of state security apparatus, something which is of particular relevance for societies emerging from authoritarian rule. Experience in East Central Europe and the Balkans suggests that these institutions, and struggles over their control by the executive, have exercised influence in the political life of several transitional countries.

The quality of democracy is closely linked to the nature of controls, oversight, and accountability that democratically elected governments and their electorates wield over the entirety of the state security apparatus including the intelligence sector. Security and intelligence institutions possess the capacity to directly affect the quality of political discourse and governance; they are indispensable for collecting information and providing intelligence on threats to societal and state security, but those same powers and the secrecy under which they operate pose risks to individuals' privacy, liberty, rights to freedom of expression and of association.

The EU proclaims itself a community of states, one that is not only aimed at building a common market but, as a precursor, is built on common values of democracy and respect for human rights. These fundamental values are reflected in the Copenhagen criteria but they were almost never explicitly invoked in terms of intelligence governance, despite continuing governance challenges linked to the intelligence sector in a number of former communist states. The enlargement process and EU foreign policy towards its neighbouring regions, insofar as intelligence is concerned, has prioritized measures to bolster security of EU member states against transnational crime and migration originating in candidate states over the consolidation of democratic controls over security actors.

Conflict in former Yugoslavia and the associated sanctions regime affected the wider Balkan sub-region. Conflict compounded the challenges of transition, creating dilemmas of nation and state identity, and fostered underground economies, strengthening organized crime and corruption there and in neighbouring states. Reform in Balkan states has generally been more drawn out, complicated and more subject to competing international interests in the rebuilding of internal security institutions and the strengthening of anti-corruption measures. The fact that Western Balkan states are going through a process already experienced by the East Central European states suggests that multilateral actors, especially the EU, have had, in theory, the opportunity to develop more effective and coherent approaches in support of intelligence and internal security reform. While the EU developed more stringent conditionality for candidate states beginning with Romania and Bulgaria with particular attention to their capacities to combat organized crime, this does not appear to have been matched by EU efforts in oversight and accountability of intelligence services. Conversely, the lack of local ownership of this prioritization may also threaten the sustainability of reforms.

Similarly, East Central European state experiences indicate that the prospect of gaining NATO membership may have spurred certain reforms in intelligence governance, but that these were not aimed at increasing the democratic control or accountability or good governance of the intelligence sector. Implementing NATO's requirements for the handling of classified information by new member states required the rolling-back of freedom of information provisions in several states aspiring to NATO membership. The still partially obscured history of participation by intelligence actors in certain states (Poland, Lithuania, Romania especially) in extraordinary rendition points to another area to study in terms of the impact of external actors and agendas in instrumentalizing the intelligence sector and failures in intelligence oversight and accountability.

Finally, there are some important challenges to the comprehensiveness of insights on contemporary intelligence governance that can be drawn from analysis conducted by academics and other outsiders. Academic observers can more readily access and assess information on the legislative framework and constraints on institutional powers, whether mandates are clear and appropriate, transparency regarding general structure, mechanisms for parliamentary oversight and their missions and legitimacy in the eyes of the public. Students of contemporary intelligence encounter difficulties in accessing reliable information on other factors that are likely to be important in the democratization of intelligence governance, such as organizational culture, norms and professional ethos among intelligence personnel. But ever more information becomes available from the opening of archives, media reports, parliamentary investigations, leaks, and accounts by former insiders and whistle-blowers which all open the window slightly wider. Two decades of scholarship on democratic transitions and the role of precursor regimes and their legacies suggests that the past offers a key to understanding the future. Therefore students of intelligence can learn much from careful study of the communist-era institutions and approaches towards internal security in the East Central European and the Balkan states, in terms of how these may have influenced pathways towards democracy and towards the governance of intelligence.

Intelligence, Crisis, and Democracy: Institutional Punctuations in Brazil, Colombia, South Africa, and India

MARCO CEPIK AND CHRISTIANO AMBROS

ABSTRACT This article analyzes why institutional crises are bound to happen and how they impact on national intelligence systems' development. Punctuated Equilibrium theory is reviewed and employed to explain one institutional crisis in each of Brazil, Colombia, South Africa, and India. In Brazil, the case study is the fall of the Brazilian Intelligence Agency (ABIN) director in 2008, following the Satiagraha operation conducted by the Federal Police Department (DPF). In Colombia, the 2009 wiretapping scandal known as *chuzadas* is examined. In South Africa, the investigation in Project Avani (2006–8) is reviewed. Finally, in India the case study is the intelligence crisis following the Mumbai terrorist attacks in 2008. We found that institutional crises are inevitable because there are tensions between security and democracy, both being co-evolutionary dimensions of successful contemporary state building. However, the impacts of such crises vary across the four cases pending on three variables: (1) degree of functional specialization inside the national intelligence system; (2) degree of external public control over the national intelligence system; (3) whether effectiveness, legitimacy or both were the main drivers of the crisis. Our analysis of the four case studies suggests that the amount of positive institutional change in the aftermath of an intelligence crisis is greater in countries with more functional specialization and stronger external control mechanisms.

Introduction

Occasional poor performance, analytical failures, and even scandals are expected during the life span of any intelligence organization regardless of the type of political regime, power capabilities, or economic development levels in different countries. Institutional crises, however, are more serious and rare in the sense that they may lead to the destruction of an intelligence organization or the government it serves. Whenever such a crisis occurs, the normative cry from political, academic, and media circles tends to treat them as severe pathologies to be cured through proper reforming therapy.[1]

To avoid the pure normative outsider Scylla and the official cynical Charybdis, one needs to be realistic about the inevitable tensions between political processes at the national level and the dilemmas of international security. In that sense, all national intelligence systems are involved in a permanent quest for effectiveness and legitimacy.[2]

Are some national intelligence systems more inclined to experience crises than others? Is the resulting change after a crisis anything more than a brief agitation on the surface of a deep behavioral, attitudinal, and institutional complex system characterized by structural stasis? The obvious answer for both questions is yes. Nonetheless, we still need to explain why and how, providing some empirical corroboration. The hypothesis is that all national intelligence systems evolve in a non-linear way, implying both distinct national trajectories and a great amount of historical discontinuity in any given country. Because of cumulative pressures for change resulting from such discontinuities (or punctuations) in the institutionalization process, internal

---

[1]To affirm that failures, scandals, and even crises are inevitable does not imply that those involved with them should not be held responsible for their acts and choices. We take seriously the ethical dilemmas associated with intelligence activities, but they are not the focus of this article. For a balanced discussion of such issues, we direct the reader to Michael Herman, *Intelligence Services in the Information Age* (London: Frank Cass 2001) pp.201–27; Peter Gill and Mark Phythian, *Intelligence in an Insecure World* (Cambridge: Polity Press 2012) pp.125–47; Michael Andregg, 'Ethics and Professional Intelligence' in Loch K. Johnson (ed.) *The Oxford Handbook of National Security and Intelligence* (Oxford: Oxford University Press 2010) pp.735–55. For a brief introduction to this topic in the United States, see Chapter 13 of Mark Lowenthal, *Intelligence: From Secrets to Policy*, 4th ed. (Washington, DC: CQPress 2009). Roy Godson, *Dirty Tricks or Trump Cards: US Covert Action and Counterintelligence* (Washington: Brassey's 1995) pp.120–83, also covers ethical aspects of counterintelligence and covert actions.

[2]See Thomas Bruneau and Florina Cristiana (Cris) Matei, 'Intelligence in the Developing Democracies: The Quest for Transparency and Effectiveness', in Johnson (ed.) *The Oxford Handbook of National Security and Intelligence*, pp.757–73. We are mindful about the intrinsic limitations of a strict institutionalist approach towards the study of intelligence, but we also could argue that being governmental agencies, intelligence services are power-based institutions and should be analyzed as such. Of course, taking into account even the simplest relations between formal and informal aspects of institutional life would require another sort of comparative exercise. A better synergy between culturalist, contextual, and institutionalist research programs in the field of Intelligence Studies is necessary, even if beyond the scope of this article. See Amy Zegart, *Spying Blind: The CIA, the FBI, and the Origins of 9/11* (Princeton, NJ: Princeton University Press 2007); Marco Cepik, 'Preface' in Russell G. Swenson and Suzana C. Lemozy (eds.) *Democratización de la función de inteligencia: El nexo de la cultura nacional y la inteligencia estratégica* (Washington, DC: JMIC 2009); Peter Gill, 'Theories of Intelligence' in Johnson (ed.) *The Oxford Handbook of National Security and Intelligence*, pp.43–58; Stephen Welch, 'Political Culture: Approaches and Prospects' in Philip H.J. Davies and Kristian C. Gustafson (eds.) *Intelligence Elsewhere: Spies and Espionage outside the Anglosphere* (Washington, DC: Georgetown University Press 2013) pp.13–26.

functional specialization and external accountability are crucial to identify which national intelligence systems are better equipped to use successive crises to achieve better equilibria between effectiveness and legitimacy.[3]

In order to demonstrate how the mechanism works, this article is divided into four sections. The next section offers a cursory introduction to the Punctuated Equilibrium theory and its usefulness to analyze intelligence crises.[4] In this case, what Richard Betts wrote about the study of intelligence failures applies to the study of intelligence related institutional crises: 'case studies of intelligence failure abound, yet scholars lament the lack of a theory of intelligence'.[5] Consequently, this article is part of an ongoing conversation among colleagues from many quarters towards a more theoretically and comparatively oriented research in the field of Intelligence Studies.[6]

---

[3]On the impact of institutional designs, see, among others, Robert E. Goodin (ed.) *The Theory of Institutional Design* (Cambridge: Cambridge University Press 1996); Bert A. Rockman and Kent Weaver, *Do Institutions Matter?* (Washington, DC: Brookings Institution 1993); Kathleen Thelen et al., *Structuring Politics* (NY: Cambridge University Press 1993); and George Tsebelis, *Veto Players: How Political Institutions Work* (Princeton, NJ: Princeton University Press 2002).

[4]Notice that S.J. Gould and N. Eldredge, 'Punctuated Equilibria: The Tempo and Mode of Evolution Reconsidered', *Paleobiology* 3 (1977) pp.115–51, developed their punctuated equilibrium theory to explain discontinuous rhythms in the process of formation of species in geological time scales, not to explain even the whole evolutionary biology. However, in Section V (*For a General Philosophy of Change*) of their article, the authors also pointed out the similarities between their model and other criticisms to the slow and continuous evolution (p.145). Marxian theory of history and Kuhnian approaches towards Scientific Revolutions make good examples of such critical perspectives, but even they are dealing with huge scale social processes. Punctuated Equilibrium (PE) theory had a significant impact in many disciplines, including Sociology, Linguistics, and Political Science. Of course, when Political Science uses PE theory, the time frame for considering alternative states of equilibrium and transformation is measured in days, weeks, months, years, centuries, and millennia at most. Albert-Laszlo Barabási, *Burst* (NY: Dutton 2010) explains why this adaptation from the original geological time scale is correct. For the evolutionary dynamics in general, see Martin A. Nowak, *Evolutionary Dynamics* (Cambridge, MA: Belkap-Harvard Press 2006). For an introduction to the complex adaptive systems literature, see John H. Miller and Scott E. Page, *Complex Adaptative Systems* (Princeton, NJ: Princeton University Press 2007). For an introduction to the study of scale-free networks, see Albert-Laszlo Barabási, *Linked* (NY: Plume 2003).

[5]See Richard K. Betts, 'Analysis, War, and Decision: Why Intelligence Failures are Inevitable' in Peter Gill, Stephen Marrin and Mark Phythian, *Intelligence Theory: Key Questions and Debates* (NY: Routledge 2009) p.20.

[6]About theory in Intelligence Studies see, among others, Michael Herman, *Intelligence Power in Peace and War* (Cambridge: Cambridge University Press 1996); Gregory Treverton, Seth Jones, Steven Boraz and Phillip Lipscy, *Toward a Theory of Intelligence: Workshop Report* (Santa Monica, CA: Rand Corporation 2006); Michael Warner, 'Building a Theory of Intelligence Systems' in Gregory Treverton and Wilhelm Agrell (eds.) *National Intelligence Systems: Current Research and Future Prospects* (Cambridge: Cambridge University Press 2009); Peter Gill, Stephen Marrin and Mark Phythian, *Intelligence Theory: Key Questions and Debates* (NY: Routledge 2009); and Gill, 'Theories of Intelligence', pp.43–58. Regarding intelligence failures, we direct the reader to Richard K. Betts, *Enemies of Intelligence: Knowledge and Power in American National Security* (NY: Columbia University Press 2007);

In the third section, recent intelligence related institutional crises in South Africa, Brazil, Colombia, and India will be briefly discussed. Regarding Brazil, the case in point will be the fall of the Brazilian Intelligence Agency (ABIN)[7] director in 2008, following the *Satiagraha* operation conducted by the Federal Police Department (DPF). In Colombia, the 2009 wiretapping scandal (*chuzadas*) and the proposed demise of the Administrative Department of Security (DAS) are reviewed. The South African investigation (2006–8) in Project Avani, and the later transfiguration of the Ministry of Intelligence Services into the Ministry of State Security, are examined. The current situation of intelligence governance in India will be illustrated via the National Counter-Terrorism Center project and its pitfalls.

Why these countries? First, all four are regional military powers, and India and Brazil aspire to be treated as global great powers. Second, they present roughly comparable levels of economic and social development. Third, each of them has a political regime classified as fully democratic according to regular procedural criteria. Two of them are newer democracies emerging from long-lasting authoritarian regimes that nowadays experience lower levels of political violence (Brazil and South Africa), and two of them are older democracies living with higher levels of internal political violence and militarized interstate disputes (India and Colombia). Holding constant regime type, economic development, and international clout (regional powers), three commonly used independent variables, one can enjoy a better qualitative observation of national intelligence systems' institutional differences, as well as the interplay between those features and actual results of intelligence-related crises.[8]

Finally, the fourth section draws some conclusions and identifies limitations as well as further research possibilities.

Intelligence Systems and Punctuated Equilibrium Theory

As a specialized set of formal institutions comprised of people, organizations, and procedural rules, national intelligence systems are strategic resources and a regular part of contemporary government machinery in most countries.[9] Even so, there is significant variation in the way intelligence systems are

---

Ephraim Kam, *Surprise Attack: The Victim's Perspective* (Cambridge, MA: Harvard University Press 2004); and Robert Jervis, *Why Intelligence Fails? Lessons from Iranian Revolution and the Iraq War* (Ithaca, NY: Cornell University Press 2010). An article aiming at analyzing intelligence crises is J. McCreary and R.A. Posner, 'The Latest Intelligence Crisis', *Intelligence and National Security* 23/3 (2008) pp.371–80.

[7]When referring to intelligence agencies or any governmental bodies, we will use the full name in English, and the acronym following the official language of the country.

[8]The case of Indonesia is also comparable to the ones discussed here. See Peter Gill and Lee Wilson, 'Intelligence and Security-Sector Reform in Indonesia' in Davies and Gustafson (ed.) *Intelligence Elsewhere*, pp.157–79.

[9]See Marco Cepik, *Espionagem e democracia: Agilidade e transparência como dilemas na institucionalização dos serviços de inteligência* (Rio de Janeiro: Editora FGV 2003); Treverton and Agrell (eds.) *National Intelligence Systems*; Davies and Gustafson (eds.) *Intelligence Elsewhere*.

designed, located within the state apparatus and provided with missions, resources, and authority in different countries. As Leigh[10] states:

> Some states (for example, Bosnia and Herzegovina, the Netherlands, Spain and Turkey) have a single agency for security and intelligence (both domestic and external). Others have distinct agencies for domestic and external intelligence and security, with either separate or overlapping territorial competences, as in the United Kingdom, Poland, Hungary and Germany. More rarely, a state may have a domestic security agency but no acknowledged or actual foreign intelligence agency; Canada is the exemplar of this approach. A further variable is that either intelligence or security services may have either a more pro-active mandate or be restricted to the gathering and analysis of information.

Furthermore, most national intelligence systems evolved over the last centuries through great historical discontinuity.[11] Causal explanations of national intelligence systems' evolution tend to combine different blends of functional-utilitarian, power-based, and path dependence arguments.[12] We have no feud with functional-utilitarian and power-based explanations. Path dependence explanations, however, are inclined to overemphasize increasing returns over long stretches of time, positive feedbacks, and lock-in mechanisms of institutional life.[13] Despite the presence of concepts such as critical junctures, conflicts, and regime breakdown, permanence plays a much bigger role than discontinuity within this approach.[14]

---

[10]Ian Leigh, 'The Accountability of Security and Intelligence Agencies' in Loch K. Johnson (ed.) *Handbook of Intelligence Studies* (NY: Routledge 2009) p.67.

[11]See Herman, *Intelligence Power in Peace and War*; Cepik, *Espionagem e democracia*; Stuart Farson, Peter Gill, Mark Phythian and Shlomo Shpiro (eds.) *Handbook of Global Security and Intelligence: National Approaches* (Washington, DC: Praeger 2008); Treverton and Agrell (eds.) *National Intelligence Systems*.

[12]See Amy Zegart, *Flawed by Design: The Evolution of the CIA, JCS and NSC* (Stanford, CA: Stanford University Press 1999); Marco Cepik, 'Sistemas nacionais de inteligência: Origens, lógica de expansão e configuração atual', *Dados – Revista de Ciências Sociais* 46/1 (2003) pp.75–127; Priscila Brandao, *Serviços secretos e democracia no Cone Sul* (Niteroi, RJ: Editora Impetus 2010); Eduardo Estevez, 'Comparing Intelligence Democratization in Latin America: Argentina, Peru, and Ecuador Cases', paper prepared for the IPSA-ECPR (International Political Science Association – European Consortium for Political Research) Joint Conference, USP, São-Paulo-SP, Brazil, 2011.

[13]P. Pierson, 'The Limits of Design: Explaining Institutional Origins and Change', *Governance* 13 (2000) pp.475–99.

[14]The prevalence of gradualist explanations rest in what Niles Eldredge and Stephen Jay Gould ('Punctuated Equilibria', p.145) once called a deep-rooted ideological preference, which was well captured by the statement attributed to Linnaeus – *natura non facit saltum* (nature does not make leaps). According to Eldredge and Gould's own theory of biological evolution published in the 1970s, reproducing species actually reveal little evolutionary change most of the time in a geological scale, lingering in a state called stasis (equilibrium). Stasis is characterized by incremental genetic changes, but it is interrupted (punctuated) by events (crises) producing

In order to explain change and discontinuity we need a Punctuated Equilibrium (PE) theory.[15] Let us begin by defining a crisis as a non-routine period of serious threat and uncertainty with respect to previously existent essential characteristics of an institutional set. Hence, a crisis is somehow more acute, general, and profound than occasional bad performance or partial failure. In turn, by equilibrium we mean the sort of 'self-reinforcing resting point' characteristic of a balanced status, as affirmed by Thermodynamics or Economics.[16]

Although a tendency towards equilibrium exists, endogenous and exogenous sources of change are permanently creating different equilibria.[17] According to physicist Albert-László Barabási, crises are more than exogenous perturbations pressed upon otherwise stable systems and trajectories.[18] Crises are inevitable because reality itself is complex and self-organized in networks, all the way from atoms and cells to human societies and the whole universe. And change rarely is produced by smooth adaptation because of another feature of human behavior: the power-law relations. A layman's definition of a power-law relationship could abridge it as follows: any event whose frequency varies according to an attribute such as size follows a power-law.[19]

Let us explain. To affirm gradual evolution as the normal development path for intelligence systems would require one to assume that human

---

transformation (disequilibrium), a process of speciation known as cladogenesis. Cladogenesis is the relatively abrupt process by which a species splits into two different ones, rather than gradually transforming into another (which is also known as phyletic gradualism).

[15] As pointed out by Kathleen Thelen: 'Increasing returns cannot tell the whole story because, in politics, losers do not necessarily disappear and their "adaptation" to prevailing institutions can mean something very different from "embracing and reproducing" those institutions, as in the worlds of technologies and markets'. Kathleen Thelen, 'How Institutions Evolve: Insights from Comparative Historical Analysis' in James Mahoney and Dietrich Rueschmeyer (eds.) *Comparative Historical Analysis in the Social Sciences* (Cambridge: Cambridge University Press 2003) p.231.

[16] Ibid.

[17] For the purposes of this article, we decided to use punctuation, crises, and disequilibrium as parts of a sequential process (burst) resulting in qualitative change (transformation).

[18] See Barabási, *Linked*, and Barabási, *Burst*.

[19] A technical definition of power-law as a polynomial relationship exhibiting scale invariance properties, as well as further elaboration of its huge implications and applications to many types of natural critical events, can be found in Didier Sornette, *Critical Phenomena in Natural Science: Chaos, Fractals, Self-Organization and Disorder*, 2nd ed. (Berlin: Springer-Verlag 2006). It is also relevant to note: 'Power functions are part of a class of probability distributions that are leptokurtic – they have strong central peaks and fat tails. The statistical signature of a disproportionate response model such as the friction model is straightforward: in response to a Normal distribution of real-world inputs, the decision-making process transforms the data by reducing those values below some threshold and by amplifying those values above the threshold. Such distributions are often called "fat tailed" or "extreme value" distributions and are not uncommon in many natural processes where friction models operate'. Frank R. Baumgartner, Christian Breuning, Christoffer Green-Pedersen, Bryan D. Jones, Peter B. Mortensen, Michiel Nuytemans and Stefaan Walgrave, 'Punctuated Equilibrium in Comparative Perspective', *American Journal of Political Science* 53/3 (2009) p.607.

behavior is idiosyncratic, random, and unpredictable. A random logic of distribution of human actions over time would mean that the intensity and timing of these activities would follow a periodicity consistent with regular and linear patterns, therefore resulting in gradual and smooth change.[20] Since most social phenomena do not follow random patterns (e.g. wars, wealth distribution, Internet communication, and daily life activities), gradualist explanations can only capture part of the relevant institutional story.[21]

Alternatively, the root of 'burstiness' in human behavior can be located in our own decision-making process based on ordering priorities. Indeed, according to Barabási, 'if we set priorities, our response time becomes rather uneven, which means that most tasks are promptly executed and a few will have to wait forever'.[22] And we are forced to set priorities due to our naturally limited ability to process many possible tasks in a limited period of time. Given time constraints and the complexity and limitations of human decision making, 'power laws and burstiness become unavoidable'.[23]

Rare events and long delays are critical in the process. Those are the outliers in a string of events. They are not the tasks done quickly, but rather those long waiting in 'to-do' lists. These 'low priority' tasks are the ones often causing punctuations in a pattern of events because they tend to be the most difficult ones to be performed, or take longer to be processed, being chronically postponed with critical consequences.

In the field of policy analysis, Incrementalism is the functional equivalent of path dependence explanations of institutional evolution. It sees adaption as the decision makers at various levels of the government interact with many interest groups and other relevant actors through democratic channels, being able to efficiently translate social inputs into policy decisions and output values with normal distributions.[24]

---

[20]'Current models of human dynamics in areas such as risk assessment and communications assume that human actions are randomly distributed in time and are well approximated by Poisson process'; Barabási, *Burst*, p.38. The distinct applications and meanings of Poisson Process and Poisson Distributions in Statistics and Probability Theory are beyond our expertise. Suffice to say that events in a stochastic Poisson process take place continuously and autonomously of one another, as a collection of random variables with discrete probability distribution. For further elaboration, see Richard Durret, *Essentials of Stochastic Processes* (Berlin: Springer-Verlag 1999).

[21]'There's nothing smooth or random in the way life expresses itself, but bursts dominate at all time scales, from milliseconds to hours in our cells; from minutes to weeks in our activity patterns; from weeks to years when it comes to diseases; from millennia to millions of years in evolutionary processes. Bursts are an integral part of the miracle of life, signatures of the continuous struggle for adaptation and survival'; Barabási, *Burst*, p.240.

[22]Ibid., p.124.

[23]Ibid., pp.124–5.

[24]To be fair, the incrementalist/pluralist approach tends to be more concerned with power distribution among social groups and how their unequal access and influence affect the government decision process. See Charles Lindblom and Edward J. Woodhouse, *The Policy Making Process*, 3rd ed. (Upper Saddle River, NJ: Prentice Hall 1992).

However, there are important homologies between the limited attention span and bounded rational information processing capacity observed in human individuals and those observed in social aggregates acting collectively, from social groups to firms, government agencies, markets, and the whole political system.[25] By linking them with policy analysis, an important research program has been established by the Punctuated Equilibrium theory.[26]

Since government institutions can only allocate partial attention and efforts to a limited and conflicting assortment of problems at a time, Punctuated Equilibrium theory predicts that agenda setting, decision making, and policy outputs are much more inherently fractured than understood by the incrementalist tradition. The various types and amounts of political inputs and the consequent policy outputs are incongruent because of the same causal mechanisms hindering people and government responses to new issues.[27]

To explain such mechanisms, think about these mismatches between problems and solutions as caused by institutional costs. As pointed out by Jones, Sulkin, and Larsen,[28] there are four types of institutional costs involved in making decisions: decision costs, transaction costs, information costs, and cognitive costs. All of them act similarly on the capacity of government institutions to process information, but they vary along the policymaking cycle, as well as among distinct government institutions.[29]

In the policymaking cycle, and with adaptations in the intelligence cycle, it is common to identify four overlapping and recurring stages: agenda setting,

---

[25] Edmund T. Rolls, *Memory, Attention and Decision-Making* (Oxford: Oxford University Press 2008) is a very thorough book on emotion, information processing, memory, perception, attention, and decision making, using a multidisciplinary approach to understand how the human brain works.

[26] The main propellants in that research program are Frank R. Baumgartner and Bryan D. Jones. In the fourth part ('Agenda and Instability, Fifteen Years Later') of Frank R. Baumgartner and Bryan D. Jones, *Agendas and Instability in American Politics*, 2nd ed. (Chicago, IL: The University of Chicago Press 2009), the reader can find not only a review of their main claims and findings since their book was first published in 1993, but also a proposition regarding the importance of what the authors call *disruptive dynamics* in public policy, which is close to what we call crisis in this article. We also refer the reader to James L. True, Bryan D. Jones and Frank R. Baumgartner, 'Punctuated Equilibrium Theory: Explaining Stability and Change in Public Policymaking' in Paul A. Sabatier (ed.) *Theories of Policy Process*, 2nd ed. (Boulder, CO: Westview Press 2007) pp.155–87. In order to understand the role of information processing in the Punctuated Equilibrium approach in Political Science, it is important to review Herbert Simon's contribution regarding Bounded Rationality. Herbert Simon, Massimo Egidi, Robin Marris and Riccardo Viale, *Economics, Bounded Rationality and the Cognitive Revolution* (Cheltenham: Edward Elgar 2008).

[27] Examples of political inputs are plentiful, from changed preferences to election results, from new social actors to technological innovations and media coverage from intelligence.

[28] B.D. Jones, T. Sulkin and H.A. Larsen, 'Policy Punctuations in American Political Institutions', *American Political Science Review* 97/1 (2003) pp.151–69.

[29] An earlier consideration of decision costs in the intelligence cycle was Loch K. Johnson, 'Decision Costs in the Intelligence Cycle' in A. Maurer, M. Tunstall and J Keagle (eds.) *Intelligence: Policy and Process* (Boulder, CO: Westview Press 1985) pp.181–98.

decision making, implementation of policy outputs, and evaluation of results and impacts.[30]

According to Baumgartner et al.,[31] the institutional costs of collective action increase along the policy cycle because of cascading effects of the same universalistic cognitive limitations already mentioned.[32] Besides the horizontal stages in policymaking, it is also important to consider vertically nested parts or networks of a given polity. To avoid further distinctions, let us divide the government institutions between a political macro-system and a number of political subsystems.[33]

The political macro-system encompasses major government institutions and their leaders.[34] It is concerned with prominent, urgent, and far-reaching issues, processing them serially. Alternatively, various types and numbers of parent and subordinated government agencies and their specialized bureaucracies comprise political subsystems. Government agencies in distinct subsystems process specific issues in parallel. They also compete for jurisdiction, budgets, power, and attention from the macro-system. Established issues in the agenda and the new issues are therefore supported by distinct institutions and players. The resulting institutional friction or burstiness adds to the explanation of why crises are inevitable and how they happen, with expected results that are not randomly distributed.

Friction is not a concept arbitrarily taken from Mechanical Engineering by the Punctuated Equilibrium theory. First, it is useful to remember that friction between two surfaces moving in contact to each other converts kinetic energy into heat. Even more important, friction in complex non-linear systems such as networks 'cause the linkage between inputs and outputs of the system to be

---

[30] For a critical stance against the 'stages heuristics', see references in Paul A. Sabatier (ed.), *Theories of Policy Process*, 2nd ed. (Boulder, CO: Westview Press 2007) pp.6–8. For a brief summary of various classifications of policymaking stages, see Wayne Parsons, *Public Policy: An Introduction to the Theory and Practice of Policy Analysis* (Cheltenham: Edward Elgar 1995) pp.77–81.

[31] See Baumgartner et al., 'Punctuated Equilibrium in Comparative Perspective'.

[32] Note that institutional constraints, including limited ability to adapt and to process issues are not the same as what was originally called 'goal displacement' by Robert Merton, 'Bureaucratic Structure and Personality', *Social Forces* 17 (1940) pp.560–8, when people in complex and bureaucratic organizations start to value means over ends, when formalistic goals become more important than the main substantive goal of an organization. For a refutation of Merton's argument, see James Q. Wilson, *Bureaucracy: What Government Agencies Do and Why They Do It* (NY: Basic Books 1989) pp.50–71.

[33] See Vidar W. Rolland and Paul G. Roness, 'Mapping Organizational Units in the State: Challenges and Classifications', *International Journal of Public Administration* 33/10 (2010) pp.463–73, to better understand the classification of State's organizational units.

[34] Another important research program that is also related with PE Theory is organized around the Operational Code Analysis. For a review, see Stephen G. Walker, 'Operational Code Analysis as a Scientific Research Program: A Cautionary Tale' in Colin Elman and Miriam F. Elman (eds.) *Progress in International Relations Theory: Appraising the Field* (Cambridge: BCSIA 2003) pp.245–76.

disproportionate - underresponse because of friction, then overresponse in response to built-up pressures'.[35]

In government, friction is the retarding force holding together the macro-system and the subsystems in ever-precarious states of equilibria. The transforming forces are the dynamic political processes from outside and inside the system pressing for change in the priority order of tasks and issues to be decided upon. Such attention change does not occur in response to any momentary increase in transforming forces. Change is, rather, the uneven result of built-up pressures overcoming thresholds not fixed in time or space, but sensitive to context and types of subsystems.[36]

When the transforming forces exceed the tension threshold (crisis), thus forcing emergent issues to be dealt with promptly, they push a cascade of activities and changes that risk overloading the political system. The higher the institutional costs for change, the more punctuated the resulting transformation tend to be. In other words, bursts will be more intense and when change occurs it tends to be relatively extreme.[37]

To sum up, crises do offer opportunities for institutional transformation as common sense articulates, but there are associated challenges related to the appropriateness of the results themselves. The 'fit' (and survivability) of any new institutional arrangement cannot be normatively guaranteed *ex ante*, but they need to be judged afterward by their efficiency, effectiveness, legitimacy, and own ability to adapt and endure. Despite the best management techniques available, no one can fully control the results of a crisis, as demonstrated by the case studies in the next section.

An Intelligence Crisis for all Seasons?

National Intelligence Systems are just one of many networked political subsystems linked with the macro-system in any given polity.[38] At the same

---

[35] See Baumgartner et al., 'Punctuated Equilibrium in Comparative Perspective', p.606.

[36] Jones, Sulkin and Larsen, 'Policy Punctuations in American Political Institutions', p.155.

[37] 'The issue may be systematically tracked and a specialized agency or bureau may even be created to focus on it. Attention to the problem becomes institutionalized, and this may induce a second inefficiency. Not only is government slow to pay attention to new policy problems, but, once established, policies may be continued long after the severity of the problem which justified them in the first place has declined. Reactions to improvements in the state of the world, by reallocating attention or resources to other areas with more severe problems, or more rapidly growing ones, are slow'; Baumgartner et al., 'Punctuated Equilibrium in Comparative Perspective', p.608.

[38] There are tentative uses of PE theory to explain war and armed peace (see Bahar Leventoglu and Branislav Slantchev, 'The Armed Peace: A Punctuated Equilibrium Theory of War', *American Journal of Political Science* 51/4 (2007) pp.755–71, as well as terrorism and homeland security (see David B. Cohen and Alethia Cook, 'Institutional Redesign: Terrorism, Punctuated Equilibrium, and the Evolution of Homeland Security in United States', paper presented at the Annual Meeting of Political Science Association, 2002). It is certainly our fault, but the authors are not aware of literature connecting Punctuated Equilibrium theory and Intelligence Studies.

time, intelligence is also just one of many informational flows recurring at all stages of any policymaking cycle.[39] Even recognizing its potential impact over various stages of policymaking (including implementation) in distinct sectors of government, one could say that intelligence is mainly about providing input to strategic, operational, and tactical decisions in the national security realm of foreign policy, defense policy, and law enforcement. Intelligence matters, but it is auxiliary, both as a power-based subsystem as well as a type of information flow.[40]

Due to its connection with National Security, intelligence tends to form a closed type of networked political subsystem. Secrecy, specialized and compartmentalized knowledge, powers, and unique techniques have always been self-constructed to be distinctive from other political subsystems. Even in democratic contexts, intelligence subsystems are hardly considered as equals in comparison to other highly insulated and specialized bureaucracies like Central Banks, Armed Forces, or Diplomatic Services.[41]

Therefore, another important feature of intelligence is the dominance of specialized bureaucrats from within agencies that are part of the Executive branch.[42] Because of high access costs, the Legislative and the Judiciary, along with all other policy subsystems and even more the civil society, tend to avoid the politics of the intelligence subsystem policymaking. When decisions in a subsystem are dominated by a relatively small number of participants who share a common understanding regarding the agenda, not only is access restricted, but also new ideas emerge only with difficulty.[43]

Considering that institutional crises are the non-linear results of the friction ratio between retarding and transforming forces exceeding a tension threshold that is different for each subsystem, the higher the tension threshold, the greater the burst during a crisis, and the more punctuated the policy and/or the institutional results will be. Hence, one should expect crises in intelligence to be more intense than in other policy subsystems because the

---

[39]Many in the field of Intelligence Studies would accept the dual nature of intelligence (as information and power). Unfortunately, few try to pursue the theoretical consequences. Gill and Phythian, *Intelligence in an Insecure World*, provide exemplary effort in that direction. Note how the authors treated intelligence systems as complex networks, taking into account actors such as state agencies, business firms, organized crime, and others.

[40]For a more complete and accurate description, see Treverton and Agrell, *National Intelligence Systems*, as well as Herman, *Intelligence Power in Peace and War*.

[41]See Russell Swenson and Suzana Lemozy (eds.), *Intelligence as a Profession in the Americas: New Approaches*, 2nd ed. (Washington: JMIC Edition 2004).

[42]See Zegart, *Flawed by Design*.

[43]'All these things give government agencies room to maneuver. Presidents and member of the Congress listen to bureaucrats because they cannot afford to do otherwise. Armed with expertise, extraordinary incentives, shrinking mechanisms and public appeals, government agencies do not have to remain the servile subjects of their political masters (...) While institutional incentives push presidents toward action, institutional constraints work to hold them back. Although it is possible in theory to ignore the bureaucrat's interests and concerns, it is impossible to do so in practice. Agency's officials hold more cards than the statute suggest'; Zegart, *Flawed by Design*, p.52.

tension threshold is higher. If emerging issues like institutional reform remain unattended and return to the bottom of the list of priorities after the crisis ends, transforming forces come back faster to the same previous level, which is close to exceeding the tension threshold again. In other words, crises in the national security sector also tend to recur more than in other policy domains.[44]

The claims made in the previous paragraphs cannot be tested by observing just one intelligence-related crisis in each country (Brazil, Colombia, South Africa, and India). For that we would need to compare a greater number of crises in various countries and times. Moreover, we would need to compare crises in different types of subsystems, not only in intelligence. Nevertheless, the four cases allow for a preliminary assessment of the conceptual framework advanced in this article. By evaluating the variation across the four cases studied, we will try to assess the correspondence between intelligence institutional designs and intelligence crises results.[45] We shall start by examining the Brazilian intelligence system and its crisis of 2008.

Brazil: Slow and Harmonic Evolution, or Just Lengthy Stasis?

The current Brazilian Intelligence System (SISBIN) was established in 1999 by Public Law no. 9.883. The same law created the Brazilian Intelligence Agency (ABIN), which was designated as the central organ of the SISBIN. The agency is responsible for intelligence collection, analysis, counter-intelligence, information security, counterterrorism, training, and doctrinal development.

Between 1999 and 2008, it is important to highlight five institutional developments in Brazil's intelligence sector. First, the ABIN was placed under the authority of the Institutional Security Cabinet (GSI), a ministry-level position in the office of the President of the Republic.[46] Second, the National

---

[44]Institutional reform can be seen as a low-priority issue: 'the chief executive faces severe time constraints. Presidents have at most eight years to achieve their major domestic and international policy goals and secure their place in history. While bureaucratic reforms may be important, even instrumental, in achieving those goals, it is not something for which great leaders are likely to be remembered'; ibid., p.48.

[45]Marina Caparini, 'Comparing Intelligence Democratisation in East Central Europe and the Western Balkans', paper prepared for the IPSA-ECPR (International Political Science Association - European Consortium for Political Research) Joint Conference, USP, São-Paulo-SP, Brazil, 2011, is a good and recent example of a comparative exercise on intelligence democratization designed to observe commonalities between East Central Europe and the Western Balkans intelligence reform processes. About the logic of comparison and research using Most Similar System Designs (MSSD), see Paul Pennings, Hans Keman and Jan Kleinnijenhuis, *Doing Research in Political Science: Comparative Methods and Statistics* (London: Sage 2003).

[46]The subordination of the ABIN to the GSI is interpreted by some (Roberto Numeriano, *A inteligência civil do Brasil, Portugal e Espanha,* doctoral thesis (Recife 2007); Jorge Zaverucha, 'De FHC a Lula: A militarização da Agência Brasileira de Inteligência', *Revista de Sociologia Política* 16/31 (2008) pp.177–95) as evidence of the maintenance of political

Congress halfheartedly established the Joint Commission for the Intelligence Activities' Control (CCAI). Third, more ministries and specialized bodies were formally included in the SISBIN. Fourth, law enforcement intelligence was organized at the federal and state levels as a Public Security Intelligence Sub-System (SISP). Lastly, military intelligence was also reorganized as a Defense Intelligence System (SINDE).

Therefore, since 2008 the SISBIN has included the GSI/ABIN, the Ministry of Defense, the Ministry of External Relations, the Presidential Advisor's Office (Casa Civil, which is responsible for the Amazon Protection System), the Ministry of Justice, the Ministry of Regional Integration, the Ministry of Science and Technology, the Ministry of Environment, the Ministry of Health, the Ministry of Social Development, as well as the Ministry of Labor. Although many distinct intelligence organizations exist in Brazil, their missions and jurisdictions are overlapping and the whole national intelligence system (SISBIN) is characterized by low functional specialization.[47]

Three main bodies are responsible for the oversight and external control of intelligence activities in Brazil. In the executive branch, there is the Office of the Comptroller General (CGU). The Brazilian Court of Audit (TCU) has investigatory powers over civilian and military intelligence budget expenditures. In the legislative branch, there is a Joint Commission for External Control of Intelligence Activities (CCAI), but it has been facing difficulties since its inception in 2000. For instance, even in 2013, almost 14 years later, it was still not able to get its internal rules approved by National Congress, nor does the Commission have a proper budget, personnel, and secure infrastructure. Its activities are intermittent, directed by whatever appears in the media rather than by any regular effort from the Parliamentarians. As a result, the level of actual external control over intelligence in Brazil could be regarded as weak.[48]

As the institutional context is presented, it is relevant to mention that the 2008 intelligence crisis was not the first one since 1999. Actually, in the first nine years of its existence the ABIN had had five different Directors-General. Even so, the 2008 institutional crisis was the largest, not only bringing about the firing of the ABIN's fifth Director-General, but also drawing considerable attention from the political system more generally.

---

prerogatives of the military in the civilian democratic regime. On the other hand, to Marco Cepik and Thomas Bruneau, 'Brazilian National Approach Towards Intelligence: Concept, Institutions and Contemporary Challenges' in Farson et al., *Handbook of Global Security and Intelligence*, p.11: 'the case for subordinating ABIN to GSI, although this is a distortion of the spirit of the 1999 law (since the director of ABIN is a civilian whose name must be approved by the Senate and the head minister of GSI is an Army general appointed by the President of the Republic), is justified by the need to guard the President from the daily managerial demands and the potential crises resulting from scandals and/or tensions inherent to the relation between intelligence and democracy'.

[47]See Cepik and Bruneau, 'Brazilian National Approach Towards Intelligence'.

[48]See Brandao, *Serviços secretos e democracia no Cone Sul*; Joanisval Brito Gonçalves, *Atividade de inteligência e legislação correlata* (Niterói, RJ: Impetus 2010).

DEMOCRATIZATION OF INTELLIGENCE

The 2008 crisis was about legitimacy, not about the effectiveness of intelligence in Brazil. It all started with the *Satiagraha* operation, launched in 2004 by the Department of Federal Police (DPF) with the aim of investigating corruption, money laundering, and embezzlement of public funds. In July 2008, a major DPF operation resulted in arrests of powerful private sector people, including banker Daniel Dantas, president of Opportunity Group. The grant of *habeas corpus* to Dantas by the then President of the Federal Supreme Court (STF), Justice Gilmar Mendes, was followed by heated debate in the media and official circles, and it was condemned by many voices.

As the public outcry grew stronger, Justice Mendes claimed that the Office of the Federal Supreme Court Presidency had been wiretapped and was being illegally monitored by the ABIN since the court order to release the accused banker. The then Defense Minister Nelson Jobim (himself a former Federal Supreme Court judge) went public to strongly assert that the ABIN possessed equipment to intercept telephone calls, although this was barred by the 1999 intelligence law. The equipment in question had been acquired through the Public Purchasing Commission of the Army, on behalf of the GSI. During his testimony on the Parliamentary Commission of Inquiry created to investigate the wiretapping allegations in the House of Deputies (the lower chamber of the National Congress), Jobim told the commission that he had advised President Luis Inacio Lula da Silva to remove the top brass of the ABIN. However, his claims about the ABIN's illegal wiretapping capability were weakened after an independent investigation proved the equipment was designed not for communications interception, but rather to detect and neutralize illegal interception attempts.[49] The Defense Minister changed his statement after that, then denouncing an allegedly irregular participation of ABIN agents in the *Satiagraha* operation run by the DPF.

Given the escalating crisis between the Executive and the Judiciary, President Lula was forced to sack the ABIN's Director Paulo Lacerda in December 2008. Paulo Lacerda was a former Federal Police Department director who had been in charge of the ABIN since October 2007. After his fall, an intelligence officer from the ABIN, Wilson R. Trezza, was appointed as interim Director.

In 2009, the President established a Joint Ministerial Committee to review the allegations of improper collaboration between ABIN and the Federal Police in ongoing criminal investigations. The committee was coordinated

---

[49] According to Ariel Macedo de Mendonça, *A proposta de reformulação do Sistema Brasileiro de Inteligência* (Rio de Janeiro: ESG 2010) p.116, two weeks before Jobim's testimony, the Army acquisitions office released an official statement saying that the ABIN's equipment was only for the location of wiretapping attempts, not to conduct wiretapping. The same conclusion was reached by the National Institute of Criminology of the Federal Police Department in mid-September 2008. According to the same source, even the manufacturer, US Electronic Research International, issued a technical report confirming that the equipment, called Omni-Spectral Correlator (Oscor 5000), was only capable of detecting transmitters for counter-surveillance purposes.

by the GSI and had representatives from the GSI, ABIN, Ministry of Justice, Ministry of Defense, Ministry of Foreign Affairs, Ministry of Planning, Budget and Management, and the Strategic Affairs Secretariat (SAE). By April 2009, a Federal Court ruled that cooperation between the ABIN and other intelligence agencies is legal and proper under the Public Law 9883/1999 provisions and SISBIN operational agreements. From that point onwards the Joint Committee dedicated itself to review the priorities in the National Intelligence Policy, as well as the ABIN's role, and all the main institutional features of the SISBIN. The conclusions and recommendations of the Joint Committee were not made public. In any case, by the end of 2009, the ABIN's acting director Trezza had been officially appointed by the President, and his name was approved by the National Congress, as required by law, becoming the ABIN's sixth director in less than 10 years. For all practical purposes, the intelligence related portion of the *Satiagraha* crisis was over without major institutional consequences.[50]

It is noteworthy that all intelligence crises in Brazil since 1999 have been related to the lack of jurisdictional clarity among SISBIN agencies regarding their missions, priorities, and degree of subordination to the ABIN's formal role as the central agency.[51] Yet, intelligence reform has been a low-priority issue for the Brazilian political system since the transition to democracy was completed more than 20 years ago. Likewise, all crises were also driven by legitimacy concerns. Even so, the National Congress failed repeatedly to address the lackluster record of the CCAI.

The absence of clear mandates and missions among SISBIN agencies is the result of unresolved disputes between established bureaucracies coupled with the low priority given to the problem by politicians. During his short term as Director-General, Paulo Lacerda was pursuing better integration and consolidation of the SISBIN through the creation of a Department of SISBIN Integration (DISBIN).[52] In that sense, his fall may have contributed to the restoration of *status quo ante*, even if the department still exists. As for the CCAI and the National Congress, the intelligence crises are recurrent but minor in political terms, mainly because their national security consequences are not considered too pressing by the political elites.

---

[50] By September 2013, Mr Trezza remained the ABIN's director in the midst of another intelligence crisis, prompted by Snowden's leaked documents including ones on US National Security Agency (NSA) spying on Brazil. See 'As Brazil's Uproar over NSA Grows, US Vows to Work through Tensions' <http://edition.cnn.com/2013/09/11/world/americas/brazil-nsa/index.html> (accessed 11 September 2013).

[51] Soon after president Dilma Rousseff took office, a group of ABIN Intelligence Officers delivered a letter to the new incumbent, complaining about the subordination of the ABIN to the GSI and demanding closer access to the President. See 'Abin repudia controle militar em carta a Dilma e rejeita ser "Tropa do Elito"' <http://www.estadao.com.br/estadaodehoje/20110208/not_imp676571,0.php> (accessed 24 July 2011).

[52] See Carlos Ataides, 'La visión de Brasil sobre la Comunidad de Inteligencia Sudamericana y la Experiencia de la ABIN en los servicios de Inteligencia del Estado' in Freddy Velez Rivera (ed.) *Inteligencia estratégica y prospectiva* (Quito: FLACSO-SENAIN-AECID 2011) pp.127–36.

This relaxed attitude towards intelligence reform defies understanding in a country where 43,909 homicides were committed in 2009 alone.[53] Besides, Brazil's international role is rapidly increasing, and the country prepares itself to deal with big international events like the football World Cup in 2014, and the Olympic Games in 2016. Both factors indicate that intelligence effectiveness issues will soon add pressure to reform the intelligence sector in Brazil.

Colombia: Between Politicization and Counter-Insurgence, Hazardous Intelligence

Following the new Constitution of 1991, a National Intelligence System (SINAI) was formally established in Colombia. Although a lot has changed since President Ernesto Samper issued the Presidential Decree 2,233, in December 1995, that was the first time the Political System tried to make sense of intelligence as an important subsystem in Colombia.[54]

According to Presidential Decree number 3,600, issued by President Uribe in 2009, there were seven main intelligence agencies in Colombia. The General Intelligence Directory of the Administrative Department of Security (DAS) is the main intelligence organization in the country. There are two more major civilian agencies, the Intelligence Directory (DIPOL) of the National Police, and the Treasury's Unit of Information and Financial Analysis (UIAF). The main military intelligence units are the respective directories of the Army, Navy, and Air Force. The general staff of the Armed Forces also has its own Directory of Intelligence and Counterintelligence, which is the seventh distinct intelligence unit. All of them have been part of the SINAI since 1995. Despite the formal existence of a National Intelligence System, Colombia is characterized by low functional specialization with two basic distinct public perceptions regarding intelligence. One is related to the traditional politicization and corruption identified with the DAS and its main competitor, the DIPOL. Another *ethos* is the all-encompassing counter-insurgency role of the Colombian armed forces. Both of them are prone to produce Human Rights abuses and poor performance in terms of building state capacity. Especially in a country like Colombia, where prolonged armed

---

[53] See UNODC, *The Global Study on Homicide* (Vienna: United Nations Office on Drugs and Crime 2011).

[54] As Steven Boraz, 'Colombia' in Farson et al. (eds.) *Handbook of Global Security and Intelligence*, pp.130–45, points out, Samper's term as president (1994–8) was a very troubled one, mainly because of the strained relations with United States. For a thorough review of intelligence in Colombia, see Alexander Arciniegas, 'Inteligencia en democracias: La crisis del servicio de inteligencia colombiano' in M. Cepik (eds.) *Inteligência governamental: Casos nacionais e desafios contemporâneos* (Niterói, RJ: Impetus 2011) pp.97–114; Steven Boraz, 'Establishing Democratic Control of Intelligence in Colombia', *International Journal of Intelligence and Counterintelligence* 19/2 (2006) pp.84–109; Boraz, 'Colombia', 2008; and Douglas Porch 'Taming a "Dysfunctional Beast"' – Reforma in Colombia's Departamento Administrativo de Securidad', *International Journal of Intelligence and Counterintelligence* 22/3 (2009) pp.421–51.

conflict, high rates of violent crime, and the exportation of illegal drugs have combined to form a rather complex situation in the last decades.

Although military intelligence was also associated with power abuses, scandals, and crises in Colombia during the counterinsurgency campaign against the Revolutionary Armed Forces of Colombia (FARC), our focus here is the role of DAS during Uribe's presidency (2002–10). Since its formation in 1960, the intelligence component of the DAS has been involved in recurrent scandals. There are cultural, historical, and institutional causes in Colombia for this recurring problem. One of these causes is the high organizational centrality of the President in the Colombian intelligence system and the resulting politicization of the main intelligence agencies, which undermines both the legitimacy and the effectiveness of Colombian intelligence. 'The proximity between DAS ... and the President politicized it and focused its intelligence missions in the political survival of the President. The lack of oversight manifests an attitude that intelligence is above the law'.[55]

DAS-related scandals recurred in Colombia from 2005 to 2009, the time frame this article is concerned with. In 2005, for instance, the links between the DAS Director, Jorge Noguera, and paramilitary leaders raised great debates about the morality, the organization and the professionalism of the agency. Under the Noguera administration, the DAS was accused of extinguishing paramilitary crimes data, promoting electoral fraud to ensure that Uribe supporters would be elected, wiretapping investigations of police and offering lists of unionist and left-wing teachers to paramilitary groups. Another serious complaint was a plan, supported by the Director's right-hand man, Enrique Ariza, to construct an intelligence arrangement inside the DAS, which would be paid for by the paramilitaries to operate for them. This was all part of a bigger scandal known as *parapolítica* in Colombia.[56]

In 2009, the crisis became even more serious as the practice known in Colombia as *chuzadas* (illegal communications interceptions) threatened to compromise Uribe's entire coalition. In January, the DAS counterintelligence department destroyed various box files, computer hard-drives, tapes, and transcriptions. They contained the result of years of espionage against judges, prosecutors, human rights defenders, political opposition, Supreme Court judges, ministers, journalists, police, and military officers. One month later this deed was made public by magazine 'Semana' and the TV channel 'Bogotá Notícias Uno'. Evidence to support the reports was found by a series of inspections in DAS buildings ordered by the Office of the Attorney General. The discoveries ranged from illegal wiretapping to false propaganda against Uribe opponents in 2006 elections.

After judicial investigations, dozens of people and at least 10 important members of the Uribe government were prosecuted, including three former directors of the DAS.[57] Jorge Noguera (director from 2002 to 2005) was declared ineligible (*inhabilitado*) for 18 years. Andres Peñate (director from

---

[55] Porch, 'Taming a "Dysfunctional Beast"', p.445.
[56] Boraz, 'Colombia', p.137.
[57] Porch, 'Taming a "Dysfunctional Beast"', p.422.

2005 to 2007) was also declared ineligible for eight months on the grounds that he failed to denounce the illegal activities. Maria del Pilar Hurtado (director from 2007 to 2008) became a fugitive wanted by the Colombia Justice. In December 2010, the government of Panama granted political asylum to Ms Hurtado, who could directly implicate former president, Alvaro Uribe.

Because of the 'bursting' effects of the *parapolítica* and *chuzadas* scandals to the legitimacy of the intelligence sector in Colombia, as well as because of the 2010 elections, President Uribe announced legal and administrative intelligence reforms. The new legal framework was introduced to the National Congress as Law Project 1288 on 5 March 2009. Meanwhile, President Uribe signed Executive Decree 3,600 on 21 September 2009, with the same provisions. The main improvements brought by the regulations were the establishment of a more delimited scope for intelligence and counterintelligence activities, supervision systems and operations control, better information security procedures, more accountable intelligence budget, as well as identity protection and personnel security for the intelligence services and units.[58] Another Law Project (number 189) was sent by the government to the National Congress on 8 October 2009. Basically, the new law would suppress the DAS, transferring its intelligence functions to a new Central Intelligence Agency (ACI).[59]

Trying to boost the effectiveness of the intelligence was a subsidiary goal, to be achieved through better coordination. The Presidential Decree 3,600 also established the mandate of a Joint Intelligence Council (JIC) to coordinate the analysis of all information obtained by any agency through the establishment of an Interagency Center for Information Analysis and Fusion (CEFAI).[60] In practice, the JIC operates primarily as a forum where intelligence agency leaders deliberate about tactical and operational matters, like target selection or specific covert collection operational planning. This lack of strategic clout may be caused by overreliance on the only other intelligence tradition Colombia has besides political intelligence, that is, the US inspired and financed intelligence support for counterinsurgency military operations.[61]

In 2011, the Constitutional Court ruled the Law Project 1288 as unconstitutional on the grounds that a statutory law was necessary. Such a statutory law project was sent by President Santos to the National Congress

---

[58] < http://www.secretariasenado.gov.co/senado/basedoc/ley/2009/ley_1288_2009.htm> (accessed 27 October 2011).

[59] As of October 2011, the DAS continued to exist in its previous incarnation. See <http://www.das.gov.co> (accessed 13 October 2011).

[60] Arciniegas, 'Inteligencia en democracias', p.104.

[61] According to Porch, 'Taming a "Dysfunctional Beast"', p.442: 'this probably contributed to the international outcry that surrounded *operación fénix*, the killing of FARC's "foreign minister", Raúl Reyes, on Ecuadorian soil in February 2008. Much of the ruckus was orchestrated by Venezuela's President Hugo Chavez, certainly, but the focus on HVTs appears to have blinded President Uribe to the strategic repercussions of his "tactical" action'.

in 2011, with much more detailed regulations for intelligence and counterintelligence. The legislative proceedings of the project were progressing well as of October 2011, but to avoid the multiple veto points of Colombian politics the Santos government issued the Presidential Decree 4057 (31 October 2011) to eliminate the DAS altogether, a process scheduled to be completed by October 2013.[62]

South Africa: A Stress Test for the External Control Mechanisms

The intelligence laws of 1994, the White Paper on Intelligence of 1995, and the 1996 South African Constitution defined the basic features of the post-Apartheid South African national intelligence system.[63] The three parliamentary acts of 1994 are of particular interest. The Intelligence Services Act 1994 created the National Intelligence Agency (NIA) for domestic intelligence and the South African Security Service (SASS) for foreign intelligence. The National Strategic Intelligence Act 1994 determined the activities of the members from the National Intelligence Structure, which includes the NIA, the SASS, the Crime Intelligence component of the South African Police Service (SAPS), and the Intelligence Division of the South African National Defence Force (SANDF). Furthermore, it established the National Intelligence Coordinating Committee (NICOC), a senior council bringing together the heads of the services. This Act also created the Ministry of Intelligence, with direct authority over the NIA and the SASS. The Minister was responsible for the supervision and general superintendence of the intelligence services, policy formulation, guidance and direction of transformation processes, and the general conduct of intelligence.[64] Finally, it is important to mention the Committee of Members of Parliament and Inspectors General of Intelligence Act 1994, which created the Office of the Inspector-General of Intelligence (OIGI) and the parliamentary Joint Standing Committee on Intelligence (JSCI).

The post-Apartheid mandates, functions, agencies, and controls of the South African national intelligence system rapidly converted South Africa into a model for democratic governance of developing countries,[65] with intelligence legislation and governance arrangements favorably comparable

---

[62]The full text of executive decrees, law projects, and legislation is available at <http://www.senado.gov.co/az-legislativo>. The full text of the Colombian Constitutional Court rule (Sentencia C-913/10) is available at <http://www.corteconstitucional.gov.co> (accessed 12 October 2011).

[63]This is not as obvious as it seems. During the context of profound political change, as during the transition to democratic regimes, the intelligence subsystem usually is marginalized or even excluded from the democratization and security sector reform agendas. For an interesting view about the constitution as a primary frame of the maintenance and the transformation of South Africa's Intelligence, see Laurie Nathan, 'Intelligence Bound: The South African Constitution and Intelligence Services', *International Affairs* 86 (2010) pp.195–210.

[64]See <www.gov.za/ministry/intelligence.php> (accessed 23 July 2011).

[65]Lauren Hutton, 'Looking Beneath the Cloak: An Analysis of Intelligence Governance in South Africa', ISS Paper 154 (2007) pp.1–24.

with those in more established democracies.[66] However, the new system was not free of institutional frictions. First, to implement the *Batho Pele* process in the intelligence services was at least as hard as doing it in the Police or Armed Forces.[67] Changing deeply ingrained organizational cultures formed in the historical context of the Apartheid regime and the struggle against it proved very challenging for the new South Africa. As a result of this political and historical structure, a secretive intelligence mindset and the belief that bending the rules can enhance effectiveness are features of South Africa's intelligence culture.[68]

Though the effectiveness of South African intelligence services has never been an item of public questioning, there were several reports criticizing the misconduct of intelligence officers or questioning the legality of specific acts. The NIA, in particular, was accused on several occasions of illegal spying, partisan involvement, political interference, and the use of overly intrusive methods.[69] The legitimacy issues peaked in 2005, breaking the tension threshold as the biggest crisis of contemporary South Africa's intelligence history erupted.

In 2005, Ronnie Kasrils, the then minister of intelligence, received a complaint from a senior member of the African National Congress (ANC) about the NIA's illegal surveillance operations. Kasrils requested the Inspector General to investigate the case, which found that 'the National Intelligence Agency (NIA) had conducted illegal surveillance and that the Director General of the Agency, Billy Masetlha, had unlawfully intercepted the communication of ruling party and opposition politicians'.[70]

The origins of this case were in Project Avani, an intelligence project aimed to estimate the impact of the ANC's presidential succession dispute on the stability of the country. Through this project the NIA had allegedly intercepted emails from high-profile political figures purportedly conspiring to thwart Jacob Zuma's bid to become the ANC president. After investigations by the Joint Standing Committee on Intelligence (JSCI) and

---

[66]Keneth Dombroski, 'Transforming Intelligence in South Africa' in Thomas Bruneau and Steven Boraz (eds.) *Reforming Intelligence: Obstacles to Democratic Control and Effectiveness* (Austin, TX: University of Texas Press 2007) pp.241–68. See also Nathan, 'Intelligence Bound', pp.195–210.

[67]*Batho Pele* is a Sesotho word meaning 'People First'. It was an initiative launched in 1997 to transform the South African Public Service at all levels. In the Armed Forces and the Intelligence it also meant to amalgamate the former enemy organizations into a new and cohesive system.

[68]For a historical analysis of South Africa's intelligence services since the Apartheid period and during the transition towards the democratic regime, see Dombroski, 'Transforming Intelligence in South Africa', pp.241–68, and also Kevin O'Brien, 'South Africa' in Farson et al. (eds.) *Handbook of Global Security and Intelligence*, pp.619–48.

[69]See Greg Hannah, Kevin O'Brien and Andrew Rathmell, *Intelligence and Security Legislation for Security Sector Reform*, Technical Report Prepared for United Kingdom's Security Sector Development Advisory Team (Rand Report, June 2005).

[70]Laurie Nathan, 'Lighting up the Intelligence Community: An Agenda for Intelligence Reform in South Africa', *African Security Review* 18/1 (2009) pp.91–2.

the Office of the Inspector-General of Intelligence (OIGI), the Inspector-General concluded that the emails had been fabricated and recommended disciplinary action and criminal charges against those responsible. Minister Kasrils fired two senior NIA officials found responsible for the mischief and President Mbeki dismissed Masetlha in March 2006.[71]

Although the crisis was in a part a result of the lack of proactive oversight of intelligence activities, it also constituted an important stress test to the *ex post* functioning of oversight and external control mechanisms.[72] The Inspector General, the Ministry of Intelligence, and the JSCI performed well and played a vital stabilizing function to the intelligence subsystem by helping it to improve and adapt. However, as the intelligence related crisis was also a manifestation of the internecine conflict within the ANC between the Mbeki and the Zuma camps, the crisis continued to evolve.

In 2006, among other emergency measures, Kasrils summoned a special commission to review legislation related to intelligence.[73] The Ministerial Review Commission on Intelligence, consisting of the Chairperson Mr Joe Matthews, Dr Frene Ginwala, and Mr Laurie Nathan, after long comparative research into intelligence control mechanisms and a series of discussions with government and top officials of the South African government, submitted the final report in August 2008. The recommended reforms concerned intelligence adherence to the constitution; the Intelligence White Paper; ministerial control and responsibilities; the mandate of the NIA; and intrusive measures and transparency.

One month after the final report's submission, on 25 September, Kasrils resigned from his post in solidarity with President Mbeki, who had resigned from the Presidency the day before, after he was recalled by the African National Congress's National Executive Committee. However, 'on the eve of his departure Kasrils declassified the commission's report, resulting in an unprecedented public disclosure of classified intelligence policies. The NIA attempted unsuccessfully to block the publication of the report'.[74]

---

[71] Nathan, 'Intelligence Bound', p.199.

[72] For a historical analysis of South African intelligence accountability mechanisms, see Kevin O'Brien, 'Controlling the Hydra: A Historical Analysis of South African Intelligence Accountability' in H. Born, Lock Johnson and Ian Leigh, *Who's Watching the Spies? Establishing Intelligence Service Accountability* (Washington, DC: Potomac Books 2005); Hutton, 'Looking Beneath the Cloak', pp.1–24; Lauren Hutton, 'Intelligence and Accountability in Africa', ISS Policy Brief no. 2 (2009).

[73] 'In the wake of the crisis Kasrils took three measures aimed at preventing further acts of illegality, all of them expressly promoting the constitution as the primary basis for the good conduct, socialization, and reform of the intelligence services. First, he issued a statement entitled "Five principles of Intelligence service professionalism" (...) Second, Kasrils instructed the intelligence chiefs to develop a civic culture education programme for the services in order to promote and entrench a culture of respect for the constitution and the rule of law'; Nathan, 'Intelligence Bound', p.201. See more about these measures in Ronnie Kasrils, 'To Spy or Not to Spy? Intelligence and Democracy in South Africa' in Lauren Hutton (ed.) *To Spy or Not to Spy? Intelligence and Democracy in South Africa* (Pretoria: ISS Monograph 157 2009).

[74] Nathan, 'Lighting up the Intelligence Community', p.93.

South African public attention was focused on the government crisis; as a result, the final reports were not utilized as a pressing instrument to recall the intelligence reform to the political agenda of the macro-system. When intelligence reform finally came a year later, it was not what the Commission had in mind.

Through Proclamation number 59 of 2009, the new President Jacob Zuma established the State Security Agency (SSA).[75] The new agency, led by its first director Ambassador Mzuvukile Maqetuba, was placed under the authority of the Minister of State Security (formerly known as the Minister of Intelligence Services). The new organization brought together as departments of the SSA the main agencies of the former intelligence dispensation. The former National Intelligence Agency (NIA) became the Domestic Branch, the former South African Secret Service (SASS) became the Foreign Branch, and the South African National Academy of Intelligence (SANAI) became the Intelligence Academy. The organizational structure of the SSA also comprises the National Communications branch, which brought together the former National Communications Centre (NCC), the former Office of Interception Centres (OIC), and the Electronic Communications Security Pty Ltd (COMSEC).

The new SSA priorities were distilled by President Zuma and the new Minister of State Security, Dr Siyabonga Cwele, in a series of public addresses in 2010 and 2011. Unsurprisingly, the SSA intelligence priorities are terrorism, sabotage against critical infrastructure, subversion, counter-espionage, border management, corruption, and organized crime.

More important, the rationale for the centralizing approach of this reform was presented by Minister Cwele on the occasion of the Parliament budget vote in Cape Town, in June 2011:

> (1) The development of an integrated and focused multi-source collection capability that advances our national (sic) and mitigate against threats identified in the National Intelligence Estimate. (2) The development of a highly effective and target driven counterintelligence capability to defend our country's national interests; and (3) These priorities will be supported by focused skills development, improved analytic and technical capabilities, good corporate governance, accountability and an organizational culture that carefully balances secrecy required to achieve our mandate and openness based on sound values of commitment to democracy, loyalty and professionalism.[76]

The intended goals of that reform were directed more at improving effectiveness than legitimacy. Basically, they represented a departure from an

---

[75] Additional Proclamations 912, 913, 914, and 915 were made to address each of the former independent agencies as they were transformed into SSA branches. The proclamations were made under the Presidential authority provided by the National Intelligence Act, 1994 <http://www.ssa.gov.za> (accessed 10 September 2013).

[76] Address by the Minister of State Security, Dr Siyabonga Cwele on the occasion of state security budget vote, 2 June 2011 <http://www.nia.gov.za> (accessed 23 September 2011).

institutional design inspired by the New Public Management vogue, which was deemed inefficient and ineffective in the case of Defense and Intelligence in South Africa. However, since the Parliamentary Joint Standing Committee on Intelligence (JSCI) and the Office of the Inspector-General of Intelligence (OIGI) have also grown stronger after the prolonged crisis, the net effect seems, counter intuitively, to be a better equilibrium between legitimacy and effectiveness it the South African intelligence system.

India: A More Powerful System after Mumbai with Even Fewer Democratic Controls

The Intelligence Bureau (IB), the Research and Analysis Wing (RAW), and the Defence Intelligence Agency (DIA) constituted the core of the Indian national intelligence system until 2008.[77] The IB is responsible for collecting and disseminating intelligence on all matters related to internal security, including law and order, counterterrorism, counterinsurgency, VIP security, and counterintelligence. Initially, the IB was also responsible for external intelligence. Due to a lack of intelligence analysis on China and Pakistan prior to India's 1962 and 1965 wars, then Prime Minister Indira Gandhi created the Research and Analysis Wing (RAW) as India's first civilian foreign intelligence agency in 1968. Thus the RAW became responsible for collecting and disseminating intelligence related to external security, including political, military, economic, scientific, and technological issues. The RAW is subordinated to the Prime Minister, while the IB answers to the Minister of Home Affairs. The DIA, created by the 2002 reform, was the result of a series of military demands for better organization among the intelligence agencies. Directly subordinated to the Ministry of Defense, the DIA analyzes and assesses military intelligence from the perspective of the armed forces as a whole and also coordinates the directories of military, air force and naval intelligence.[78]

The Joint Intelligence Committee (JIC) is responsible for coordinating and integrating all source analysis. The JIC is subordinate to the National Security Advisor (NSA), which serves the National Security Council (NSC), the highest inter-ministerial body for decision and coordination of strategic policies in India. Under the direct authority of the NSA, there is also the National Technical Research Organization (NTRO), which is a relatively autonomous agency responsible for reconnaissance missions and surveillance satellites. The NTRO also has direct authority over an All India Radio Monitoring Service (AIRMS). The Aviation Research Center (ARC), in turn, used to be a department of the RAW before growing such in size and importance as to become independent from the Wing. Being responsible for aerospace platforms as well as reconnaissance and surveillance aircraft, the ARC is now a direct subordinate of the NSA and aims at collecting and analyzing imagery.

---

[77] See Robert Henderson, *International Intelligence Yearbook*, 2nd ed. (Washington: Brassey's 2004).

[78] See Rahul Roy-Chaudhury, 'India' in Farson et al. (eds.) *Handbook of Global Security and Intelligence*, pp.211–29.

The three Armed Forces have their own intelligence sector: the Directorate of Military Intelligence (DMI), the Directorate of Naval Intelligence (DNI), and the Directorate of Air Intelligence (DAI). The most relevant agency within the Armed Forces is the DMI, which has its own Signals Intelligence Directorate (SID) – Indian's largest *sigint* agency – and for *imint*, the Defence Image Processing and Analysis Centre (DIPAC). Moreover, the DMI is also responsible for India's *humint*, mainly in the border regions with Pakistan and Bangladesh. The Joint Cipher Bureau (JCB) is another agency subordinated to the Ministry of Defence: its primary function is supplying the government with values and codes intercepted and solved. The JCB is also responsible for signals intelligence and cipher activities and for providing coordination and direction to other military service organizations with missions similar to the SID.[79]

India's vast intelligence system has evolved over the years by increasing its level of functional specialization, mainly in response to failures. Before the Mumbai attacks, the previous broad reform of the intelligence system had been in 2002 and resulted from a 1999 report by the Kargil Review Committee (KRC) – the first official report made public on an intelligence failure. The main goals of this reform were to improve the system's surveillance capacity and to avoid security failures like those reported by the KRC. The most important innovations settled by this rearrangement were the reorganization of military intelligence through the creation of the Defence Intelligence Agency (DIA), and the technical update of captured image and signals, economic intelligence, and counterintelligence data.[80]

However, the terrorist attacks of 26 November 2008 in Mumbai unleashed a new intelligence and security-related crisis. The combined attacks left at least 172 victims. Evidence suggests that Lashkar-e-Taiba (LeT), a terrorist group based in Pakistan, was responsible for the attack. The group landed on the beaches of Mumbai with a captured Indian fishing boat and used small weapons – such as automatic rifles, pistols, machine guns, and grenades – to perform multiple simultaneous attacks in different locations. The complexity of the attack, the audacity and ambition of the objectives, the diversity of the targets, and the length of the raid – it took about 60 hours until the Indian security forces were able to neutralize the terrorists – led to public criticism and perception of a major intelligence failure.

According to a study performed by the RAND Corporation,[81] the Mumbai attacks underscored several weaknesses in the structure of counterterrorist security of India. Among the key weaknesses were the failures of intelligence, especially regarding the lack of coordination between the central intelligence agencies – RAW and IB – and the local police; and problems of coastal surveillance including the lack of personnel, equipment, and appropriate

---

[79]IBPUS, *India: Intelligence & Security Activities and Operations Handbook*, 4th ed. (Washington, DC: International Business Publications 2008) p.55.
[80]Rahul Roy-Chaudhury, 'India', 2009.
[81]Angel Rabasa et al., *The Lessons of Mumbai* (Santa Monica, CA: RAND Corporation 2009) pp.9–12.

resources of the Coast Guard. The response was also too slow, as the first local army contingent arrived at the attacks location five hours after they had started, and the special unit of the National Security Guard (NSG), the 'Black Cat Commandos', began the first operations of search-and-rescue (SAR) only after a delay of nine hours. Local police were passive in the face of the situation; lacking adequate counterterrorism training and not knowing exactly what to do, their weapons and personal protection were also much poorer than those of the terrorists.[82]

Furthermore, the 2008 terrorist attack in Mumbai was not the deadliest. In July 2006, a series of simultaneous bomb attacks in the city's train system killed nearly 190 people. However, despite its magnitude, the attack of 2006 and other previous attacks were not able to draw the attention of the macro-political system to the internal security problems. The main difficulties in capturing the attention of the political system for security reforms are inter-agency disputes and legal uncertainties as to the jurisdiction of each federal and state level entity. Up to 2008, relatively few initiatives had been taken by the federal government, for internal security is the responsibility of each state government.

According to Fair,[83] the factors that explain why the Mumbai attacks were able to trigger reform processes in homeland security and intelligence, unlike the other attacks, are the clear foreign nature of the attack itself and blanket coverage by the media; the strong mobilization of the Indian corporate elite in connection with the need for India to deal with national security; the regional and global strategic context in which the event was inserted, and the initiative of specific political leaders.

Days after the Mumbai attacks, Home Minister Shivraj Patil resigned his position and was replaced by then Minister of Finance C. Chidambaram. On 11 December 2008, with the support of Prime Minister Manmohan Singh, Chidambaram announced a series of proposed reforms to internal security, including the creation of a Coastal Command, the establishment of 20 counterterrorism training centers, a counterterrorism task force with units deployed in various states, the creation of a national agency to investigate terrorist activities, and the tightening of anti-terrorist laws.[84] Just six days later, the lower house (Lok Sabha) and the upper house (Rajya Sabha) of the National Congress approved amendments to the Indian Unlawful Activities (Prevention) Act 1979 'to incorporate more stringent provisions for search and arrest of suspected terrorists, filing of charge sheet, speedy trial in a special court, power of detention (up to 180 days), public prosecutor's plea to be heard before granting bail, and so on'.[85] It also established the National Investigation

---

[82] For a more detailed description of the relationship between intelligence and security in India see N.C. Ashtana and Anjali Nirmal, *Intelligence and Security Management* (Jaipur: Pointer 2004), especially parts IV and V.
[83] C. Christine Fair, 'Prospects for Effective Internal Security Reforms in India', 2011 <http://ssrn.com/abstract=1885488> (accessed 20 August 2011).
[84] Ibid.
[85] Subhash Sharma and Devendra Mishra, 'Terrorism: Problem and Prospects', *The Indian Police Journal* 58/3 (2010).

Agency (NIA) to be responsible for counterterrorism intelligence. Despite the establishment of NSG units in different cities (Mumbai, Kolkata, Bangalore, Chennai, and Hyderabad), problems of equipment, transportation, and logistics have yet to be addressed.

Although several similar changes were examined, suggested, and even enacted into law in 2002, many of them only became effective after the 2008 attacks in Mumbai. An example of this is the operational activation of the Multi-Agency Centre (MAC), whose primary function is improving interagency cooperation through the analysis and dissemination of information to the integrated agencies in real time.

The National Intelligence Grid (NATGRID) is part of the 2008 reform project, being a large nationally integrated database that can be accessed by all security agencies in the country. The NATGRID, originally scheduled for 2011, was finally approved by the Cabinet Committee of Security and entered into operation in 2012. Considering the efforts to improve inter-agency information flow, the Crime and Criminal Tracking Network and Systems (CCTNS), expected to complete by 2015, will connect India's 16,000 police stations in order to improve crime control and respond to the challenges of counterterrorism.

Another major project launched by Chidambaram was the National Counter-Terrorism Center (NCTC), which was supposed to start operation in late 2010. The NCTC would be responsible for directly coordinating the activities of the NIA, NTRO, JIC, and NSG, while the RAW, ARC, and CBI would cede part of their staff and resources to the new agency.[86] The objective would be to centralize counterterrorism-related intelligence efforts to increase the effectiveness and the capacity to cooperate among agencies.

The creation of the NCTC was the biggest challenge for the proposed Chidambaram reforms, for it would establish a new power configuration, both in the macro-system of Indian government and in the subsystem of security agencies. The empowerment of the Ministry of Home Affairs is grounded on the argument that it is necessary for the Ministry to focus exclusively on internal security. This ended up weakening the role and relevance of the NSA, who previously reported directly to Prime Minister, but now would start to attend daily meetings at the Ministry of Home Affairs. Creating the NCTC further weakens the NSA, since it would lose the direct and exclusive command of the JIC, NTRO, and ARC. Essentially, from day one the central intelligence agencies in India tried to block the creation of the NCTC. For example, the RAW did not accept the transfer of part of its staff and resources and was unwilling to lose its direct channel of communication with the Prime Minister. Also, the IB did not accept losing its role of protagonist in the fight against terrorism. Besides, the NCTC did not emerge until 2013 because of strong opposition from non-Congress state chief ministers.[87]

---

[86]Fair, 'Prospects for Effective Internal Security Reforms in India', p.25.

[87]Ibid, p.26. See also 'Centre May Make Fresh Attempt to Push NCTC' <http://articles.timesofindia.indiatimes.com/2013-07-09/india/40467981_1_anti-terror-body-nctc-national-counter-terrorism-centre> (accessed 14 September 2013).

Chidambaram was harshly criticized for what was perceived as his failure to tackle left-wing Naxalite-Maoist insurgency and to prevent the July 2011 Mumbai bombings, and when he finished his stint as Home Minister and became Finance Minister again in 2011, the NCTC had lost its main political support.

Although the reforms were not completed, the new institutional configuration of internal security in India promoted by Chidambaram may increase the effectiveness of the intelligence services. But it also has contributed to further weakening of external control mechanisms of intelligence and security agencies, which may, in the long term, compromise the legitimacy of the system.

Conclusion

After reviewing intelligence-related institutional crises in Brazil, Colombia, South Africa, and India, we can summarize the results of our observations in Table 1.

As explained by Punctuated Equilibrium theory, institutional crises are inevitable due to the complex nature of networked agents' (individuals or institutions) decision processes, enhanced by tensions between security and democracy. Crises affect the evolution of national intelligence systems by increasing the demand for better effectiveness and legitimacy. However, the actual change resulting from each of the intelligence related crises studied here depended on the degree of functional specialization already present in the system, as well as the degree of external public control. The kind of issue (legitimacy or effectiveness) causing the breaking of a tension threshold between retarding and transforming forces was also important, but not decisive.

In South Africa, a more established mechanism of democratic external control provided for a more balanced result concerning the legitimacy and effectiveness requirements when President Zuma decided to engage in the wholesale transformation of the intelligence system profile. At the same time, a higher degree of functional specialization made the national intelligence system better prepared to adapt itself and improve its effectiveness. South Africa has experienced the biggest institutional impact coming out of an intelligence crisis among the four cases.

In stark contrast, Colombia had a low degree of functional specialization among its virtually independent intelligence services, a very low level of external control, and long-standing concerns about legitimacy due to established practices of political espionage and obscure links with paramilitaries and drug traffickers. The *chuzadas* case was not the first intelligence-related crisis to bring into question the legitimacy of the DAS and the need to reform Colombian intelligence. Unfortunately, despite great political turmoil associated with the intelligence crisis, the higher friction rate and the delay of another attempt to reform the system indicate that a new intelligence crisis looms further down the Colombian road.

Brazil and India, the bigger players, showed a more mixed picture. In Brazil no one seems to worry much about intelligence effectiveness, as long as the

Table 1. Intelligence Crises and Institutional Change in Four Countries.

		Brazil	Colombia	South Africa	India
Independent variables	Degree of functional specialization inside the national intelligence system before the crisis	Low	Low	High	High
	Degree of external public control over the national intelligence system before the crisis	Medium	Low	High	Low
	Main driver of the intelligence crisis: Legitimacy (L) or Effectiveness (E)	L	L	L	E
Dependent variable	Amount of institutional change in the aftermath of the intelligence crisis	Low	Low	High	Medium

SISBIN members play by the democratic rules of the game. The country is characterized by a low level of functional specialization among its intelligence agencies, as well as by a weak presence of external control mechanisms, and punctuated attention to legitimacy issues concerning specific operations, attitudes, or particular institutional arrangements (the role and the proper place of the ABIN, for instance). The 2008 crisis, despite the fall of another ABIN Director-General and renewed public discussion about intelligence in the national political macro-system, has yet to bring any institutional change. The emergent issues associated with South America integration, greater global involvement, and big events to be held in the country from 2012 to 2016, combined with the strong managerial profile of President Dilma Rousseff and renewed political conflicts in the streets, may transform intelligence effectiveness into a more prominent item of the Brazilian policy-making agenda.

In India nobody seems to worry much about intelligence legitimacy. Its national intelligence system is bigger and much more differentiated, presenting a higher level of functional specialization. However, the main intelligence agencies in India are simply not accountable to Parliament. On top of a low degree of external control, an intelligence crisis driven by effectiveness concerns regarding counterterrorism capabilities was followed by partially frustrated reforms, despite the amount of technical, budgetary, organizational, legal, and political clout brought by Union Minister of Home Affairs, P. Chidambaram.

In the four cases, the transformational burst generated by the crisis was difficult to turn into substantial changes. The NATGRID delays and the opposition towards NCTC in India, the failed reforms in Colombia, and the institutional *stasis* in Brazil illustrate the point. Again, the unanticipated turn reforms experienced in South Africa is the outlier case in our study. Unfortunately, the more common result regarding intelligence systems seems to be a high rate of crisis recurrence.

Much more comparative research is necessary to assess intelligence systems in various countries, effectively testing if less functionally differentiated and less democratic controlled ones are more prone to crisis and learn less from its recurrent crises.[88] Punctuated Equilibrium theory is just one of the tools available to those committed to such an endeavor in the years ahead.

Acknowledgements

We are very thankful to Marina Caparini, Eduardo Estévez, Peter Gill and the anonymous reviewers of *Intelligence and National Security* for the insightful comments on earlier versions of this article. We also would like to express our gratitude to Airton Martins for his generous help throughout the editing process. Ana Julia Possamai, Bruno Kern, Gustavo Moller, Marjorie Stadnik, and Pedro Marques also gave much valued input. Peter Gill and Michael Andregg deserve extra thanks for their patience with our delays. The Brazilian National Research Council (CNPq) has supported our research on governmental intelligence for many years now, including this article.

---

[88]Warner, 'Building a Theory of Intelligence Systems', p.37.

Comparing Intelligence Democratization in Latin America: Argentina, Peru, and Ecuador Cases

EDUARDO E. ESTÉVEZ

ABSTRACT This article aims to contribute to the understanding of the intelligence democratization process in new democracies comparing three South American countries: Ecuador, Peru, and Argentina. With a background of authoritarian legacies ('political police' style intelligence agencies controlled by the military) under particular political circumstances and changing strategic environments, these countries experienced disparate trajectories, prescriptions, and outcomes in their efforts to reform their intelligence communities. Drawing on new institutionalism, historical moments and relevant events shaping the dynamics of intelligence democratization are highlighted for each case, depicting failures and successes, and identifying drivers of change.

Introduction

Characterized as a 'Sisyphean effort', democratization of intelligence is not an impossible undertaking,[1] but certainly not an easy one. Since the 1980s, Latin American democracies engaged in reinstating democratic values and practices and on holding the military accountable, while eventually reviewing their violent pasts. Concurrently, most of these countries are still overcoming the authoritarian legacy of intelligence agencies that acted as 'political police', even performed criminal activities affecting human rights on grounds of national security, counterterrorism, or plainly regime protection. According to a recent assessment, South American intelligence agencies

---

[1]Thomas Bruneau and Cris Matei, 'Intelligence in the Developing Democracies: The Quest for Transparency and Effectiveness' in L.K. Johnson (ed.) *The Oxford Handbook of National Security Intelligence* (Oxford: Oxford University Press 2010) p.771.

confront two types of dilemma:[2] old ones such as lack of legitimacy, de-professionalization, absence of national intelligence systems, militarization, policialization,[3] and politicization; and modern ones such as foreign interference, remilitarization, privatization of intelligence, and failed or unfinished reforms.

The process of intelligence democratization, immersed in the political arena of new democracies, is sometimes overlooked. Scholars of intelligence studies considered it essential to focus on comparative research,[4] and called for systematic studies on the relationship between politics and intelligence.[5]

This article contributes to the understanding of this process, comparing three South American countries: Ecuador, Peru, and Argentina. Under particular historical and political circumstances, and changing strategic environments, these countries experienced disparate trajectories, prescriptions, and outcomes in their efforts to change their intelligence communities.

Democratization of intelligence requires a framework enabling elected civilian authorities to exert control while concurrently maximizing effectiveness.[6] Regional political actors tend to approach intelligence democratization from a legal lens. This conceals aspects linked to the implementation of renewed culture and practices. Beyond legal frameworks democratically enacted, the process involves a number of actors, decisions, actions, and outcomes. This article draws on new institutionalism/historical institutionalism perspectives in order to explain the pathway to change.

The cases under comparison share similarities (for example, language, political culture, authoritarian legacies, democratic transitions, political and economic instability), but also exhibit differences in the role intelligence agencies played during dictatorship and in the efforts to put them on the right

---

[2]C. Maldonado, 'Dilemas Antiguos y Modernos en la Inteligencia Estratégica en Sudamérica', *Security and Defense Studies Review* 9/1–2 (2009) pp.50–1. For an account on legislation, see José M. Ugarte, 'América Latina, Actividad de Inteligencia y su Control. El Estado de la Cuestión', paper prepared for the 2010 Meeting of the Latin American Studies Association, Toronto, Canada, 6–9 October 2010. Also see José Manuel Ugarte, *Actividad de Inteligencia y Democracia en América Latina* (Madrid: Editorial Académica Española 2011); and C. Sancho Hirane, 'Democracia, Política Pública de Inteligencia y Desafíos Actuales: Tendencias en Países de Latinoamérica', *Inteligencia y Seguridad: Revista de Análisis y Prospectiva* 11 (2012) pp.67–102.

[3]Refers to when the police and their investigations against organized crime predominate and have 'strategic intelligence' range; Maldonado, 'Dilemas Antiguos y Modernos en la Inteligencia Estratégica en Sudamérica', p.50.

[4]K. O'Connell, 'Thinking about Intelligence Comparatively', *Brown Journal of World Affairs* 11/1 (2004) p.189; Peter Gill, 'Knowing the Self, Knowing the Other: The Comparative Analysis of Security Intelligence' in L.K. Johnson (ed.) *Handbook of Intelligence Studies* (NY: Routledge 2006) pp.82–90.

[5]Len Scott and Peter Jackson, 'Journeys in Shadows' in L. Scott and P. Jackson (eds.) *Understanding Intelligence in the Twenty-First Century: Journeys in Shadows* (London: Routledge 2004) p.21.

[6]F.C. Matei and T. Bruneau, 'Intelligence Reform in New Democracies: Factors Supporting or Arresting Progress', *Democratization* 18/3 (2011) pp.602–30.

path. In fact, timing was not the same. Historical moments of the democratic period shaped the dynamics of intelligence democratization; relevant events will be highlighted, depicting failures and successes, and identifying drivers of change. Finally, the article draws some preliminary conclusions.

A Brief Conceptual and Methodological Discussion

Peter Gill raised the importance of the historical perspective and theoretically informed comparative studies.[7] Considering that there are neither total successes nor total failures, Tom Bruneau and Cris Matei proposed some factors that support or arrest progress[8] which are helpful tools for the understanding of the intelligence sector development.

How are intelligence services democratized in new democracies? As a bureaucracy isolated by the constraints of secrecy, intelligence services are 'total institutions'.[9] Formal and informal resistance to change may arise. Thus, the institutional impact of changes may be difficult to trace. Path dependence theory, and institutional change, can be a basis to understand in greater depth the intelligence democratization process. New institutionalism and path dependence have been applied in comparative studies of intelligence and security apparatuses.[10] For process tracing, several questions are suggested: What are the steps from an intelligence service of the authoritarian regime to a service fully embedded in a democratically adopted framework? How did political leaders develop the democratic framework to change intelligence institutions, policies, practices, and even culture?

Key Concepts

What follows is a brief review of core concepts that inform the approach selected for this study. Path dependence involves conditions where legacies[11] are relevant,

---

[7]Gill, 'Knowing the Self, Knowing the Other', pp.88–9. See also the map for theorizing and researching intelligence developed by Peter Gill and Mark Phythian, *Intelligence in an Insecure World* (Cambridge: Polity Press 2006).
[8]Matei and Bruneau, 'Intelligence Reform in New Democracies'.
[9]Erving Goffman, *Asylums: Essays on the Social Situations of Mental Patients and Other Inmates* (NY: Doubleday 1961). Other authors used Goffman's concept, for example, regarding military bureaucracy. K.E. McCoy, 'Beyond Civil–Military Relations: Reflections on Civilian Control of a Private, Multinational Workforce', *Armed Forces and Society* 36/4 (2010) p.679.
[10]Priscila Carlos Brandão, *Serviços Secretos e Democracia no Cone Sul: Premissas para uma Convivência Legítima, Eficiente e Profissional* (Niterói: Editora Impetus 2010). L.P. Markowitz, 'Unlootable Resources and State Security Institutions in Tajikistan and Uzbekistan', *Comparative Political Studies* 44/2 (2011) pp.156–83; this author used the process-tracing method. See also Amy Zegart, *Flawed by Design: The Evolution of the CIA, JCS and NSC* (Stanford: Stanford University Press 1999).
[11]'Decisions taken in the past, established ways of thinking and routines [that] impact on the present', J. Beyer, 'The Same or Not the Same – On the Variety of Mechanisms of Path Dependence', *International Journal of Social Sciences* 5/1 (2010) p.1.

thus tending to institutional stability.[12] Concerning institutional change, the typology developed by Wolfgang Streeck and Kathleen Thelen[13] offers us two modes that are of interest for this article: 'conversion'[14] and 'layering'.[15]

Periods of stability may be shaken by punctuated changes: 'critical junctures',[16] 'significant changes',[17] or 'starting points'.[18] What determines the outcome is the interaction between causal mechanisms – for example, conversion and layering – and context.[19] It is significant to consider 'periodizing based on important moments in those layers of the contextual environment that are likely to be most relevant to the process and outcome of interest'.[20] Finally, 'process tracing' is relevant for comparative politics because it explains the outcomes by identifying key events, processes, or decisions that link causes with outcomes.[21]

Studying the Process of Intelligence Democratization

We need to elucidate to what extent the outcomes were due to gradual or punctuated change. In short, to understand the dynamics of stability and change, to detect starting points, significant events, critical junctures, and outcomes, we need to pass through the legacies and the process of democratization, and to identify the actors – agents of change – who were aware of the opportunities for change.

To know the status of the process, it is useful to observe the progress of the following topics: respect/violation of rights of citizens; use/misuse

---

[12]T.C. Boas, 'Conceptualizing Continuity and Change: The Composite-Standard Model of Path Dependence', *Journal of Theoretical Politics* 19/1 (2007) pp.33–4.

[13]Wolfgang Streeck and Kathleen Thelen, 'Introduction: Institutional Change in Advanced Political Economies' in W. Streeck and K. Thelen (eds.) *Beyond Continuity. Institutional Change in Advanced Political Economies* (Oxford: Oxford University Press 2005) pp.1–39. Other modes are displacement, drift, and exhaustion.

[14]Conversion means that institutions '[A]re redirected to new goals, functions, or purposes ... as a result of new environmental challenges, to which policymakers respond by deploying existing institutional resources to new ends'; ibid., p.26.

[15]Layering '[I]nvolves active sponsorship of amendments, additions, or revisions to an existing set of institutions. The actual mechanism for change is differential growth; the introduction of new elements [that] crowd out or supplant by default the old system'; ibid., p.23.

[16]Constituting branching points, triggering events that initiate processes of institutional or policy change; J.W. Hogan and D. Doyle, 'The Importance of Ideas: An A Priori Critical Juncture Framework', *Canadian Journal of Political Science* 40/4 (2007) pp.883–910.

[17]James Mahoney, 'Conceptualizing and Explaining Punctuated versus Incremental Change', paper prepared for the Annual Meetings of the American Political Science Association, Washington, DC, 2–5 September 2010, p.9.

[18]T.G. Falleti and J.F. Lynch, 'Context and Causal Mechanisms in Political Analysis', *Comparative Political Studies* 42/9 (2009) pp.1154–6.

[19]Ibid., p.1151.

[20]Ibid., p.1159.

[21]Tulia G. Falleti, 'Theory-Guided Process-Tracing in Comparative Politics: Something Old, Something New', *American Association of Political Science Newsletter*, Fall 2006.

of secret expenses; intelligence failures endangering democracy; democratic regulations; effectiveness of parliamentary control; consistency between intelligence policy and activities; access to archives of repression; media and judicial controls; changes in intelligence culture and practices; and intelligence community reliability in the international community.[22] It is important to verify also related changes in the military and police sectors.

Structural determinants also need to be considered: strategic environment, politicization, securitized domestic context, and military influence may shape the outcomes. Outcomes of such a process may be changed levels of transparency, control and effectiveness,[23] autonomy, and penetration.[24]

Roots and Common Legacies

A common feature of the countries under analysis is the legacy of military interventionism. In the context of the cold war in Latin America, 'national security doctrine' emerged as:

> [A]n idea, a doctrine, and an institution, designed to bridge the traditional division between the interest of the state abroad and those of the state at home, and to merge the culture of everyday life with that of the defense of the national interest.[25]

Linking issues such as state, development, counterinsurgency warfare, and defense, the doctrine was the ideological framework sustaining military interventions in politics.[26] Dictatorships turned their focus of attention inside societies, towards domestic security, looking for adversaries and enemies, aiming to preserve the regime. Intelligence services were instrumental for such purposes. In all three countries, 'political police' style intelligence agencies were controlled by the armed forces, oriented toward the internal enemy and the domestic political sphere.

As shown below, military regimes had substantial differences in their historical and political situations, for example, while Peru and Ecuador had progressive military regimes, Argentina had a neoliberal one.

---

[22] Eduardo E. Estévez, 'Argentina's Intelligence in the Twenty-First Century/After Twenty-Five Years of Democracy', paper delivered at the 51st International Studies Association Annual Convention, New Orleans, 17–20 February 2010.
[23] Bruneau and Matei, 'Intelligence in the Developing Democracies', p.771.
[24] See Peter Gill's typology of security intelligence services, P. Gill, 'Securing the Globe: Intelligence and the Post-9/11 Shift from "Liddism" to "Drainism"', *Intelligence and National Security* 19/3 (2004) pp.468–70.
[25] Bill Mc Sweeney, *Security, Identity, and Interests: A Sociology of International Relations* (Cambridge: Cambridge University Press 1999) p.20.
[26] See D. Pion-Berlin, 'Latin American National Security Doctrines: Hard- and Softline Themes', *Armed Forces and Society* 15/3 (1989); J. Patrice McSherry, *Incomplete Transition: Military Power and Democracy in Argentina* (NY: St Martin's Press 1997).

In a context of petroleum bonanza, the Ecuadorian military regime (1972–9) was an experiment in military reformism; a 'progressive' military engaged in a nationalist revolution characterized as 'radical praetorianism'.[27] Although they remained authoritarian, these regimes were not very repressive and did not persecute parties or labor unions: '[r]adical praetorianism [appeared] like enlightened despotism'.[28] With impressive rates of economic growth, after proposing the Integral Plan for transformation and development for 1973–7, and restructuring the agrarian sector, the military regime did not transform the country. Ecuador adopted a stockholder mentality and bureaucracy grew.[29] After the uprising of 1 September 1975 against the military regime, a slow process of democratization began; three years later, elections took place. Meanwhile in 1978, the military amended their organic law, conditioning the future president to designate a military officer as defense minister.[30] After 1979 when democracy was restored, the military remained a significant factor in politics, maintaining a planning vocation on the social and political,[31] acting as a monitor of *continuismo*.[32]

Peru has a long record of military involvement in politics. The last experience was the military regime of 1968–80. Military nationalism conceived development as a condition for a cardinal objective, security; all variables, including the protectionist economy, industrialization, and nationalization of resources, were dependent on that.[33] Military reformism intended to modernize the archaic society and to reduce external dependence; its aim was to remove internal and external barriers to achieve a harmonious development, a 'humanist revolution'.[34] With a cautious attitude toward popular participation, the regime of General Juan Velasco Alvarado (1968–75) was characterized by its paternalism, in which the people were mere spectators of the transformations. It shared common features with 'radical praetorianism'.[35] While, in the late 1970s, the military regime of General Francisco Morales Bermúdez (1975–80) tightened the actions against the

---

[27]Alain Rouquié, *The Military and the State in Latin America* (Berkeley: University of California Press 1987) p.327.

[28]Ibid., p.330.

[29]Ibid., pp.328–9; also see Rafael Correa, *Ecuador: De Banana Republic a No República* (Buenos Aires: Debate 2010) pp.35–7.

[30]Rouquié, *The Military and the State in Latin America*, p.362.

[31]T.C. Bruneau, 'Ecuador: The Continuing Challenge of Democratic Consolidation and Civil-Military Relations', *Strategic Insights* 5/2 (2006); B. García-Gallegos, 'El 20 de Abril: Presente y Pasado de un Proyecto Militar Corporativo', *Iconos. Revista de Ciencias Sociales* 23/September (2005) p.95.

[32]Juan Pablo Pitarque, 'An Armed Forces Anomaly: Key Ingredients to Ecuador's Democratic Consistency', Council on Hemispheric Affairs-COHA, Washington DC, 4 August 2010 <http://www.coha.org/an-armed-forces-anomaly-key-ingredients-to-ecuador%E2%80%99s-democratic-consistency/>.

[33]Eduardo Toche Medrano, *Guerra y Democracia: Los Militares Peruanos y la Construcción Nacional* (Lima: DESCO-CLACSO 2008) p.142.

[34]Rouquié, *The Military and the State in Latin America*, p.313.

[35]Ibid., pp.330–1.

leftists through severe police repression of social protests, and increased deportations of opponents, it was far from the levels of violence observed since 1983, when the armed forces devoted to combating guerilla warfare.[36] Army intelligence services fulfilled a key political role providing the doctrinaire frame for the reformist ideas that accompanied General Velasco Alvarado in the coup of 3 October 1968.[37]

Argentina's history of authoritarian rule began in the 1930s and culminated in the Military Junta that ruled from 1976 to 1983, widely known due to the 'disappeared'.[38] This regime, known as 'National Reorganization Process', imposed a strict market economy, executed the 'dirty war' against subversion, and became engaged in the South Atlantic conflict of 1982 with the United Kingdom concerning the Malvinas Islands.[39] To be brief, the 'dirty war'[40] was the maximization of the conjunction of state resources for the implementation of a systematic plan, where intelligence agencies became essential instruments.[41] The monitoring and infiltration actions in the education sector illustrated the scope of military intelligence activities.[42]

Peru: From Crisis to Change?[43]

The recent intelligence history of Peru moves from an abusive and illegal use of the intelligence apparatus for political and corruption purposes in the case of the administration of President Alberto Fujimori (1990–2000) and his advisor and virtual intelligence chief Vladimiro Montesinos, a period in which intelligence services co-ruled as instruments of control,[44] to the recent

---

[36]Comisión de la Verdad y Reconciliación (CVR), 'Los Períodos de la Violencia' in *Informe Final*, vol. I, 1 (Lima: CVR 2003) p.56.

[37]Fernando Rospigliosi, *Montesinos y las Fuerzas Armadas: Cómo Controló Durante una Década las Instituciones Militares* (Lima: Instituto de Estudios Peruanos 2000) p.193.

[38]For a historical perspective of the last century, see Luis A. Romero, *A History of Argentina in the Twentieth Century* (Buenos Aires: Fondo de Cultura Económica 2006).

[39]The United Kingdom refers to them as the 'Falkland Islands'. De facto president Lieutenant-General Leopoldo Galtieri's order to recover the Malvinas by military means took place on 2 April 1982.

[40]See Wolfgang Heinz, 'Determinants of Gross Human Rights Violations by State and State-Sponsored Actors in Argentina 1976–1983' in W.S. Heinz and H. Frühling (eds.) *Determinants of Gross Human Rights Violations by State and State-Sponsored Actors in Brazil, Uruguay, Chile, and Argentina (1960–1990)* (Den Haag: Kluwer Law International 1999) pp.593–737.

[41]An example is the participation of SIDE personnel in the clandestine detention center known as 'Automotores Orletti'. See Centro de Estudios Legales y Sociales (CELS), 'Justicia por los Crímenes de la Dictadura' in *Informe sobre la Situación de los Derechos Humanos en Argentina 2007* (Buenos Aires: CELS 2007) footnote 37.

[42]See Martin Edwin Andersen, *Dossier Secreto: El Mito de la Guerra Sucia* (Buenos Aires: Editorial Planeta 1993) pp.222–6.

[43]This part is based on an unpublished paper by this author: 'Intelligence in Peru: The Tortuous Quest for Democratization', June 2010.

[44]Rospigliosi, *Montesinos y las Fuerzas Armadas*, p.190.

efforts to put intelligence agencies under democratic control, while simultaneously reforming the police and defense sectors.

The mechanism of change in Peruvian intelligence democratization is 'incremental policy change': the conversion mode – old institutions with new purposes – best explains the new arrangements. The creation of the National Directorate for Intelligence (DINI) by law in 2006 appeared to be a punctuated change leading to a reform. The reform process recognizes some of the factors mentioned earlier. Those that arrest progress include the complexity of the intelligence reform process, lack of institutions and resources, competing priorities, legacies of the non-democratic past, and resistance and reluctance to reform. Lack of civilian expertise is also relevant in addition to the atmosphere of corruption (a legacy of the Fujimori-Montesinos era). Factors that support progress include the willingness of decision makers to democratize intelligence, foreign assistance, and the increased perception of the emerging threats of terrorism increasing the awareness of the need for effectiveness.

Early History

Peruvian intelligence services were born in the second half of the twentieth century in the context of military professionalization.[45] The National Intelligence Service (SIN) was formally established in January 1960 during the Presidency of Manuel Prado Ugarteche; the National Intelligence System (SINA) was created in 1970. In 1984, during the democratic transition, President Fernando Belaúnde Terry dictated the SINA and SIN laws.[46] The SIN had no authority to perform operational tasks.[47] During the 1980s, Peru experienced an increase in military intervention in politics[48] which finally erupted in the 1992 coup d'état. During his tenure, President Alan García (1985–90) attempted, with limited success, to exert civilian control over the military and the police; at the same time, internal armed conflict escalated.[49] This unexpected conflict began in May 1980, lasting until 2000. Its leading actor was the Communist Party of Peru Shining Path (*Partido Comunista del Perú Sendero Luminoso*) which promoted a prolonged people's war strategy with the purpose of destroying and replacing the democratic political system.[50] [51]

Legacy of the Fujimori-Montesinos Era

During Fujimori's administration, the militarization of the countersubversive fight was evident after legislative decrees of 'pacification' signed by the end of

---

[45] Ibid., p.191.
[46] Legislative Decrees No. 270 and No. 271 of 1984.
[47] See Sentencia Fujimori, 'Capítulo V. El Servicio de Inteligencia Nacional', Corte Suprema de Justicia de la República, Sala Penal Especial, EXP. N° A.V.19–2001 Parte II–Capítulo V–p.259.
[48] Rospigliosi, *Montesinos y las Fuerzas Armadas*, p.146.
[49] Comisión de la Verdad y Reconciliación (CVR), 'Las Fuerzas Armadas' in *Informe Final*, vol. II, 1.3 (Lima: CVR 2003) p.272 and ss.
[50] Ibid., p.248.
[51] Abimael Guzmán, leader of Shining Path, was captured on 12 September 1992.

1991.[52] President Fujimori, with military support, performed the auto-coup of 5 April 1992; Montesinos played a fundamental role in the preparation of the takeover.

The legacy consisted of an intelligence apparatus characterized by the 'stigma' of a non-democratic past, a military monopoly, and lack of professionalism. In the 1990s, under the influence of Montesinos, intelligence was subject to strong changes. Intelligence activities covered all fields and levels of national activity: ministries, public offices, regional and local governments; the SIN was also authorized to perform operations.[53] Exempt from democratic controls, the SIN of Montesinos exerted its vast power to pursue political enemies, to violate human rights, and to commit acts of corruption.[54] It conducted espionage on the military and the opposition, controlled the military intelligence, became involved in political campaigns, controlled media, and significantly increased its budget and staff.[55] Montesinos substantially modified the military intelligence arrangements; from the SIN, he ran special operations outside of the chain of command, a parallel structure for dirty jobs.[56]

The intelligence apparatus of that period was a hybrid type, with high levels of penetration of society and low autonomy because of extensive subordination to the regime but definitely not of any democratic standard.

The legacy described above was the critical juncture that generated the need to devise changes. Executive decisions, special commissions, legislative action, expert involvement, and other tools were among those chosen to promote change. The starting point differs from those seen in the other cases. In fact, the regression that the intelligence sector suffered during the Fujimori-Montesinos era is unique in the region and added a major difficulty or obstacle to change.

The New Democratic Administration's Prioritization of Intelligence

The revelation of a video showing Montesinos in an act of corruption prompted President Fujimori to promulgate a law that deactivated the SIN.[57] After Fujimori abandoned power[58] and democracy was restored, work began

---

[52]Rospigliosi, *Montesinos y las Fuerzas Armadas*, p.117.
[53]Legislative Decree No. 746 of November 1991 and Decree-Law No. 25,635.
[54]E. Obando, 'La Reestructuración de la Inteligencia en Perú: Sus Avances y sus Problemas', *Inteligencia y Seguridad, Revista de Análisis y Prospectiva* 5 (2008–2009) pp.55–6. For a study on Montesinos's bribes see John Mcmillan and Pablo Zoido, 'How to Subvert Democracy: Montesinos in Peru', CESifo Working Paper No. 1173, April 2004 <http://ssrn.com/abstract=520902>.
[55]Rospigliosi, *Montesinos y las Fuerzas Armadas*, p.202; Carlos Basombrío, 'La Inteligencia como Erosionador de la Democracia: El Caso Montesinos' in FLACSO-Chile, *Reporte del Sector de Seguridad en América Latina y el Caribe* (Santiago de Chile: FLACSO 2007) p.133.
[56]CVR, 'Las Fuerzas Armadas', pp.354–5.
[57]Law No. 27,351 of October 2000.
[58]In 2009 after trial, Fujimori was found guilty of human rights violations. See Jo-Marie Burt, 'Guilty as Charged: The Trial of Former Peruvian President Alberto Fujimori for Human Rights Violations', *The International Journal of Transitional Justice* 3/3 (2009) pp.384–405.

to democratize intelligence. During the provisional Government of Valentín Paniagua (November 2000–July 2001), the whole intelligence community was replaced by law. The National Intelligence Council (CNI) became the new governing body.[59] This was the starting point from which the new democratic administrations prioritized an intelligence revamp and the need to review the past. These significant events are explained below.

In June 2001, President Paniagua created the Commission on Truth and Reconciliation (CVR) to investigate crimes and human rights violations committed by terrorist organizations, state agents, or paramilitary groups during the Fujimori regime.[60] In August 2003, the CVR issued its public report. As illustrated by Lisa Laplante, the report:

> [I]dentified conditions and causes of not only the political violence but also the social and political factors that silenced victims and witnesses of these atrocities. Through this diagnosis, the [CVR] left Peru with a road map that, if it chooses, can guide democratic reform to erect protections against future atrocities.[61]

The report, for example, mentions the *Grupo Colina*, a special operations Army detachment controlled by the SIN of Montesinos, involved in clandestine and illegal repression.[62] The Barrios Altos massacre – 15 citizens murdered, 3 November 1991 – and the University of Cantuta case – nine students and a professor abducted and murdered, 18 July 1992 – were among actions perpetrated by this group.

The report recommended the implementation of democratic civilian control of military intelligence services, limiting them to the production of defense intelligence, and called for a legal framework strengthening CNI's role. In addition, it recommended the strengthening of the intelligence agencies of the Peruvian National Police and the Ministry of the Interior, and to define the police constitutionally and legally as a non-militarized civilian institution.

In 2002, elected President Alejandro Toledo (2001–6) appointed for the first time a civilian, sociologist Juan Velit, as CNI chief, later replaced by Fernando Rospigliosi, a journalist and sociologist who was in charge of a police reform. Their goal was to put the intelligence agencies under civilian and democratic control, and looked for expert international assistance;[63] in

---

[59]Law No. 27,479 of 11 May 2001.
[60]Supreme Decree No. 065 of 2 June 2001.
[61]L.J. Laplante, 'The Peruvian Truth Commission's Historical Memory Project: Empowering Truth-Tellers to Confront Truth Deniers', *Journal of Human Rights* 6/4 (2007) pp.448–9.
[62]See Comisión de la Verdad y Reconciliación (CVR), 'La Década del Noventa y los Dos Gobiernos de Alberto Fujimori' in *Informe Final*, vol. III, 2.3 (Lima: CVR 2003) appendix, pp.130–58; Also see J. Robles Montoya, 'El Accionar del Grupo Colina como Deformación de las Actividades de Inteligencia', *AA Inteligencia* 1/2 (2008) pp.10–19.
[63]See P. Heymann and J. Ellis, 'Reforming Intelligence in Peru. An International Effort to Promote Change', *Harvard Review of Latin America* 2/1 (2002) pp.26–9; also Andrés Gómez

the words of Velit, they were building a new intelligence service.[64] Among other measures, they undertook a purge of analysts and agents of the former SIN, and terminated the strategic intelligence courses of the SINA, and the Army intelligence.[65] Later, after institutional resistance to change, and the appointment of retired military officers in 2004 to lead the CNI and the system, the brief effort to establish civilian control ended.[66]

In 2004, a presidential decision established the Special Commission of the CNI Restructuring. The focus was directed towards the establishment of democratic controls, including judicial, congressional, and Executive controls, in addition to matters of efficiency, protection of rights, and transparency.[67] The Commission recommended that a majority of the Congress ratify the intelligence chief proposed by the Executive, the secret expenditures be controlled by a congressional committee, and the establishment of judicial control for special intelligence operations.

In July 2001, Toledo's administration launched a police reform headed by Minister of the Interior Rospigliosi[68]; and created the Special Commission for the Restructuring of the Peruvian National Police. In February 2002, the commission issued its report characterizing the national police as militarized, isolated from the community, politicized, with high levels of corruption, and a negative citizen perception.[69] The reform found institutional obstacles, lack of political support, and budgetary limitations. In 2003, a process of regression began and, by mid 2004, the reform was abandoned.[70] Notably, unlike the CNI, the General Directorate of Intelligence (DIGIMIN)[71] of the

---

de la Torre Rotta, 'Peru: Frustrations in Attempts to Reconstruct its Intelligence System' in R. Swenson and S. Lemozy (eds.) *Intelligence Professionalism in the Americas*, revised ed. (Washington, DC: Joint Military Intelligence College's Center for Strategic Intelligence Research 2004) pp.200–3.

[64]'Inteligencia Sin Espejismos', *Caretas*, No. 1722, Lima, 23 May 2002.

[65]Arturo Vigil Dávila, 'Así Se Produjo el Arrasamiento del Sistema Nacional de Inteligencia. Gobierno de Toledo Desapareció Arma de Inteligencia y el Irreemplazable Curso de Inteligencia Estratégica', *Reporte Perú*, May 2009.

[66]See G. Costa, 'Two Steps Forward, One and a Half Steps Back: Police Reform in Peru, 2001–2004', *Civil Wars* 8/2 (2006) p.221; also Gómez de la Torre Rotta, 'Peru', p.190.

[67]Obando, 'La Reestructuración de la Inteligencia en Perú', pp.59–63.

[68]Gino Costa replaced Rospigliosi until January 2003; later Rospigliosi returned to the post (July 2003–May 2004).

[69]Comisión Especial de Reestructuración de la Policía Nacional del Perú, 'Informe de la Comisión Especial de Reestructuración de la Policía Nacional del Perú', Ministerio del Interior, Lima, 22 February 2002.

[70]Reform accomplishments included police professionalization, establishment of neighborhood boards to improve police-community relations, creation of a ministerial Office of Internal Affairs, legislation on disciplinary system, and creation of the National System of Citizen Security for participation in crime prevention. See Costa, 'Two Steps Forward, One and a Half Steps Back', pp.215–30.

[71]According to Legislative Decree No. 370 of 1986, the Ministry of the Interior's organic law, DIGIMIN is responsible for the direction, coordination, and centralization of the information of the police forces and political authorities and for the production of intelligence.

Ministry of the Interior retained qualified and experienced personnel, thus maintaining a high operational capacity.[72]

The final report of the Commission on the Integral Restructuring of the Armed Forces, published in April 2002,[73] recommended several changes to constitutional and legal arrangements and measures to be implemented by the Ministry of Defense. The CVR report also called for a defense reform.[74] Military reform achieved only modest results; armed forces continue to respond to cold war standards, which is dysfunctional for current security concerns.[75]

The establishment of the CNI, the SIN's successor, was not a successful renovation that provided a modern, professional, and democratically driven intelligence service. Toledo's administration of the intelligence sector featured instability in the CNI leadership, politicization, and lack of high-level intelligence; under these circumstances, the expected reform vanished.[76] As stated by a local analyst: 'There is no doubt that in the matter of intelligence, in Peru there is nothing "to reform" and still less "to restructure"; the system must be totally reconstructed'.[77]

A Road to Change: The New Legal Framework

The frustrated experience was not an obstacle preventing the Peruvian Congress from playing a fundamental role to promote transformation.[78] In December 2005, Law No. 28,664 was adopted. It followed some recommendations of the Special Commission of the CNI Restructuring. The law established a new national intelligence system. The following are the substantial contents of this law.

The National Intelligence System (SINA) comprises the National Intelligence Council (COIN), the National Directorate for Intelligence (DINI), the intelligence services of the Defense and Interior sectors, and the General Directorate for Security and Defense Affairs of the Ministry of Foreign Affairs. The objective of the intelligence activity is to provide,

---

[72] Jorge Serrano Torres, 'Comentario Invitado' in R. Swenson and S. Lemozy (eds.) *Democratización de la Función de Inteligencia – El Nexo de la Cultura Nacional y la Inteligencia Estratégica* (Washington DC: National Defense Intelligence College Press 2009) pp.xlvii–xlviii.

[73] 'Informe de la Comisión de Reestructuración Integral de las Fuerzas Armadas', *El Peruano Diario Oficial*, No. 7972, Lima, 20 April 2002, pp.221639–43.

[74] For a detailed description of the defense reform agenda, see Carlos Basombrío and Fernando Rospigliosi, *La Seguridad y sus Instituciones en el Perú a Inicios del Siglo XXI. Reformas Democráticas y Neomilitarismo* (Lima: Instituto de Estudios Peruanos 2006) pp.17–44.

[75] Toche Medrano, *Guerra y Democracia*, p.283.

[76] See J. Robles Montoya, '¿El Gobierno Tiene Inteligencia?', IDEELEMAIL No. 316, 27 September 2003; and 'CNI: SIN Inteligencia', IDEELEMAIL No. 350, 19 March 2004.

[77] Gómez de la Torre Rotta, 'Peru', p.196.

[78] A. Gómez de la Torre Rotta, '¿Quién Vigilará a Nuestros Vigilantes? (Reinventando a Juvenal ante el Foro de Roma en Perú y Sudamérica)', *Inteligencia y Seguridad, Revista de Análisis y Prospectiva* 5 (2008–2009) p.46.

through the SINA, to the President and the Council of Ministers, timely and useful knowledge on current and potential threats and risks that may affect national security and constitutional order. Seven *principles* guide the intelligence activity: legality, legitimacy, democratic control, relevance, restricted circulation (of information), specialty, and planning.

The SINA is defined as the ensemble of institutions of the State functionally linked, acting in a coordinated manner in the production of intelligence and counterintelligence. Under the guidance of the DINI, SINA components must standardize their selection, evaluation, and training as well as doctrine and working procedures. COIN is the top collegiate body of the SINA, responsible for guiding intelligence and counterintelligence and reviewing the annual plan. The DINI is responsible for (1) the production of intelligence and counterintelligence in the non-military domains of national security; (2) directing, coordinating, centralizing, integrating, processing and disseminating intelligence that is provided by the components of the system; and (3) ensuring intelligence sharing between system components. The DINI Director is also the SINA's higher-ranking officer and presides over the COIN.

The National School of Intelligence is responsible for training analysts and counterintelligence staff. Regarding secrecy, the law establishes the classification categories, the obligation to secrecy, penalties, and a procedure for declassification. The law establishes a procedure for special operations, which require prior judicial authorization, and provides the definition and scope of reserved expenditure and the basis for the accountability of DINI special resources. Supreme Decrees No. 025 and 026 of 2006 approved, respectively, SINA and DINI regulations; Supreme Decree No. 064 of 2007 approved the personnel bylaw.

Finally, the law established the Congressional Intelligence Committee with powers to control SINA activities, to require classified information, to investigate ex officio, to supervise the annual plan, and to request an annual secret report. The law does not provide for congressional control of intelligence budgets or military intelligence.

Outcome

In general terms, it is remarkable that attempts to reform the areas of intelligence, police, and security and national defense of Peru were preceded by and/or driven by restructuring commissions established in the Executive that issued relevant recommendations, in many cases later adopted by law. Academic involvement in both the design and implementation of the reforms was also an important element. However, their impact was dissimilar and, as in the case of the police reform, the objectives were later abandoned.

Effective civilian leadership has been sporadic. Congress took significant actions sanctioning a law with a clear democratic profile and several reform bills are under study. The military still heavily influence the intelligence sector and are not prevented from performing domestic intelligence. Although there were no insurmountable obstacles to promote changes in civil-military relations and in the military and intelligence sectors, the main impediment was the incomprehension of politicians and their lack of decision for transformations.[79]

An unintended consequence that raised media concerns was the proliferation of private intelligence companies, hiring retired military officers, performing illegal espionage activities, getting involved in turf wars, and making use of classified information.[80] In 2007, a case of navy intelligence officers selling information to private intelligence companies was the subject of a congressional inquiry.[81]

Yet, as during the last century, Peruvian intelligence maintains a domestic-oriented profile.[82] As one analyst puts it: 'during recent years, the Peruvian intelligence community has been reduced to ashes, by both autocrats and democrats, and still it is expected to rise like the Phoenix, to defend the Peruvian society from emerging and complex threats, and enlighten the decisions that rulers must make'.[83]

Ecuador: From Crisis to Crisis

For decades, Ecuadorian intelligence and security sectors were relatively stable. This was the case for the period under military rule that culminated in 1979, as well as during the democratic period until the mid-2000s. Neither the main intelligence agency – the National Directorate of Intelligence (DNI), under the General Secretariat of the National Security Council[84] – nor military and police intelligence agencies were subject to any serious restructuring attempt during this period. It was not until the late 2000s that intelligence democratization in fact began to develop.

Two stages are clearly distinguished in the recent history of intelligence and democracy: before and after the Correa Presidency. The first one clearly indicated path dependence, without change. The main change related to the beginning of President Luis Correa's tenure (2007–present). Correa took the opportunity presented by the Angostura case (discussed below) in 2008 to gain support for reform. Presidential decisions were supported by the expert advice of special commissions, and backed by legislative action.

The factor that supports progress is undoubtedly the willingness of decision makers to democratize intelligence, while those that arrest progress include legacies of the non-democratic past, reluctance to reform, lack of civilian expertise, and the negative influence of foreign intelligence services.

---

[79]Basombrío and Rospigliosi, *La Seguridad y sus Instituciones*, p.327.
[80]Obando, 'La Reestructuración de la Inteligencia en Perú', pp.67–8.
[81]See 'Pleno del Congreso Aprobó Informe de Inteligencia con 14 Meses de Atraso. Fuga de Información de la Marina a Empresas Privadas', *El Comercio*, 17 October 2008.
[82]Obando, 'La Reestructuración de la Inteligencia en Perú', p.65.
[83]Serrano Torres, 'Comentario Invitado', p.xlii; translation by the author.
[84]See National Security Law of 1979.

Early History

The following paragraphs illustrate the antecedent condition. The maintenance of military structure and its domain in the 'strategic areas' conditioned the transition of power in 1979 in Ecuador; political parties did not envisage the urgent need to build a strong (doctrinal, political, and legal) civilian rule over the military. On the contrary, the legislature in particular ceded positions, leaving aside the exercise of its legislative and oversight functions in military matters.[85]

Ecuador's emerging democracy falls among those countries that choose to preserve the existing intelligence apparatus, therefore maintaining the doctrinal approaches of the cold war period. Issues such as effectiveness, transparency, and political control of intelligence were absent from the political agenda for several decades of democracy. Yet, under the legal framework for national security, intelligence developed professionally in support of the armed forces mission within the defense structure. In this regard, an analyst who recommended improving the system argued that intelligence should not be an exclusive element of the defense sector, but should serve the State as a whole.[86]

Intelligence in a Context of Political Crises and Military Influence

The turbulent democratic period that began in 1979 suffered several scandals related to intelligence, including human rights abuses, confronting domestic unrest, and military border conflicts. A brief mention of the economic policies that prevailed previously helps to illustrate the context. The administrations of Osvaldo Hurtado, León Febres Cordero, Rodrigo Borja, Sixto Durán Ballén, and more recently Abdalá Bucaram, Jamil Mahuad, and Alvaro Noboa, applied neoliberal reforms. In 1995, after a secret budget scandal, Vice-President Alberto Dahik resigned; he could not justify in court the diversion of secret funds for his personal use. In February 1997, the Assembly removed President Bucaram. Under a growing economic crisis, such policies led to social protest and the emergence of a new actor, the indigenous groups.[87] This culminated in February 2000 when President Mahuad was overthrown by a military-indigenous coalition.[88]

The border issue was one of a number of significant events involving intelligence affairs and changes in the strategic environment: there was ambivalence between an active and defensive role on the border with Peru

---

[85] García-Gallegos, 'El 20 de Abril', pp.101–2.

[86] Jaime Castillo Arias, 'La Cultura Nacional y su Influencia en la Estructura de Inteligencia Nacional en el Ecuador' in Swenson and Lemozy, *Democratización de la Función de Inteligencia*, p.107. Castillo Arias, an Ecuadorian colonel, was then Assistant Director of the Army Intelligence Directorate.

[87] See Natalia Leon Galarza, *Ecuador: La Cara Oculta de la Crisis. Identidades Políticas y Protesta en el Fin de Siglo* (Buenos Aires: CLACSO 2009) Introduction.

[88] See M.E. Andersen, 'Ethnic Politics, Defense, and Security in "Latin" America', *Joint Force Quarterly* 58/3 (2010) pp.19–21, based on anthropologist Brian Selmeski.

and a tacit toleration on the border with Colombia. From 1941 until 1998, the Ecuadorian administration's attention was directed towards the border with Peru.[89] In 1995, the historical border conflict with Peru escalated into war. The struggle reflected the military superiority of Ecuador. On 26 October 1998, Peruvian President Fujimori and Ecuadorian President Mahuad signed peace accords under international supervision.[90]

Security problems on the northern border relate to the protection of strategic areas where the oil industry is located, indigenous and social protests related to this, the incursions of FARC (*Fuerzas Armadas Revolucionarias de Colombia*) troops and crime. To face these challenges, the Ecuadorian armed forces had to change their strategy and move from a regular warfare scenario on the southern border to one of irregular combats on the northern border;[91] 'the army is concentrated in the north, where social conflict surrounding the country's oil industry is combined with destabilizing influences spilling over the border from Colombia'.[92]

Since 1979, Ecuadorian intelligence was assessed as operating in a highly institutionalized framework, which was explained by the long period of professionalization and political autonomy of the armed forces.[93] As claimed by Bonilla and Camacho, from the mid-1990s the challenges facing the intelligence agencies came from political instability and major tensions on its borders.[94] In fact, there was no intelligence community serving the political level; the DNI was not functional for the needs of a modern State.[95] DNI weaknesses included: lack of specialists in the production of political-strategic intelligence, lack of training of its staff, limited technological innovation, inadequate organic and functional structure, and lack of legal framework for a national system of intelligence.[96] In short, intelligence agencies maintained

---

[89] Juan Carlos Ruiz and Rocío Pachón, 'Seguridad en Ecuador: Paradojas, Ambivalencias y Disyuntivas' in R. Sánchez et al., *Seguridades en Construcción en América Latina I: El Círculo de Colombia, Brasil, Ecuador, Panamá y Venezuela* (Bogotá: Centro Editorial Universidad del Rosario 2005) p.76.

[90] See Alejandra Ruiz-Dana, 'Peru and Ecuador: A Case Study of Latin American Integration and Conflict' in S. Rafi Khan (ed.) *Regional Trade Integration and Conflict Resolution* (NY: Routledge 2009).

[91] Ruiz and Pachón, 'Seguridad en Ecuador'.

[92] M. Jaskoski, 'Ecuador and Peru: Army for Rent, Terms Negotiable', *Berkeley Review of Latin American Studies* Spring (2009) p.46.

[93] Adrian Bonilla and Cristina Camacho, 'El Sistema de Inteligencia Ecuatoriano y su Contexto Político', FLACSO-Ecuador, REDES 2001, Research and Education in Defense and Security Studies, Washington, DC, May 2001.

[94] Ibid.

[95] Fredy Rivera Vélez, 'La Inteligencia Ecuatoriana: Tradiciones, Cambios y Perspectivas', in F. Rivera Vélez (ed.) *Inteligencia Estratégica y Prospectiva* (Quito: FLACSO-Ecuador/SENAIN 2011) p.54.

[96] Fabián Tobar B, 'La Dirección Nacional de Inteligencia en Apoyo a las Políticas de Seguridad y Defensa en el Ecuador ante las Nuevas Amenazas', Master's Thesis, IAEN (Instituto de Altos Estudios Nacionales), Quito, 2007, p.86 < http://repositorio.iaen.edu.ec/handle/24000/104>. The author is an Ecuadorian military officer.

their own agenda and, certainly, there was no exercise of the necessary democratic political control over them.

The Circumstances of the Change of Course

The path dependence period outlined above characterized by the stability of intelligence institutions and organizations began to end during the tenure of President Correa (2007–present). The Angostura case, and the 'Operación Montecristi', amounted to a critical juncture. It produced a punctuated change, the replacement of the DNI, the refurbishing of police and military intelligence, and the establishment of a new intelligence system approved by the Assembly. The investigation of human rights abuses of the past by a special commission was also relevant. This change of path was followed by a reform process.

In February 2007, the Commission for the Modernization of the National Police was established; in October 2007, the police was put under a state of emergency in which the government took full authority to determine organizational reforms; in March 2008, a citizen security plan was launched.[97] In 2007, the Assembly passed new defense laws improving civilian control over the armed forces.[98] The Truth Commission of Ecuador was created in May 2007 for investigating and preventing impunity regarding violent acts and violations of human rights attributed to State agents that occurred between 1984 and 1988, and other periods.[99]

A Colombian military offensive against the FARC in Ecuador's territory (province of Sucumbíos) on 1 March 2008 resulted in the killing of Raul Reyes, the FARC's spokesman and second-in-command, and provoked a major crisis. Known as the Angostura case, it had both international and domestic political impact. It required a rapid intervention of the OAS (Organization of American States), which disapproved the raid. There was a rupture of the already tense diplomatic relations between Ecuador and Colombia but they soon began to restore them.[100]

The Angostura case also promoted a denunciation of the military and police intelligence services due to indications of penetration from, and collaboration with, US intelligence. The military power was rocked by these allegations; Correa forced the resignation of the Defense Minister, the Joint Chiefs commander, the Army commander, and National Police commander. As stated by Bertha-Garcia: 'past presidents couldn't have attempted this, but

---

[97] Daniel Pontón, *Policía Comunitaria y Cambio Institucional en el Ecuador* (Quito: FLACSO-Ecuador/Abya Yala 2009) pp.64–9.
[98] National Defense Organic Law No. 74 of 19 January 2007; Armed Forces Social Security Law No. 82 of 31 July 2007; Law No. 75 of 22 January 2007 amending the Armed Forces Personnel Law.
[99] Decree No. 305 of 3 May 2007.
[100] For more on this, see the interesting article by Michael Shifter and Adam Siegel, 'Colombia and Ecuador in 2009: The Rocky Road to Restoring Relations', *EFE Anuario Iberoamericano 2010*, 23 March 2010 <http://www.thedialogue.org/page.cfm?pageID=32&pubID=2321>.

Correa has space to maneuver'.[101] In addition, a far-reaching interrogation of military and police intelligence structures, after the exposure of both organizational and technical flaws, led to an accelerated intervention in them.[102] Another case, which deepened the negative view of the role of intelligence services, was the so called 'Operación Montecristi', an incident of domestic spying on the National Constituent Assembly by officers of the intelligence group of the Joint Command of the Armed Forces.[103]

President Correa announced the reform of police and military intelligence services: in May 2008, his Minister of Defense raised this issue before the National Assembly. By Decree No. 1,080 of 15 May 2008, President Correa established the Commission to Investigate Military and Police Intelligence Services. The Commission was tasked, among other duties, to investigate and evaluate the infiltration of Ecuadorian police and military intelligence by foreign intelligence agencies, and to make recommendations on structure, policies, and legislation that needed amendments. According to this commission, the 'national security doctrine' militarized and policialized national intelligence while various Governments did not develop the DNI as the body in charge of the strategic management of the system. In November 2008, the commission issued its report recommending changes in the intelligence community. President Correa also created the Commission on Transparency and Truth Case Angostura in March 2009.[104] The case unveiled problems of delays in the delivery of information, concealment, lack of depth in the relevant analysis, disrespect of the channels of command, and few operational actions.[105] Decree No. 1,768 of 8 June 2009, issued by President Correa, restructured and replaced the DNI by the National Secretariat for Intelligence (SENAIN), under the newly created post of Minister Coordinator for Domestic and Foreign Security.

Meanwhile, the Commission unveiled the involvement of intelligence units of the police and the armed forces in illegal activities, and called attention to the persistence of the internal enemy conception as a guiding principle of national security and focus of intelligence and security functions.[106]

In its final report issued in 2010, the Truth Commission recommended the declassification of police and military archives that could contribute to the elucidation of human rights violations. It referred to, in particular, files of the Special Investigations Unit (UIES) and Public Security Bureau – formerly Politics Security Bureau – both under the National Police, of the National Security Council, and of the Special Group of Military Intelligence

---

[101]Chris Kraul, 'Ecuador Military Meets Match', *Los Angeles Times*, 2 May 2008.
[102]*Informe de la Comisión de Transparencia y Verdad Caso Angostura*, Quito, 10 December 2009.
[103]Maldonado, 'Dilemas Antiguos y Modernos en la Inteligencia Estratégica en Sudamérica', p.58.
[104]Executive Decree No. 1,646 of 25 March 2009.
[105]See *Informe de la Comisión de Transparencia y Verdad Caso Angostura*.
[106]Comisión de la Verdad, *Informe de la Comisión de la Verdad, Ecuador 2010. Sin Verdad No Hay Justicia* (Quito: Edicuatorial 2010).

Operations (GEOIM), under the Armed Forces, as well as the presidential archives.[107] It also recommended amending the public security law, allowing declassification of public records for investigating violations of human rights.[108]

New Legal Framework

The first temporary clause of the new Constitution, as reformed in 2008, provided for the approval of a law to regulate public and state security. In addition, the Commission to investigate military and police intelligence services recommended legal changes in the intelligence sector. In September 2009, the National Assembly passed the Law on Public and State Security. Following a comprehensive security concept for both the State and the inhabitants, it establishes a Public and State Security System comprising external defense, internal security, and domestic disaster spheres, with the main advisory element being the Council Public and State Security. Articles 13 through 21 detailed the new legal framework of the SENAIN and its role within the Public and State Security System.

The SENAIN is in charge of the National Intelligence System; its chief, appointed by the president, cannot be a military or police officer in active duty. Intelligence is defined as the activity of gathering, processing, and analyzing specific information on threats, risks, and conflicts affecting national security. Counterintelligence is defined as the activity performed in order to prevent or counteract intelligence operations that represent security threats or risks. The SENAIN's main responsibilities are: to develop the annual intelligence plan; to coordinate and implement the gathering and analysis of information for the production of intelligence; to coordinate, articulate, and integrate the activities and functioning of military and police intelligence with those of bodies in charge of Presidency's security; and to provide strategic intelligence in a timely fashion, to the President and the Ministry of Security Coordination.[109]

The law states that the intelligence budget figures are included in the national budget law although the detailed appropriations remain classified. The law also provides for judicial control. Prior judicial authorization is required to intercept documents or communications while performing covert operations. The SENAIN is accountable to a special committee of the Assembly and to the State General Comptroller. Finally, intelligence agencies are forbidden to obtain information, produce intelligence, or keep data on individuals because of their race, sexual preference, religion, private actions, and political ideology, or due to their membership in partisan, social, union, community, co-operative, assistance, cultural, or labor organizations. Decree No. 486 of September 2010 provides regulations for the provisions of the Law on Public and State Security.

---

[107] Comisión de la Verdad, Vol. V, p.441.
[108] Ibid., p.460.
[109] Created by Decree No. 117 of February 2007.

Outcome

Recent events leading to the reorganization of the intelligence agencies show that political leaders have had little confidence in their professionalism and loyalty. Although the agencies did not pose significant threats to democracy, their behavior, practices, and results were not those expected by the Government. The legislation is a new beginning, a first signal towards intelligence democratization. The intention to reform the intelligence community is now present on the Government agenda. A civilian was posted as the SENAIN's chief.

Unexpectedly, a crisis broke out in the incipient stage of implementation of the reform. In the context of the police rebellion (30 September 2010) and a year after its entry into force, the new legal framework was jeopardized.[110] The SENAIN suffered its first step back: the president admitted that he was not warned about the police intentions; its first civilian chief was fired a month after the rebellion. This intelligence failure was a significant event that affected the entire system.[111] An immediate consequence was the submission of a bill to the Assembly by the President amending the Law on Public and State Security, promoting the use of the armed forces in internal protection and control of public order by order of the President when facing situations of necessity.[112] Civilian control over the intelligence agencies was also reduced: retired military officers were posted as chiefs of security and intelligence. Moreover, more recently, the Government ordered by decree a profound reorganization of national police; it stipulated also that the Ministry of the Interior should assume the legal, judicial, and extra-judicial representations of the police.[113] This may present a second chance for the effective exercise of democratic civilian control over the police.[114]

It is still premature to draw conclusions from this intelligence reform endeavor. It is clear that more time is needed to determine if change is consolidated in the sector. However, it is possible to depict some preliminary thoughts on this matter. Currently, the intelligence sector is designed with low autonomy and low penetration. A recently adopted regulatory framework is in the midst of implementation. The effectiveness of the new intelligence agency was tested with negative results: President Correa was not warned about the police rebellion preparatory activities. The embryonic civilian control is challenged by the repositioning of the military in internal security and strategic intelligence areas.[115]

---

[110]'Police Rebellion Quelled in Ecuador', *Jane's*, 1 October 2010.

[111]See 'Cinco Organismos de Inteligencia Fallaron el 30 de Septiembre', *El Universo*, 4 October 2010.

[112]'Proyecto de Ley Reformatoria a la Ley Seguridad Pública y del Estado', submitted by President Rafael Correa to the National Assembly, 7 December 2010.

[113]Decree No. 632 of 17 January 2011.

[114]See 'Roce entre Alfredo Vera y la Policía', *El Comercio*, 20 January 2011; Marco Arauz Ortega (Subdirector General), '¿La Reforma Policial Llegó?', *El Comercio*, 20 January 2011.

[115]Rivera Vélez, 'La Inteligencia Ecuatoriana', p.72.

Argentina: Gradual Changes after Legislation[116]

From the mid-twentieth century, the intelligence sector comprised a powerful intelligence service under the Presidency, the services of each military branch, and those of the federal police and security forces.[117] Heavily influenced by the armed forces, the intelligence community engaged in political policing.

From 1984, Argentina's new democracy gradually made essential improvements.[118] In order to break away from the autonomy of the military, police, and intelligence sectors, Congress adopted specific legislation to establish civilian democratic controls, including the National Intelligence Law of 2001.

Argentina's democratization of intelligence had no critical juncture that would have promoted a profound change. Organizational restructuring rather than fundamental reform was the political choice. The starting point is the establishment of democracy. 'Layering' best describes the observed incremental change. Layers such as national intelligence, military intelligence, criminal intelligence, congressional role, laws, and regulations, are relevant. Each one recognizes key agents of change and disparate timings, as well as specific triggering or significant events and punctuated changes, dealing with clashes between new and old practices.

Factors that arrest progress include the complexity of the intelligence reform process, legacies of the non-democratic past, resistance and reluctance to change, insufficient political support, and tendencies to politicization. At the outset, the momentum of legislators and advisors, and later the impetus of the Executive, were relevant to advance democratization.

Early History

The military coup of 1930 may be considered as the starting point of a period characterized by the use of coercive power against opposition, a period marked by the growth of a secret state within the state lacking controls and accountability, engaged in 'surveillance, instigation, espionage, blackmail, and vetting'.[119]

---

[116]This part is based on an unpublished paper by this author: 'Intelligence Democratization in Argentina: Achievements and Challenges', June 2010; a revised version was published as 'Intelligence Community Reforms: The Case of Argentina', in P.H.J. Davies and K. Gustafson (eds.) *Intelligence Elsewhere: Spies and Espionage Outside the Anglosphere* (Washington, DC: Georgetown University Press 2013) pp.219–37.

[117]'Security forces' include National Gendarmerie (GN), Naval Coast Guard (PNA) – both intermediate forces fulfill law enforcement tasks – and Airport Security Police (PSA).

[118]See Priscila Carlos Brandão Antunes, 'Establishing Democratic Control of Intelligence in Argentina' in T. Bruneau and S. Boraz (eds.) *Reforming Intelligence: Obstacles to Democratic Control and Effectiveness* (Austin, TX: University of Texas Press 2007) pp.195–218; Eduardo E. Estévez, 'Executive and Legislative Oversight of the Intelligence System in Argentina' in H. Born, L. Johnson and I. Leigh (eds.) *Who's Watching the Spies? Establishing Intelligence Service Accountability* (Washington, DC: Potomac Books 2005) pp.160–79.

[119]L. Kalmanowiecki, 'Origins and Applications of Political Policing in Argentina', *Latin American Perspectives* 27/2 (2000) pp.37–40.

In 1946, elected President Juan Domingo Perón created an office for the Coordination of Information of the Presidency, and later established the Coordination of Information of the Ministry of War. Renamed in 1949 the Coordination of State Information, in 1951 it was replaced by the State Information Service, under the Presidency. The intelligence services of each military branch had been operating since 1946. Finally, in 1956, the State Information Secretariat (SIDE) was set up under Decree No. 776 of the military government, while in 1966, a new coordination and analytical body under the President, the National Intelligence Center (CNI), was established by law.

Sequence of Tribulations and Improvements

Elected President Raul Alfonsín (1983–9) appointed the first civilian head of the SIDE, lawyer Roberto Pena. Pena encountered resistance from the military as well as from within the agency. He appointed civilian undersecretaries, performed an unprecedented depuration of military officers,[120] and drafted a CNI reform proposal, but after a 14-month term he resigned when it was ignored. The last intelligence chief of Alfonsín's administration, Facundo Suárez, also intended to empower the CNI.

Revision of the past was central to Alfonsín's agenda. Military Junta members were arrested, tried, and sentenced for human rights violations during the 'dirty war'. The National Commission of the Disappeared, chaired by well-known writer Ernesto Sábato, issued its 'Nunca Más' report, showing data of 9000 disappearances. In 1988, Congress passed the National Defense Law No. 23,554. This law, approved by consensus, replaced the 'national security doctrine'; armed forces were allowed to confront only external aggression and internal security was to be defined by a special law. Military intelligence was banned from conducting domestic and political intelligence. Military intelligence would be produced by an agency composed of the intelligence agencies of the armed forces under the authority of the Minister of Defense.

The period was not free from tense civil-military relations, including several military uprisings; the armed forces lobbied to retain their earlier monopoly of intelligence and domestic security. Reactive measures undertaken by President Alfonsín and later by President Menem, after the unexpected ultra-leftist command attack on an army base in January 1989,[121] triggered a number of short-lived decisions – creation of a Security Council[122] and a Committee on Domestic Security[123] – that generated concern about military participation in domestic intelligence.

---

[120]See Gerardo Young, *SIDE. La Argentina Secreta* (Buenos Aires: Editorial Planeta 2006) pp.70–1.
[121]The taking of the military infantry regiment of La Tablada by the MTP (Movimiento Todos por la Patria) took place on 23 January 1989.
[122]Decree No. 83 of 25 January 1989.
[123]Decree No. 327 of 10 March 1989; Decree No. 392 of 26 February 1990.

Carlos Menem's administration (1989–99) was marked by scandals involving illegal intelligence activities, increase in secret expenditures, the impact of two terrorist bombings, and tendencies to involve the military in domestic intelligence and internal security focused in social conflict.[124] To legitimize intelligence activities, Menem's second intelligence chief tasked the SIDE to support criminal investigations, a shift of doubtful utility that contributed nothing to a renewal.[125] During Menem's administration, secret expenses were diverted to the payment of extra salaries to high officials. In December 2009, a federal court confirmed the prosecution of former President Menem, his Economy Minister, Domingo Cavallo, and other former top officials under the penal qualification of 'peculation'.[126]

The Internal Security Law No. 24,059 of 1992 was approved by consensus and established the civilian management of the police and security forces. It gave birth to the Congressional Joint Committee for the oversight of internal security and intelligence activities and agencies, and created the Directorate for Internal Intelligence under the Internal Security Secretariat, the first domestic intelligence body with democratic legitimacy.[127]

A scandal known as 'ideological surveillance' surfaced in June 1993 when an order to update intelligence files, issued by the Ministry of Interior, was leaked to the press. Intelligence elements of the Buenos Aires Provincial Police and the National Gendarmerie engaged in surveillance of students, teachers, and trade unionists.[128] As a consequence, the Internal Security Council invited legislators from the Joint Committee to a meeting. They issued a statement to the security forces reiterating the strict prohibition on collecting information and producing intelligence on people simply because of their race, religious faith, or political opinion, or their adherence to principles of trade union, youth, student, cooperative, welfare, or cultural movements, as well as the legitimate activity that they performed. This scandal demonstrated the democratic deficit regarding the implementation of controls over domestic intelligence.

In 1993, a bill on intelligence introduced by majority Senator Eduardo Vaca informally released for consideration by the Executive was subject to legislative negotiations. While the majority draft followed the existing centralizing approach, the opposition draft proposed a de-centralizing approach, with ministerial, parliamentary, and judicial controls. In August 1994, the Senate approved the majority bill but, in December 1995, it did not pass the lower chamber.

---

[124] For more details, see J.P. McSherry, 'National Security and Social Crisis in Argentina', *Journal of Third World Studies* 17/1 (2000).
[125] Young, *SIDE*, pp.115, 180.
[126] 'Prosecution for Menem and Cavallo Confirmed', *Télam*, National News Agency of Argentina, 22 December 2009.
[127] Its legal basis was complemented with Regulatory Decree No. 1,273 of 1992.
[128] See 'La Orden para el Espionaje Ideológico', *Clarín*, 7 July 1993, pp.6–7; also *La Nación*, 2 July 1993.

A first terrorist bombing affected the Israeli Embassy (17 March 1992); a second one struck the Jewish Community Center (AMIA) (18 July 1994), both in Buenos Aires and attributed to Hizbollah. In 1995, the government developed a regional strategy on counterterrorist cooperation. The Triborder Tripartite Command, created in May 1996 to operate in the area between Puerto Iguazú (Argentina), Foz de Iguazú (Brazil), and Ciudad del Este (Paraguay), composed of police officers from those countries, was tasked to exchange information and perform counterterrorist actions.[129] These bombings evidenced the limited capacity of anticipation of the intelligence services.[130] Eventually, Decree No. 815 of 2005, signed by President Kirchner, acknowledged responsibility of the Government's failure to prevent and to properly investigate the AMIA bombing.

In November 1998, the officers responsible were prosecuted after revelations that the Air Force's intelligence agents performed surveillance on graphics media journalists and a women's NGO.[131] In June 2000, a judge revealed that the Army's Information Collection Center 141 was performing intelligence activities against political parties, trade unions, and university groups in the province of Cordoba.[132]

De Santibañes, the first intelligence chief of Fernando De la Rúa administration (2000–1), introduced changes in the SIDE: a thousand personnel were discharged; secret expenditures were cut; qualified personnel were hired; and a new organizational structure was established.[133] In late 2000, in the context of the scandal of the alleged payment of bribes in the Senate, the General Trusteeship of the Nation (Sigen) reported that SIDE declared expenditure had not been made and therefore it had funds available to finance operations without control; De Santibañes resigned on 21 October.[134] Congress reopened the consensus-building process on intelligence legislation the following year and a team of about 40 people, including legislators, intelligence experts, and advisors, drafted a unified proposal.[135] The Executive

---

[129] Argentina Government, 'Report of the Argentine Republic on its implementation of Security Council resolution 1373 (2001)', Document S/2001/1340, Security Council, United Nations, 31 December 2001, pp.10–11 <http://www.unhcr.org/refworld/pdfid/46d571621.pdf>.

[130] The social crisis of December 2001 in the context of a political and economic crisis that prompted the resignation of President De la Rúa, was not anticipated.

[131] Sergio Moreno and Adriana Meyer, 'Espías de Muy Corto Vuelo', *Página 12*, 6 March 2000.

[132] 'El Ejército Hizo Tareas de Espionaje en Córdoba', *La Nación*, 12 June 1999.

[133] Florencia Fontán Balestra, 'Towards a Democratic Control of Argentina's Intelligence Community', International Center for Criminal Justice, Harvard Law School, 2000, pp.24–46. See also, 'El Servicio de Inteligencia Estatal', editorial, *Clarín*, 8 February 2000.

[134] See Laura Zommer, 'La Sindicatura Le Apunta a Santibañes', *La Nación*, 19 October 2000.

[135] J. Garreta, 'El Diseño de un Nuevo Marco Jurídico Regulatorio para la Actividad de Inteligencia del Estado en la Argentina', *Security and Defense Studies Review* 2/2 (2002/2003) pp.268–82. See also Elsa Llenderrozas, 'Del Espionaje Domestico a la Inteligencia Estratégica: Los Caminos hacia una Ley de Inteligencia', Center for Hemispheric Defense Studies, REDES 2001, Washington, DC, 22–25 May 2001.

referred it to the Senate and Congress passed the National Intelligence Law No. 25,520 in December.

From 2002 until present, a distinctive secrecy policy was outlined. President Nestor Kirchner (2003–7) issued several presidential decrees on the relief of legal obligations to preserve secrecy and the disclosure of intelligence information in a case-by-case basis upon a judicial request.[136] This affected cases of human rights abuses during the dictatorship, corruption, use of intelligence funds, terrorist-bombing investigations, and crimes committed by police officers. In December 2003, Congress passed Law No. 25,873 on Data Retention, later regulated by Decree No. 1,563 of 2004, tasking telecommunications and Internet service providers to devote resources to the seizure of communications and for their remote observation upon judicial requirement. Known as the 'spy law', and due to the threat to privacy, it caused alarm in the media and public opinion. President Kirchner issued Decree No. 357 of 2005 suspending its application[137] and, finally, in February 2009 the Supreme Court of Justice declared it unconstitutional.[138]

In 2005, the National Aeronautical Police (PAN), under the Air Force, was involved in a drug trafficking scandal.[139] President Kirchner prompted a reform, transferring the PAN from the Ministry of Defense to the Ministry of Interior, renaming it the Airport Security Police (PSA)[140], a new security force governed by Law No. 26,102 of 2006. As regards intelligence, the PSA contributes to the development of criminal intelligence. In March 2006, the Center of Legal and Social Studies reported that the Navy was performing illegal domestic intelligence activities at the Almirante Zar base in Chubut province.[141] President Kirchner initiated a far-reaching reform of military intelligence. It included a comprehensive restatement of its doctrine, the resumption by the Ministry of Defense of the control of the military intelligence community, and the reformulation of the cycle of military intelligence planning.[142] In 2010, President Cristina Fernández de Kirchner

---

[136]See Eduardo E. Estévez, 'Developments of the Democratization of Intelligence in Argentina: Trends in Secrecy Policy – Implications for Comparing Transitional Settings', paper prepared for the 4th European Consortium for Political Research Conference, Pisa, Italy, 6 September 2007.

[137]For example, see Gustavo Ybarra and Lucas Colonna, 'Sigue en Vigor la Polémica "Ley Espía"', *La Nación*, 2 May 2005.

[138]Halabi, Ernesto c/P.E.N.-ley 25.873 dto. 1563/04 s/amparo ley 16.986, Corte Suprema de Justicia de la Nación (H.270.XLII), Fallo, Buenos Aires, 24 February 2009.

[139]Alejandra Dandan, 'Las Valijas Salieron por un Mecanismo Aceitado', *Página 12*, 15 February 2005.

[140]Decree No. 145 of 22 February 2005.

[141]For more details see Centro de Estudios Legales y Sociales (CELS), 'Políticas de Defensa y Control Civil' in *Informe sobre la Situación de los Derechos Humanos en Argentina 2007* (Buenos Aires: CELS 2007). Also see CELS, 'El Efecto, en el Plano Judicial y Político, de la Denuncia Penal por la Inteligencia Ilegal en la Base Almirante Zar de Trelew', CELS, Buenos Aires, March 2007.

[142]See *Memoria Anual Detallada del Estado de la Nación 2008*, Jefatura de Gabinete de Ministros, Buenos Aires, 1 March 2009, pp.85–94.

(2007–present) issued Decree No. 4 declassifying information on the actions of the Armed Forces during the last dictatorship as requested by a judge who is investigating violations of human rights.[143]

Main Features of the Legal Framework

The National Intelligence Law of 2001 establishes the National Intelligence System, comprising three agencies: the Secretariat of Intelligence (SI), the National Directorate for Criminal Intelligence (DINIC), under the Ministry of Security,[144] and the National Directorate for Strategic Military Intelligence (DINIEM), under the Defense Ministry. The SI, the main agency, manages the system and produces national intelligence. The DINIC is tasked with the production of criminal intelligence and co-ordinates the intelligence activities of the national police and security forces, and the 23 provincial police forces.

To prevent political intelligence, the law provides for the protection of rights and guarantees through several safeguards. The system must adjust strictly to the Constitution and legislation in force. Prohibitions include the collection of information and intelligence on individuals, and the exercise of influence on the domestic sphere, foreign policy, public opinion, and media.

The law empowers the President to determine the national intelligence policy. In addition, it provides for secret expenditure control mechanisms, judicial authorization for wiretaps, and includes doctrinal definitions, and criminal and personnel provisions. Decree No. 950 of 2002 provided regulations for the provisions of the law. The Congressional Joint Committee for the Oversight of Intelligence Activities and Agencies, created by the law, oversees, among others, the legality of intelligence activities, policy, and management, system effectiveness, personnel education plans, secret budget, and expenditures.

This legislation did not bridge the clash between centralizing and de-centralizing approaches to the intelligence structure. The ministers of Security and Defense share some competencies regarding executive control and accountability with the SI, which concentrates the most. The legal scheme is thus a hybrid, combining a centralized-prone pattern at the top, with a de-centralized-prone pattern at the second level.[145]

Outcome

In the late 1980s, the impulse was in the legislature; the executive merely followed. The intelligence sector remained expectant, while the military lobbied against changes and even performed illegal operations. Until the 2000s, intentions to reform the area were normally scandal and politically driven. Following the passage of the law in 2001, the Executive assumed a

---

[143]Information on the Malvinas war and on strategic military intelligence was excluded from declassification.
[144]Created in December 2010.
[145]See José M. Ugarte, 'Nueva Ley de Inteligencia', *La Nación*, 14 December 2001; Estévez, 'Executive and Legislative Oversight of the Intelligence System in Argentina', pp.171–2.

greater role in promoting reforms. A second generation of reforms concerned the military, airport security, and secrecy policy, this last one a major step in terms of transparency. In comparison with the 1990s, legislative oversight in the 2000s was not characterized by its effectiveness.[146] Recent legislative initiatives by the opposition propose changes in the intelligence law aimed at increasing democratic controls and transparency.

A significant step for the exercise of democratic control was the appointment of civilians as intelligence heads, a practice that remains until present. Regional improvements in intelligence cooperation coordinated by civilian officials in collaboration with intelligence agents, was also important.

From time to time democratic leaders insisted on assigning a domestic role to the military, thereby going against the legal plexus that sustains the civil-military relations model chosen by the Argentine democracy.[147] In spite of the legal prohibition, until the reform of 2006, military intelligence engaged in illegal domestic intelligence. Illegal wiretaps continued to generate public concern.[148] Discretionary use of secret funds also prevailed as a practice. Court cases on such misuses show that institutional balances can work. However, as a subject of controversy, the intelligence sector has not yet gained public confidence. Since 1984, intelligence and domestic politics, illegal wiretappings, militarization of intelligence, debates on intelligence legislation, and scandals were topics followed by journalists. During the 2000s, two major national newspapers[149] were critical of the intelligence sector and human rights NGOs have also exposed concerns and blunders. The new law has not yet induced significant changes in culture and practices. Intelligence democratization is still a pending issue.

Concluding Discussion

In the intelligence sector, decision-making rationalities, doctrines and practices developed in the (authoritarian) past impact on the present, reproducing them, thus reinforcing the vitality of those legacies even under democratic rule.[150] This institutional development based on path dependence tends to stability through a positive feedback, reproducing the institutional system. Institutional changes remain absent. Nevertheless, it is also possible

---

[146]See Jaime Rosemberg, 'Mucho Misterio y Escasa Actividad en la Comisión que debe Controlar la SIDE', *La Nación*, 11 August 2009; Alberto Binder, 'Perversa Inteligencia sin Control', Op-ed, *Clarín*, 24 November 2009.

[147]Ernesto López, 'Nuevos Desafíos a la Defensa y la Seguridad: El Impacto en las Relaciones Civiles-Militares, El Caso Argentino', Center for Hemispheric Defense Studies, REDES 2002, Brasilia, 7–10 August 2002, p.10.

[148]See 'Escuchas Ilegales y Cultura Política', *Clarín*, 22 December 2007.

[149]*Clarín* and *La Nación*.

[150]Authoritarian legacies can condition democratic transition and even be embedded in cultural and institutional practices of the new regime; see Paloma Aguilar and Katherine Hite, 'Historical Memory and Authoritarian Legacies in Processes of Political Change: Spain and Chile in Comparative Perspective' in P. Cesarini and K. Hite (eds.) *Authoritarian Legacies and Good Democracies* (Indiana: University of Notre Dame Press 2004) pp.191–231.

that relevant political actors take the risk of initiating a process of change, instead of assuming that institutions cannot be modified.[151] The cost of changing may be a temporary lack of intelligence effectiveness, a policy choice that entails policy and strategic risks. Policy choice here may be crucial for path dependence and change.

The analysis presented here shows more significant differences in the processes of intelligence democratization between the three cases than similarities that could be inferred from the legislation adopted or the legacies. Initiation, decisions, and implementation measures, their timing, and the results are diverse in each case. As I have sought to illustrate here, the processes of democratization do not necessarily occur immediately after restoration of democracy: this is not a sufficient condition to induce change in the intelligence sector. Democratic leaders, surely at some point or for certain reasons, need to exercise control of their intelligence agencies. The question is what kind of control and what for. Likewise, democratic regimes and politicians are not exempt from the temptation to use domestic or security intelligence for purposes other than those legitimate and democratically acceptable. As Ugarte shows, security intelligence is now moving towards the criminal dimension of domestic threats;[152] and the extent of conceptual and practical transparency of such activity remains most relevant for the governance of intelligence.

A common element that precedes intelligence democratization initiatives are abuses of human rights, committed either by military or authoritarian regimes, or under democracy. Concomitantly, revision of the past by special commissions, and eventually trials, emerge as significant events in the first steps of the process. The necessary condition of this is that political actors acknowledge the magnitude and implications of violations of human rights by security and intelligence apparatuses. Thus, transitional justice mechanisms deserve special attention.

In two cases, crises acted as critical junctures that prompted the decision to change. In one case, punctuated changes occurred in certain layers after a specific crisis. The Executive played the main role in Peru and Ecuador, creating special commissions[153] and sponsoring reforms, while in Argentina the promoter of the changes was Congress and only after 2003 did the Executive take up the momentum. Unintended consequences include politicians' insistence on reliance upon military commanders to lead the intelligence sector, and the reluctance to implement profound changes.

---

[151]G. Alexander, 'Institutions, Path Dependence, and Democratic Consolidation', *Journal of Theoretical Politics* 13/3 (2001) pp.255, 259.

[152]See José M. Ugarte, 'La Evolución de la Actividad de Inteligencia y de la Inteligencia Criminal en América Latina', paper prepared for the 2009 Meeting of the Latin American Studies Association, Rio de Janeiro, Brazil, 11–14 June 2009.

[153]See Andrés Gomez de la Torre Rotta, 'Comisiones Reformadoras de Inteligencia: Experiencias Latinoamericanas Recientes (2001–2009)', in Rivera Vélez, *Inteligencia Estratégica y Prospectiva*, pp.177–96.

In terms of political choice, we often observe a lack of political commitment to maintain over time the necessary control of the intelligence sector.

As a preliminary attempt to explain the causal mechanisms of intelligence democratization, this article shows that the process is highly complex. Further analysis is required to understand the links and interactions between new democracies and intelligence reform, between politics, policy, and intelligence, and to assess the outcomes of the process. In the early 2010s, intelligence democratization remains an ongoing process; it is still premature to assert that the intelligence agencies have been deeply reformed.

Acknowledgements

This paper was first presented at the IPSA-ECPR (International Political Science Association – European Consortium for Political Research) Joint Conference, Universidade de São Paulo, São Paulo, Brasil, 16–19 February 2011. I am most grateful to Tom Bruneau, Marina Caparini and Peter Gill for their very helpful comments on the text.

The Spies Who Came from the Tropics: Intelligence Services and Democracy in Brazil

JOANISVAL BRITO GONÇALVES

ABSTRACT Despite the emergence of Brazil as a global power, little is known about its security and intelligence services and the way they are seen by Brazilian society. This article analyzes the Brazilian perception of the role of its intelligence services and the relationship between the intelligence community (IC) and the decision makers. The historical background of intelligence in Brazil and a general overview of the Brazilian IC after the reestablishment of democracy are presented, as well as the general mechanisms of control and accountability of the secret services. Finally, there is consideration of some concerns on reforming the intelligence sector and its control and oversight apparatus.

Introduction

One of the great dilemmas in a democratic regime is how to balance effectiveness and transparency in the public administration. In the particular case of the security and intelligence services it becomes more evident: how to reconcile the work developed by the secret services (which has a natural component of secrecy) with the mandatory principle of transparency that shall motivate all the state activities? The objective of this paper is to present the case of Brazil, analyzing the Brazilian perception of the role of its intelligence services and the relationship between the Brazilian intelligence community (IC) and the decision makers.

The first part of the paper presents the historical background of intelligence in Brazil followed by a general overview of the Brazilian IC after the reestablishment of democracy. The second part is dedicated to the general mechanisms of control and accountability of the secret services. Finally, some concerns on reforming the intelligence sector and its control and oversight apparatus are discussed.

A preliminary concern is related to the fact that, nowadays, the Brazilian society has no clear perception of intelligence. Brazilians do not know enough about the country's IC and still see the secret services with prejudice (and, in some cases, with fear). This general view has its origins in the links of the IC with the authoritarian regime that ruled Brazil from 1964 to 1985. Whilst the population's perception of intelligence is not good, the politicians' comprehension of the role of intelligence is extremely bad: in the Executive and in the Legislative branches decision makers do not know the IC well, do not give them sufficient attention (with consequences for the IC budget) and, in fact, tend to see the secret services more as a threat to democracy than as a sector of the Government created to advise the decision makers and to protect the State and the society.[1]

Intelligence in Brazil: A Briefing

The history of intelligence in Brazil has its official beginning in 1927, with the establishment of the National Defense Council (CDN – *Conselho de Defesa Nacional*), later renamed the National Security Council (CSN – *Conselho de Segurança Nacional*). The CDN had among its missions to assist the President and the Executive branch with information about present or potential threats to national security. Amongst other assignments of the CDN was the development of intelligence and counterintelligence activities. However, the first civilian intelligence service[2] was only created in 1958, and was called the Federal Intelligence and Counterintelligence Service (SFICI – *Serviço Federal de Informações e Contra-Informações*).[3]

Nevertheless, the great landmark in Brazilian intelligence history is the creation of the National Intelligence Service (SNI – *Serviço Nacional de Informações*). On 31 March 1964, the military took the power, overthrowing the weak populist government of President João 'Jango' Goulart. The so-called 'Revolution of 1964' was a military intervention in the political process supported by some segments of the civilian society that resulted in an

---

[1] In 2013 President Dilma Rousseff expressed her disappointment with the effectiveness of the intelligence apparatus, particularly due to the absence of intelligence about the demonstrations in many Brazilian cities in June and during the FIFA Confederations Cup. There were also severe critics on the preparedness of the Brazilian counterintelligence concerning the cases of espionage of American agencies against Brazil leaked by Edward Snowden.

[2] The military intelligence agencies were established after World War II, and each armed service (the Navy, the Army and the Air Force) had its own intelligence organization to assist the Minister and military commanders. It is important to register that until the creation of the Ministry of Defense in 1999, each armed force had ministerial status in Brazil. Actually, for long time in Brazilian history the Minister of the Army (a four-star general) used to be extremely influential in the government.

[3] Some authors translate 'informações' as 'information'. However, we prefer the term 'intelligence', which is the most accurate translation of the Portuguese word 'informações'. Hence, the best translation of 'Serviço Federal de Informações e Contra-Informações – SFICI' is 'Federal Intelligence and Counterintelligence Service' as well as 'National Intelligence Service' for 'Serviço Nacional de Informações – SNI'. Anyway, the reader will find some texts with the names 'National Information Service' and 'Federal Information and Counter-Information Service' for the SNI and SFICI, respectively.

authoritarian regime, which was extended until 1985, when a civilian was elected (by indirect ballot) President of the Republic.[4]

With the exile of Jango and the establishment of the military government, one of the first measures of the new Administration was to produce a bill creating a new secret service to replace the SFICI. The draft was submitted to Congress and, after the regular discussion period, it was finally approved in June 1964. Thus, with Law no. 4,341, of 13 June 1964, a new intelligence service was created, the SNI.[5]

According to the Law, the SNI was a civilian federal secret service with the main function of assisting the President of the Republic on issues of intelligence and counterintelligence. As central intelligence agency in the country, the SNI also had as a mission to supervise and coordinate the State civilian intelligence and counterintelligence system. This system included intelligence directorates in other Ministries, federal agencies, public enterprises, and even inside universities, with thousands of people gathering information, producing intelligence, and reporting to the Central Agency of the SNI.

More than coordination, the relationship between the members of the National Intelligence System (SISNI – *Sistema Nacional de Informações*) and the SNI was based on subordination: the intelligence community reported directly to the SNI and received orders from the Central Agency in Brasilia. Furthermore, it was not unusual that the head of the SNI asked for information and commanded the organs of the system placed in other Ministries without consulting the Ministers to whom the organs were formally subordinated.[6]

---

[4]Although it is not the place to discuss aspects of the legitimacy of the military movement of 1964 that overthrew Jango, it is important to say that the 'military dictatorship' in Brazil was different from other authoritarian regimes in South America, particularly in the way the new regime treated the dissidents and ruled the country. For example, during the most part of the military period the Congress was seated, with congressmen chosen in periodical ballots in a two-party political system, in which there was a well-organized opposition. The military presidents had been elected by the Congress – after being chosen *de facto* by the military leaders – and had a term. Furthermore, radical and violent actions against the antagonists of the regime were infrequent. However, there were periods of huge repression and violations of civil liberties as occurred in all the other dictatorships in the continent.

[5]To see federal Brazilian legislation in Portuguese, see <www.planalto.gov.br>.

[6]There is no broad bibliography about the SNI. Important studies, however, were conducted by Alfred Stepan in the eighties [Alfred Stepan, *Rethinking Military Politics: Brazil and the Southern Cone* (Princeton: Princeton University Press 1988)], Luís Antônio Bittencourt in the nineties [Luís Antônio Bitencourt, *The 'Abertura' in Brazil: The Day-After of the Brazilian Intelligence 'Monster'*, presented to the 33rd Annual Convention of the International Studies Association, Atlanta, Georgia, April 1992], and Marco Cepik and Priscila Antunes in the first decade of this century [Priscila Antunes and Marco Cepik, 'The New Brazilian Intelligence System: An Institutional Assessment', *International Journal of Intelligence and Counterintelligence* 16/3 (2003) pp.349–73)]. Thomas Bruneau has also given attention to the civil–military relations in Brazil, producing a very good analysis of the present intelligence system Thomas [Bruneau and Steven Boraz, *Reforming Intelligence – Obstacles to Democratic Control and Effectiveness* (Austin: University of Texas Press 2007)].

Military intelligence took part in the system, but their agencies were not subordinated to the SNI authority. Actually, the military developed their own secret agencies, which became tremendously powerful. In some cases, those agencies competed with the SNI and amongst themselves, gathering information, producing intelligence and, above all, 'fighting against the internal enemy'. During the worst years of the dictatorship, the military intelligence was the core of a potent repressive apparatus that became responsible for some violent illegal actions.

However, the 'bad fame' of intelligence as an instrument of the authoritarian regime was definitively associated to the SNI, which became the best-known organization of the intelligence community. Certainly, during the military period, the SNI turned from a small agency into an extremely powerful organization in Brazil. Intended to be a civilian secret service, it became militarized: generals and colonels assumed posts of command in the service, and many analysts and agents were recruited from the armed forces. According to Alfred Stepan,[7] the SNI became a fourth military service, or even a state within the state, with structure and powers that could be compared to those of the secret services in communist regimes, such as the Soviet KGB. It differed from similar agencies in other western countries due to the ministerial rank of its chief and its monopoly over training the intelligence community. All of the intelligence community was trained in the National Intelligence School (ESNI – *Escola Nacional de Informações*), which was responsible for producing and propagating the Brazilian intelligence doctrine. Like the KGB, the SNI was responsible for foreign and domestic intelligence, gathering and analyzing information in different fields, including data about political dissidents and adversaries of the regime. Actually, the focus of the service became more and more on security intelligence and counterintelligence.

The Chief Ministers of the SNI were exceptionally influent in the government. In the context of increasingly repressive dictatorship, part of the intelligence community was used as watchdogs of the regime. Thus, the secret services were assigned to repressive operations against actual or potential adversaries of the group in power. From simple surveillance to kidnapping and torture, the state security and intelligence actions caused a huge trauma in the Brazilian society. Being central to the intelligence system, the SNI was the backbone of the military authoritarian regime in Brazil and notorious for its participation in these dreadful activities. Hence, almost two decades after the dissolution of the SNI, the present Brazilian Intelligence Agency (ABIN – *Agência Brasilieira de Inteligência*) has to deal with the stigma of the SNI. That is a problem with consequences for the agency budget, intelligence officers' morale and mainly for the present (mis)perception of intelligence in Brazilian society and among decision makers.

---

[7]Stepan, *Rethinking Military Politics*.

The Brazilian IC and the Transition towards Democracy

During the first civilian Administration after the end of the military regime, the SNI remained an important federal agency,[8] with its Minister still very close to the President. The service also resisted the great reforms conduced under the Constitution of 1988. Indeed, the new Charter did not abolish the SNI as it did to other institutions of the military period, like the National Security Council (CSN – *Conselho de Segurança Nacional*).[9] It is interesting how intelligence and the SNI stayed aside from the roll of issues of the new Constitution. In fact, there is no explicit mention to intelligence in the Constitution, that goes into other very specific matters, for example, the rules concerning the teaching of History,[10] the federal status of the secondary school Pedro II, in Rio de Janeiro,[11] and the duty of the State 'to foster the practice of formal and informal sports, as a right of each individual'.[12] The doubt about this apparent 'ostracism' of the intelligence in the new Fundamental Law remains: did it happen due to the huge influence of the SNI that intentionally did not want to be referred to in the Constitution and succeeded in being untouchable, or was it a means found by the men and women who wrote the new Charter to undermine the service by not providing for Brazilian intelligence on a constitutional level?

In 1990, on inauguration day, President Fernando Collor de Mello abolished the SNI and the SISNI. It was an announced coup de force in the intelligence community.[13] Even so, the presidential act took many people by surprise because few expected a really drastic initiative against the influential secret service. According to Thomas Bruneau, it was, undoubtedly, 'the most critical and basic reform in the Brazilian intelligence system'.[14]

With the end of the SNI and its system, intelligence became a damned art. The secret service faced ostracism.[15] The last decade of the twentieth century is known as 'the years of darkness' for intelligence in Brazil. At the same time that internally the intelligence community lost its prestige, the main enemy

---

[8] For a more detailed comprehension of intelligence in the period immediately after the military regime see Bitencourt, *The 'Abertura' in Brazil*.

[9] A very good reference to the changes promoted by the new Constitution of Brazil on the reminiscences of the military period is Wendy Hunter, *Eroding Military Influence in Brazil – Politicians against Soldiers* (Chapel Hill and London: The University of North Carolina Press 1997).

[10] 'The teaching of Brazilian History shall take into account the contribution of the different cultures and ethnic groups to the formation of the Brazilian people'; *Constitution of Brazil*, 1988, article 242, paragraph 1.

[11] 'The Pedro II School, located in the city of Rio de Janeiro, shall be maintained in the federal sphere'; *Constitution of Brazil*, 1988, article 242, paragraph 2.

[12] *Constitution of Brazil*, 1988, article 217.

[13] During the presidential campaign, Collor de Mello announced that one of his first measures as President would be to abolish the SNI and to put an end to the legacy of the military dictatorship.

[14] Bruneau and Boraz, *Reforming Intelligence*.

[15] Antunes and Cepik, 'The New Brazilian Intelligence System'.

had also disappeared with the end of the Cold War. On the one hand, with the collapse of the Soviet Union and the socialist bloc, international communism was no longer a threat. On the other hand, in the domestic field, the 'internal enemy' changed. Social movements, left-wing parties, including the communists, and groups from a broad political and social spectrum that would have been considered 'dangerous to the national interests' 10 years earlier, were now legitimate parts of the democratic process. Even words like 'subversion' and 'national security' were banished. As in many countries around the world, in Brazil it was very difficult to reshape intelligence and to establish secret services under a new post-Cold War perspective. The truth is that people were completely lost in terms of what to do with the intelligence services in a new and singular international order, marked by unipolarity in security, multipolarity in economy, new non-state organizations influencing the system, and by new threats from sources other than states.

But the 1990s were also the years of a great debate about the role of intelligence in democracy around the world. Thus, in the Executive and the Legislative branch, the discussion about the creation of a new civilian secret service for Brazil commenced. Some bills were presented by members of Congress and also by the Government. The main question was how to conceive an agency different from the SNI in terms of structure, procedures and orientation. Would a single service deal with both foreign and security intelligence or would it be better to create two separate agencies? How should intelligence officials be recruited and trained? What should be done with the remnants of the authoritarian regime still working in the service, some of them in senior positions? And, most important, how could the establishment avoid the secret service becoming a menace to democracy and to the society?

In 1995, Fernando Henrique Cardoso took office as the 34th President of Brazil. The Cardoso Administration decided to create a new secret service to fill the blank left by the abolished SNI. This new agency would be tailored to fit the Brazilian democratic regime. The service would be created by law, with a bill submitted to a complete congressional evaluation, including debates in the House and the Senate Committees, as well as in public hearings, when the civilian society could then participate and give its contribution and suggestions to the new bill. To conduct this process President Cardoso chose an Army general, Fernando Cardoso (no relation). Some months later, Fernando Cardoso was replaced by Alberto Mendes Cardoso (also no relation), also a general of the Army.

A commission at the Executive branch was created to draft the bill that would be presented to Congress. The commission analyzed different models of secret services and intelligence systems from many democracies around the world. After some months, a final draft was prepared. It created a civilian federal secret service, with no law enforcement powers, with focus on security intelligence but also responsible for foreign intelligence. The main mission of this new agency should be to assist the President of the Republic with intelligence on present or potential threats, as well as on opportunities according to national interests, under democratic principles, and in defense of the state and of the society.

The bill was submitted to Congress and approved two years later. On 7 December 1999, Law no. 9,883 was published. It created a new intelligence service, the Brazilian Intelligence Agency (ABIN – *Agência Brasileira de Inteligência*). The ABIN was supposed to be the central agency of a Brazilian Intelligence System (SISBIN – *Sistema Brasileiro de Inteligência*). Brazil began a new century of intelligence.

Brazilian IC in the Twenty-First Century: An Overview

Brazilian intelligence activities in the twenty-first century have their legal framework based on several documents.[16] First of all, there is Law no. 9,883/1999, which creates the ABIN and the SISBIN and establishes the official concepts of intelligence and counterintelligence. According to the law, intelligence is defined as 'the activity which intends to obtain, analyze, and disseminate knowledge within and outside the national territory on facts and situations of immediate or potential influence on government actions and decision processes about the protection and the security of society and the State'. That is an extremely generic definition, which is literally reproduced by the Executive Decree no. 4,376/2002 that implements the SISBIN. Despite its vagueness, the official concept in the law expresses the paramount role of intelligence in Brazil: to supply the first-rank decision makers with information about facts or situations considered significant to guarantee the security of the state and of the society. It is important to register that, for the first time, legislation establishes the protection of both the Brazilian society and state as an obligation for the intelligence system; previously, the mission of the intelligence community was to protect just the Brazilian state.

The Law no. 9,883/1999 creates the ABIN and assigns it as the central agency of the SISBIN. Other competences of the ABIN are expressed in article 4 of the referred Law: (1) planning and executing actions, including secret ones, related to collection and analysis of data to produce knowledge having as an objective to assist the President of the Republic; (2) planning and executing actions toward the protection of sensible knowledge, related to state and society security interests; (3) evaluating internal and external threats to the constitutional order; (4) promoting the development of human resources on intelligence and also the intelligence doctrine; and (5) producing studies and research to improve the effectiveness of the intelligence.

Previously assigned to be an agency directly subordinated to the President, the ABIN has been structured under the Institutional Security Cabinet of the Presidency of the Republic (GSI – *Gabinete de Segurança Institucional*), the former Military Office. The GSI has the main components of a National Security Council: 'This council is physically located next to the president's offices, and the Minister Chief has ready access to the president. The GSI serves as the permanent secretariat for a

---

[16] An excellent reference about Brazilian legal framework on intelligence is the chapter by Marco Cepik, 'Structural Change and Democratic Control of Intelligence in Brazil' in Bruneau and Boraz, *Reforming Intelligence*.

national defense council. It conducts studies, monitors and provides policy guidance on crises, develops position papers, and decree laws, among other functions, for the presidency under the leadership of the Minister Chief of State (*Ministro de Estado Chefe*)'.[17]

As the ABIN is under the GSI, there is no direct link between the Agency and the President, unlike the situation in the past with the SNI. For some experts, it could be a sign of loss of prestige of the secret service; for others, it was a way found to keep the President far from eventual scandals involving intelligence.[18] The latter argument is more plausible.

The ABIN is headed by a Director-General (DG), chosen and appointed by the President of the Republic, submitted to Senate approval. The DG is the main officer of the organization and is responsible for elaborating the internal rules to the agency, for authorizing operations and appointing other directors, including the Deputy Director-General. As the Agency is subordinated to the GSI, the DG reports directly to the Minister not to the President. So, the truth is that the Chief-Minister of the GSI is the real head of the intelligence service.

But the ABIN is just one of the several intelligence organizations composing the SISBIN. At present, there are around 20 federal agencies in different ministries (including the intelligence of the three armed forces) that are part of the system.[19] The members of the SISBIN usually belong to the Federal Administration, particularly those institutions responsible for defense, domestic security, and foreign affairs, such as the Ministry of Defense, the Ministry of Justice, and the Ministry of Foreign Relations or under other Ministries, such as Health, Labor or Environment (Figure 1). If necessary, however, adjustments can be carried out to allow organizations from other members of the federation to join the system. All these agencies integrate the planning and execution of the intelligence activities in the country and, although the ABIN is the central agency of the system, they are supposed to operate under the coordination of the GSI.[20]

---

[17] Thomas C. Bruneau, Florina Cristiana Matei and Sak Sakoda, 'National Security Councils: Their Potential Functions in Democratic Civil–Military Relations', *Defense & Security Analysis* 25/3 (2009) pp.255–69 (p.262).

[18] According to Cepik ('Structural Change and Democratic Control', pp.156–7), when subordinating the ABIN to the GSI, 'the government tried to justify this decision (...) citing the need to guard the president from the daily managerial demands and potential crises resulting from scandals and tensions inherent to the relation between intelligence and policymaking'. However, Cepik continues, in practice 'the subordination of ABIN to GSI corresponded to a number of responsibilities that GSI had acquired over time because of the trust the president had in General Alberto Cardoso'. But the fact is that even within Lula da Silva's Administration, the ABIN remained subordinated to the GSI.

[19] For the main characteristics of the SISBIN see Cepik, 'Structural Change and Democratic Control'.

[20] That is a really amazing situation. According to the Law, the central agency of the SISBIN is the ABIN, which has amid its attributions 'planning, executing, coordinating, supervising and controlling the country's intelligence activities' (Law no. 9,883/1999, article 3). Nevertheless, Executive Decree no. 3,376/2002 puts the GSI as the 'coordinator of the federal intelligence activities' (Executive Decree no. 3,376/2002, article 4, item II).

Figure 1. The Brazilian Intelligence System – An Overview.

Following the general commandments of the Law, the competences of the SISBIN are gathering and disseminating information (and intelligence)[21] 'necessary to the decision-making process of the Executive branch', as well as protecting information 'against access of unauthorized people or agencies'. The system has also as its fundamental elements preserving national sovereignty and defending the rule of law and the dignity of the human being.

Relationships in the system are based on cooperation, not on subordination, as in the former SISNI. The members of the SISBIN have plenty of autonomy to conduct their activities and share intelligence with others and with the ABIN in particular, within the limits of the law and while maintaining secret classified information that is transmitted. Cooperation with foreign agencies is supposed to be centralized in the ABIN. However, the police, the military and other attachés who deal with intelligence issues report directly to their own agency or service, not to the ABIN. In recent years, the ABIN has started to organize a net of intelligence attachés in some American and European countries.

In terms of the relationship between the State and intelligence agencies it is also important to notice that, despite the legal framework defining the activities of the IC (the SISBIN) in general terms, and of the ABIN in particular, the legislation concerning intelligence is extremely simple. It does not present a clear mandate to the agencies, gives no support to the IC activities and is not clear in terms of the mission and guarantees to the services and the intelligence officials and agents. Even the mechanisms of control and accountability of the IC are not entirely clear in the legislation. Consequently the services can carry out their basic missions only with difficulty.

The consumers of intelligence are both military and civilian. While the ABIN and the majority of the SISBIN have the main function to support the Executive branch with intelligence, the final consumers being the President and Ministers, the military services have their own consumers (the

---

[21]Information here can be understood as raw intelligence.

Commanders of the Armed Forces and their general-staff), but they can also provide the President with intelligence (throughout the Minister of Defense).[22] One interesting point: despite the President being the ultimate consumer of intelligence, all of the production developed by the ABIN goes first to the Minister of the GSI (a four-star general), who becomes a real 'filter' of the knowledge that goes to the Chief of the Government. The main IC civilian agency is, therefore, subordinated to a military one.

Another important point is the concept of an IC in Brazil. This idea was extremely effective during the SNI times, when a broad net of organizations was established under the orientation of the SNI's Central Agency, trained by the sole Intelligence School and guided by the same doctrinal principles. With the debacle of the SNI in the early 1990s, the System was annihilated and the idea of formal IC turned to an informal IC, with people linked more by personal relations than by official ones. During the 1990s, the community continued to get together, but without general guidelines and with weak formal connections.

One of the central aspects of the conception of the SISBIN is to improve the coordination within the Brazilian IC. Compared with the former SISNI (that operated under hierarchical principles), relationships within the SISBIN are conducted by coordination.[23] There are mistrust and communication problems among the intelligence agencies and sometimes it is difficult to share information for bureaucratic reasons. The consequence is that the IC continues to cooperate by informal means, based mainly on personal relationships. This is a problem for the institutional development of the system.

Access to information within the system is based, universally, on the 'need to know principle' (*princípio da compartimentação*). The intelligence produced is shared with other partners of the SISBIN according to guidelines produced by agency directors. The law establishes that the information must be shared, but not how it must be done. And the consumers of intelligence are only in the Executive branch. Obviously, in order to proceed with their review and oversight functions, the Judiciary and the Legislature can ask for information and are supposed to have access to the intelligence produced by the secret services. The main question about this issue under discussion now in Brazil is how far the judges and parliamentarians shall go in terms of access to the services' production. A bill is also in discussion in Congress related to the rights of access to classified documents, particularly those produced by the IC.

Probably all of these problems with the role of the intelligence services in Brazil are related to the lack of an intelligence culture in the Brazilian society. This absence is associated with misperceptions in terms of national security and defense issues. Two-and-a-half decades since the end of the authoritarian period, Brazilian society still associates national security, defense, and intelligence with the military and with repressive practices. Fortunately, this

---

[22]The Ministry of Defense has its own department of intelligence.

[23]In 2008, a Department was created inside the ABIN to coordinate the relations amongst the members of the System (the Departamento de Integração do SISBIN – DISBIN [*Department for Integration of the SISBIN*]).

perspective is changing but it is a slow process that involves changes in the way the people (and their representatives) see the State security and intelligence apparatus: from an organized structure to support the State (sometimes against the individuals) to new institutions created to defend the State and the society under democratic principles.

However, notwithstanding all of the difficulties, Brazilian intelligence has changed a lot in the last two decades. The transition from an authoritarian-based model to a modern democratic apparatus happened around a decade after the political transition. Presently, the stigma of the dictatorial past remains with the secret services, which make efforts to show to the Brazilian society (and also to themselves) that they have really changed. Indeed, important changes are expected in the near future including in the control system.

Intelligence Control and Accountability in Brazil

In terms of control and accountability, the Brazilian intelligence system is formally under several mechanisms of review and oversight. According to Peter Gill,[24] there are four levels at which both the managerial control and the external oversight of the bureaucracy should be practiced. The first is internal to the agency and is based on guidelines with the director of the agency as the main controller. The second level, also internal, is within the Executive branch and is conducted by a minister or special boards. Usually, Commissions of Inquiry are placed under the Executive guidelines. External control is conducted by institutions outside the Executive branch, particularly by the Legislative branch and its committees or external committees accountable to Parliament. In the fourth level is the citizen's oversight, in which political parties, the press and other public interest groups are the main actors.

In Brazilian intelligence, at the first level is the director of the service, for example, the Director-General of the ABIN or the chiefs of the military intelligence services. For example, Presidential Decree no. 6,408/2008 establishes the main functions of the Director-General of the ABIN: elaborating and proposing the internal rules to the Agency and present them to the Minister of the Institutional Security Cabinet; planning, directing, guiding, supervising, evaluating and controlling the execution of the projects and activities of the ABIN; and exercising administrative and functional control of the agency.

There is also the Executive control, which is under the Minister – in the case of the ABIN, that is the Minister of Institutional Security. As an advisory board to the Minister, is the Chamber of Foreign Affairs and Defense (CREDEN – *Câmara de Relações Exteriores e Defesa Nacional*). The CREDEN is responsible for supervising the accomplishment of the National Intelligence Policy and other directives to the intelligence community. Unfortunately, the CREDEN has been ineffective in recent years.

---

[24]Peter Gill, *Policing Politics: Security Intelligence and the Liberal Democratic State* (Abingdon: Frank Cass 1994). The focus of Gill's book is on security intelligence agencies, but the standards of analysis can be used in any governmental agency.

The main achievement of the Brazilian system is the external control apparatus, especially the roles of the Public Prosecutor, the Judiciary, and the Congress. The Public Prosecutor[25] is probably the most important institution for the control (both oversight and review) of public administration in the Brazilian democracy. Since the new Constitution of 1988, the Public Prosecutor has an important role as the citizen's main watchdog against misconduct of public or private officials. From an office subordinated to the Executive branch and charged to defend the administration, it has turned into an independent and autonomous institution focused on the protection of the law and defense of society's interests.[26] Presently, it is considered almost a fourth branch of the Government, a 'fourth power' autonomous from the Executive, the Legislative and the Judiciary,[27] due to the high level of the public attorneys' powers and their functional guarantees to conduct investigations.

According to article 127 of the Brazilian Constitution, the Public Prosecutor is 'a permanent institution, essential to the jurisdictional function of the State, and it is its duty to defend the juridical order, the democratic regime and the inalienable social and individual interests'. Furthermore, 'unity, indivisibility and functional independence are institutional principles of the Public Prosecution'. It operates at both federal and state levels.

The Brazilian Constitution also ensures the functional and administrative autonomy of the Public Prosecutor, and s/he may propose to the Legislative branch the creation of its offices and auxiliary services, filling them through a civil service entrance examination of tests and/or presentation of academic and professional credentials, remuneration policies, and career plans. Unlike the former Brazilian Constitutions, the Charter of 1988 established the Public Prosecutor as a professional and independent institution, and its members are regarded as protectors of the Brazilian society interests.[28]

---

[25]Like the French *Ministère Public*, the Brazilian Public Prosecutor (or Public Prosecution Service) is responsible for prosecuting criminal cases and representing the interests of society in civil litigation. For the Public Prosecution website see <http://www.mpu.gov.br/> (in Portuguese).

[26]'The 1988 Brazilian Constitution assigns to the Public Prosecution two principal responsibilities: to defend the constitutional interests of the citizens and society at a large and to ensure that the public administration, and all its respective parts, complies with its constitutional responsibilities'; Maria Tereza Sadek and Rosangela Batista Cavalcanti, 'The New Brazilian Public Prosecution: An Agent of Accountability' in Scott Mainwaring and Christopher Welna (eds.) *Democratic Accountability in Latin America* (Oxford: Oxford University Press 2003) pp.201–27 (p.203).

[27]Hugo Mazzilli, *Regime Jurídico do Ministério Público* (São Paulo: Saraiva 1993).

[28]To the Public Advocacy, the Brazilian Constitution established the Advocacy-General of the Union (AGU – *Advocacia-Geral da União*) and its equivalents in the States, Municipalities and public agencies. The AGU is the institution 'which, either directly or through a subordinated agency, represents the Union judicially or extrajudicially, and it is responsible, under the terms of the supplementary law which provides for its organization and operation, for the activities of judicial consultation and assistance to the Executive Power' (*Constitution of Brazil*, article 131, *caput*).

Amongst the guarantees of the independence of public prosecutors are:

- life tenure, after two years in office, with loss of office only by a final and unappealable judicial decision;
- irremovability, save for reason of public interest, through decision of the competent collegiate body of the Public Prosecution, by the vote of the absolute majority of its members, full defense being ensured;
- irreducibility of compensation.

Concerning intelligence, the Public Prosecutor has been important in supervising the secret services, particularly police forces' intelligence. And the prosecutors have been responsible for many investigations of irregularities committed by the intelligence community.

The Congress and the Intelligence Community

Whilst the control and oversight of public administration is constant and permanently conducted by non-partisan public prosecution, the political control of the Executive branch and the defense of public interests remains a primary function of the Legislative branch. To fulfill its constitutional control and oversight prerogatives, Congress can count on its Standing Committees and on the Parliamentary Investigating Committees.

The Parliament has an important role in terms of control and accountability of the Government. As happens in almost all democratic regimes around the world, the Legislative branch in Brazil has amongst its essential functions the prerogative to oversee the Administration, checking public policies and the expenditure of the governmental budget.

The external control conducted by Parliament has also been developed in the last two decades in Brazil. The power of Congress to supervise and oversee the other two branches of Government has grown as much as the democracy has been consolidated in the country after the end of the military period. Presently, Senators and Deputies know well their prerogatives in terms of control over the Executive and exercise them in different ways. For example, it is important to notice the increase in requests for information, public audiences and summonses of authorities, and also the establishment of temporary investigating committees in both the Senate and the House since 1988.[29]

Although there had been early attempts to control intelligence after the creation of the SNI in 1964, during the following three decades Congress made no significant intervention in terms of intelligence oversight. The formal mechanism of congressional oversight of the SISBIN was established in 1999, with Law no. 9,883/1999.

---

[29]See Leany Barreiro Lemos, 'Como o Congresso Brasileiro controla o Executivo? O uso de requerimentos de informação, convocação de autoridades e propostas de fiscalização e controle', in Mariana Llanos and Ana Maria Mustapic (eds.) *Controle parlamentar na Alemanha, na Argentina e no Brasil* (Rio de Janeiro: Fundação Konrad Adenauer 2005) pp.85–112.

According to article 6 of Law no. 9,883/1999, the intelligence activities in Brazil should be submitted to external control and Congress should create a committee to oversee the intelligence community. In November 2002 – almost a year after the Law had entered in force – the Brazilian Parliament created the Joint Committee for the Control of Intelligence Activities (CCAI – *Comissão Mista de Controle das Atividades de Inteligência do Congresso Nacional*), composed of three Senators and three members of the House of Representatives.

Notwithstanding the ABIN being based on the Canadian model of a secret service (as well as the relationship between the members of the SISBIN), the Brazilian mechanisms of external control and accountability are similar to those in the United States. Hence, the CCAI was supposed to operate like the Standing Committees of Intelligence in the US Senate and House. For example, it has prerogatives to perform oversight and not just post hoc review – as is common in Parliamentarian regimes. As other committees related to security, defense and public safety in the Brazilian Parliament,[30] the CCAI will have intrusive powers to control the intelligence community. For instance, the members of the CCAI will have total clearance to access secret documents and operations in progress. They can also invite the heads of the intelligence agencies – including the Ministers – to hearings that can be in camera or not.

The powers of the CCAI are many. However, the Committee still does not operate adequately. It has many structural and organizational problems. The Committee standing orders have not been established and there is a lack of technical resources and personnel. Additionally, due to its low prestige, sometimes it is very difficult for the Committee even to meet, because its members have other political tasks that they consider take priority. Hence, the CCAI, although a standing committee, usually meets only in reaction to crises in the intelligence community. Many parliamentarians criticize the way the CCAI is presently constituted and its work. Bills are proposed to change this situation and to establish a more effective mechanism of external legislative control.

Although it has huge operational problems, the CCAI has a symbolic role because it represents the Legislative power to control and oversee the intelligence community. It reflects the need for accountability in a sector of Brazilian public administration that had never been controlled before. The establishment of mechanisms of control and accountability under fundamental legal basis was an important step towards the transparency and democratization of intelligence in Brazil.

The Crises of 2008 and the Winds of Reform

In 2008 the Brazilian intelligence community suffered a major crisis. In early July, there was a leak to the press about a Federal Police intelligence

---

[30] For example, both the Senate and the House have a Standing Committee on Foreign Affairs and Defense Issues, and committees on public safety. These committees can oversee the public administration, including the secret services.

operation to investigate corruption, money laundering and other crimes with supposed involvement amongst public officers, politicians and the private sector. Under the name of Operation Satiagraha, police agents had intercepted several telephone conversations of politicians, ministers, bankers, public servants, lawyers and judges. Many of these targets were not under investigation and the interceptions were considered illegal.

The main problem of Operation Satiagraha is that it involved agents from the ABIN – more than 80 collaborated with the Federal Police during the investigations, which is forbidden by law. In other words, the ABIN could not participate in a criminal intelligence operation. According to the Federal Constitution, only the police forces are allowed to tap telephones. Furthermore, to engage in tapping operations, the law enforcement agents have to ask for prior judicial authorization. But the ABIN is not allowed to do this; therefore, the Brazilian federal secret service is forbidden to make use of one of the most common and useful intelligence practices.

So, in Operation Satiagraha there was illegal participation of ABIN agents in a police operation. Paulo Lacerda, then the Director-General of the ABIN, ordered ABIN officials to take part in a joint force, giving support to the Federal Police in criminal investigations of corruption related to politicians and businessmen. Apart from the fact that the investigation was using illegal means, including tapping people without judicial authorization, the problem is that the law is not clear whether or not the ABIN can really take part in this kind of operation. In this operation, people that had nothing to do with the investigation, such as the President of the Brazilian Supreme Court, the Chief-Advisor of President Lula, and Senators, had their telephones tapped and their conversations recorded. It turned out to be a great scandal, and Lacerda and the Director of the Federal Police had to face Congressmen to try to explain the irregularities.

Operation Satiagraha caused a great political turmoil in Brazil. Paulo Lacerda, many Directors and agents of the ABIN, as well as the Minister of the Institutional Security, were called to Congress to explain the involvement of the secret service in a police investigation. In August, Lacerda, the Agency's Deputy Director-General and the Director of Counterintelligence were removed by the President and the ABIN remained under direction of the then third man of the Agency, Wilson Trezza, who had administrative functions. In December 2008, Lacerda was finally dismissed, but Trezza became interim Director-General until December 2009.

In Congress, the debate about intelligence and security continued throughout 2009. In the House, a Parliamentary Committee of Inquiry was established to investigate the irregular interception of communications promoted by police officers, intelligence and private agents. During the works of the Committee, the parliamentarians discovered more than 375,000 irregular interceptions to support police investigations in 2007. The main diagnosis of the security and intelligence system was that it was completely out of control.

In this context of crisis, in February 2009, a Presidential Decree created an inter-ministerial commission to discuss intelligence, propose modifications and elaborate the draft of the first National Intelligence Policy (PNI). The group worked for months and finally presented the PNI draft to the President. In October, this was submitted to the National Defense Council (CDN) to get its members' concerns and, in December, the PNI was sent to Congress to be analyzed by the CCAI. In August 2010, it was finally approved by the CCAI with suggestions, and sent back to the Executive. However, President Lula did not sign it into law before the end of his term (31 December). At the time of writing (September 2013), the new President, Dilma Rousseff, has not signed it either.

With a PNI, there will be more clear directives to the Brazilian intelligence community. It is extremely important in terms of control and accountability. From the PNI, the national intelligence strategy can be established as well as the national and sectoral intelligence plans. The PNI will be a parameter to the controllers to check if the secret services are operating correctly.

However, it is in Congress that we can see the main changes in terms of intelligence oversight. At the end of 2008, the draft of the Standing Rules to the Joint Intelligence Committee (CCAI) was presented by Congressman Luiz Carlos Hauly. It was discussed in the Senate, at the House and in the CCAI which presented a new version (with acquiescence of Hauly) that was ready to be voted by Congress. The CCAI had many meetings (more than it has had in the former years) and the establishment of the regulations to the Committee became a priority to the Committee.

The case of the CCAI in 2009 is important to the analysis of the role of a Chair interested in the issue. On March 2009, Congressman Severiano Alves became the Chair of the CCAI. Even without a huge background on intelligence, Alves became quickly interested on the issue and decided to move the Committee on. He organized meetings with the intelligence community and visited the ABIN and other secret services. The intelligence community, for its turn, perceived in Alves someone who could be a great controller and ally.

During his period as Chair of the CCAI, Alves promoted discussion on the Standing Rules of the Committee. The CCAI also had meetings to discuss the needs of the intelligence community, for example, the ABIN budget and the recruitment of new intelligence officials. In August 2009, Alves presented a Project of Amendment to the Constitution (PEC – *Proposta de Emenda à Constituição*) to elevate the intelligence to the constitutional level. It is, without any doubt, the most important legal initiative in intelligence sector since Law no. 9,883/1999.

The PEC proposed by Alves was registered as PEC no. 398/2009. It is also known as 'the Intelligence PEC'. It amends the Constitution including five new articles on intelligence. It is the first reference to the issue in the Brazilian Political Charter. The PEC basically establishes the concept of intelligence and counterintelligence constitutionally. Additionally, it creates a coordinated Brazilian intelligence system with a central agency to conduct strategic intelligence. It also asserts the intelligence officials' prerogatives and gives them more support for their activities. For example, the preservation of the intelligence officer's identity is safeguarded with the Intelligence PEC, as well as the legal use of technical means and methods on the intelligence operations.

Nevertheless, it is precisely in terms of control and accountability that the Intelligence PEC innovates. It establishes that the control of the intelligence community shall be internal and external. In terms of external control, it focuses on the Legislative oversight. According to that, the external oversight and supervision is an attribution of Congress, and it is conducted by a parliamentary joint committee (which is presently the CCAI) and an external non-parliamentary board, the Council of Intelligence Oversight.

Hence, PEC no. 398/2009 would have created a new board to oversee intelligence. The Council would be composed of seven members, non-parliamentarians and chosen thus: two by the Senate; two by the House; one by the President of the Republic; one by the National Justice Council; one by the National Council of the Public Prosecution. They would be nominated by Congress, after being approved by the parliamentary intelligence oversight committee. The members of the Council would have a five-year term and could be dismissed only by congressional decision. They would report solely and directly to Congress and to its intelligence oversight committee.

The idea of an independent non-parliamentarian board to oversee the entire Brazilian intelligence community is based on the Portuguese and the Canadian models of controlling intelligence. However, the Brazilian Council would have more powers than its foreign counterparts. It would not have just review functions like the Canadian Intelligence Review Committee (SIRC) and the Portuguese Intelligence System Supervision Council (*Conselho de Fiscalização do Sistema de Informações da República Portuguesa*). The Brazilian Council would have functional control of the intelligence activity and be responsible for overseeing the entire system. It would develop a constant oversight to the secret services, controlling the entire community and any agency that developed intelligence within the Administration. It would also give support to the CCAI, analyzing priorities, policies and order operations proposed by the Executive. As the PEC would dispose only on the settlement of the Council, its general rules of proceedings and prerogatives would be established by law. The idea of a 'constitutionalization' of intelligence as well as the establishment of more effective mechanisms of external control were very well accepted by Congress and the intelligence community itself.

Within the intelligence community, the acceptance of the Intelligence PEC was general. As Chair of the CCAI, Alves has invited representatives of the secret services to several meetings to introduce them to the PEC and to discuss its text with them. From the GSI, from the first meeting complete support was given to the idea, which continued throughout the military intelligence and the other sectors. There was also a presentation of the project at a variety of events and seminars in various cities of Brazil and, finally, at an International Seminar on 1 December 2009.

However, in 2011, at the end of the legislature, the PEC was dead. Alves was not re-elected. In December 2012, the bill was re-introduced by Senator Fernando Collor, former President of the Republic and the Chairman of the CCAI for 2012, who had become very engaged in the intelligence community issues. The new PEC got the number 67/2012 and is under analysis by Congress.

In 2013, two important events further shook the Brazilian public opinion's of the IC. First, during FIFA's Confederations Cup in Brazil, millions of Brazilians went to the streets to protest against the Government expenditure on the Games and the corruption within the Public Administration. The IC was accused of total incapacity to produce intelligence to alert the Government about the demonstrations and the President was furious with this inefficiency of her secret services.

Second, also in June 2013, the world was informed that NSA watched more than terrorists and enemies of USA. The former National Security Agency (NSA) contractor Edward Snowden leaked many classified documents related to US espionage on foreign governments and authorities, including the President of Brazil. Rousseff had had her personal emails tapped by the Americans. There were many critics of the Brazilian counterintelligence capacity. Another Parliamentary Committee of Inquiry was established to investigate this irregular interception of communications and the role of the Brazilian intelligence and security system to prevent this. At the time of writing (September 2013), this Inquiry was still under way insofar as the Snowden case related to Brazil. Some experts in Brazil believe that these controversies could improve the prospects for PEC no. 67/2012 in Congress.

Conclusions: Towards a More Effective Transparency of the Brazilian Intelligence Community?

More than 10 years after the establishment of the Brazilian Intelligence System and the creation of the Brazilian Intelligence Agency, the Brazilian intelligence community has many challenges. Brazilian society and policymakers share a prejudice against intelligence and there is a lack of motivation within the officers. With a reduced budget and without legal support, the secret services operate in great difficulties. The result is inefficiency, ineffectiveness, and a bad reputation.

In terms of control and accountability, until recently Congress had not woken to its important role in intelligence oversight. The great majority of the parliamentarians knew nothing about intelligence. In fact, they were not interested in it. The consequence was the absence of an effective mechanism of intelligence oversight in Parliament.

However, changes are on course and 2009 represented a significant mark to the intelligence community and its oversight mechanisms. Important steps were taken in Congress and in the Executive branch: the PNI, the Standing Rules to the CCAI and the Intelligence PEC. Despite no significant advances in legislation since 2010, there are some changes expected for following years: after the PNI, the Executive intends to propose a new legal framework for the IC, with new mandates to several agencies and the creation of subsystems of defense intelligence, criminal intelligence, financial intelligence and strategic intelligence, coordinated, respectively, by the Ministries of Defense, Justice, Economy and the GSI. These issues are still under discussion inside the Executive and have met some resistance within sectors of the IC.

DEMOCRATIZATION OF INTELLIGENCE

The Snowden case will also be useful to reshape the Brazilian IC. The crises caused by this leak can promote changes on counterintelligence apparatus. Indeed, this situation was important in exposing the vulnerabilities of the State and the country to foreign espionage, particularly that related to Techint. The main conclusion: something must be done.

In terms of transparency, the IC situation is better than it was 20 years ago. However, to improve the effectiveness of this transparency it is essential to reform the legal framework and develop the mechanisms of control, particularly those related to external oversight. There is one certainty about the future of intelligence in Brazil: that the next years will see sweeping changes.

Democratic Oversight in Fragile States: The Case of Intelligence Reform in Bosnia and Herzegovina

HELGE LURÅS

ABSTRACT   In most transition countries the main aim of 'democratizing intelligence' is to weaken the authoritarian governmental structures by introducing more transparency, legality and oversight. In Bosnia and Herzegovina however, the state-building efforts driven by international parties combined formal democratization processes such as independent oversight with the strengthening and operational capacity building of previously weak-to-non-existent intelligence structures. In parallel with the descent into war when Yugoslavia collapsed in the early 1990s, the State Security Service (SDB) in the Republic of Bosnia had split into three ethnically-based outfits answering to the political and military leaders of war. 'Democratization' of intelligence in Bosnia and Herzegovina since the establishment of a unified, state-level Intelligence and Security Agency (OSA) in 2004 has followed its own unique path reflecting the fragmented nature of politics in Bosnia and the leading role of international organizations in proposing and effectuating institutional reforms. Nevertheless, in terms of habits, operational methods and values many Bosnian intelligence officers went through similar adaptations and transitions as their colleagues in countries where institutions at the time of democratic transition were too strong and authoritarian rather than, as in the case of Bosnia, being deemed too weak and ineffectual.

Introduction

This article outlines how the centralization and democratization of the intelligence and security sector in Bosnia and Herzegovina (hereafter BiH or Bosnia) was conceived, planned and implemented. The article is an insider's account of a single country reform process. The author was seconded by the Norwegian Ministry of Foreign Affairs (NMFA) to the Office of the High Representative (OHR) in BiH from 2004–8. At OHR, the author was the desk officer for intelligence reform responsible for day-to-day contact with and assessments of civilian and military intelligence structures in Bosnia and Herzegovina. Since 2008 the author has continued the contact with the intelligence structures in BiH as part of a donor support program for the intelligence and security sector in BiH run by the Norwegian Institute of International Affairs (NUPI) and funded by the NMFA.

The article aims to explain the historical and institutional background and describe the most relevant political (and international) aspects to understand what 'democratization' of intelligence amounts to in Bosnia. As with all historical processes, the interplay of forces is indeed complex and multifaceted. The article sketches events since WWII but the emphasis is on the period since 2003 when initiatives gather pace to merge the three ethno-national intelligence structures into a state-level and unified BiH Intelligence and Security Agency (OSA). The intelligence and security sector reform in Bosnia and Herzegovina since 2003 displays some of the characteristics of post-socialist transitions but have significant unique aspects as well. In most transition countries the 'democratization of intelligence' implied the weakening of the existing authoritarian governmental structures in order to make them publicly accountable. In Bosnia, authoritarian-like structures did exist prior to 'democratization' from 2003 but they were anchored in ethno-national groups and war bands rather than in the state, which had already collapsed in the early 1990s. From the Dayton Peace Agreement in 1995 forward the international parties with support mainly from the largest ethnic group – the Bosniaks – tried to assemble a Bosnian state, and from 2003 even a state-level intelligence agency, out of the ethno-national fragments that had just been involved in the most horrendous civil war. It was no easy task to assemble such an intelligence structure let alone to 'democratize' it.

To some extent, the challenges to democratizing intelligence in Bosnia were the complete opposite to those in most other transition countries. There were no state structures in Bosnia that needed to be weakened. In fact, there was not much of a state at all but rather a few symbolic state-level institutions with little constitutional powers and existing at the mercy of two sub-state entities. The state had initially no defence forces, no police and no intelligence agencies, nor were these provided for in the constitution agreed at the Dayton Peace Agreement. But some aspects of reform in Bosnia were similar to other transition countries since, upon the establishment of the state-level Intelligence and Security Agency (OSA) in 2004, quite a number of the intelligence employees had experience from intelligence work in the State Security Service (SDB) of the Socialist Federal Republic of Yugoslavia (SFRY). And SDB certainly shared with most communist intelligence agencies that its primary purpose was to preserve the regime and suppress the opposition. When SDB's branches in the SFRY's republics broke up in the early 1990s, many intelligence employees went on to serve ethno-national regimes in much the same manner as they had served the SFRY. The requirements for reform not only in terms of introducing laws and establishing parliamentary oversight but also to change the mentality and orientation of intelligence operatives, therefore, were quite similar in Bosnia even if the old state and its institutions were utterly destroyed and, from a structural point of view, needed no further weakening.

Background

Bosnia and Herzegovina (Bosnia/BiH) had been a republic within the Socialist Federal Republic of Yugoslavia (SFRY). The SFRY broke up under its own inherent contradictions in the early 1990s which put in motion a series of secessions and wars. The 1992–5 civil war in Bosnia saw intense fighting among the three main ethnic groups: the Serbs, the Muslims (now called Bosniaks) and the Croats. A US-brokered alliance was formed in 1994 between Croats and Bosniaks, and in 1995 the Dayton Accords were signed between all parties (and the neighbours), after heavy military and diplomatic involvement from the USA and its European allies.[1]

The Dayton Accords formalized the effects of ethnic cleansing but emplaced a weak state on top of two sub-state structures called 'entities'. As a result of the war, Croats and Bosniaks dominated demographically in the Federation of Bosnia, whereas Serbs made up the bulk of the population in Republika Srpska (RS). The Dayton Accords included measures for the temporary arbiter role of the international community. A body of interested parties, the Peace Implementation Council (PIC), was tasked with appointing a High Representative to oversee implementation of the Dayton Agreement. The mandate of the civilian High Representative expanded drastically with the 'Bonn powers' established by the PIC at a conference in Bonn in 1997. In subsequent years these Bonn powers have been used to impose and abolish laws, dismiss and appoint officials and instigate criminal investigations.[2]

The Dayton Accords left Bosnia an extremely decentralized state. The political-administrative decentralization as well as the corresponding identity divide was widely seen as undermining both efficiency and post-war reconciliation.[3] Western initiatives for greater centralization in BiH built up during the late 1990s but local resistance to centralization was stubborn. In the ensuing years, the international protectorate set out to shape the administrative-political system into a more unified and centralized state. Centralization was generally favoured by Bosniaks, and fiercely resisted by Serbs. Part of the Croat constituency sought to carve out a third entity from the Federation.

Intelligence Reform in the Making

Intelligence, counterintelligence and security institutions from the People's Liberation Partisan Army of Yugoslavia were operating on the territory of Bosnia and Herzegovina and other parts of Yugoslavia as early as 1941.[4]

---

[1]The presidents of Croatia and the Federal Republic of Yugoslavia (FRY), Franjo Tudjman and Slobodan Milosevic, signed the Dayton Accords on behalf of the Croats and Serbs living in Bosnia.
[2]For a list of the High Representative's decisions, see <http://www.ohr.int/decisions/archive.asp>.
[3]See for example David Chandler, *Bosnia: Faking Democracy After Dayton*, 2nd ed. (London: Pluto Press 2000).
[4]Ivo Lučić, 'Security and Intelligence Services in Bosnia and Herzegovina', *National Security and the Future* 2/1 (2000) pp.75–104.

DEMOCRATIZATION OF INTELLIGENCE

In 1946 the State Security Service (SDB) was established at the Federal Ministry of Internal Affairs.[5] The federal level of SDB set the overall intelligence priorities, but with the constitutional changes of 1974 more autonomy was delegated to the SDB branches/agencies in each of the six republics of the SFRY.[6] Alongside the SDB there was a significant military intelligence and counterintelligence capacity organized in the Second Department of the Yugoslav People's Army.

The SDB operated both within and outside the territory of Yugoslavia and had a range of tasks and customers with differing levels of access. Its primary role was to protect the sovereignty and integrity of Yugoslavia, which in practice meant serving the Communist Party, and safeguarding and consolidating its power. The SDB was a tool to keep political control and suppress opposition. Only party members could work for the SDB.[7] When three ethno-nationalist parties[8] swept aside the Social Democratic Party (renamed from the Communist Party) in elections in November 1990, the former targets of suppression by the SDB in Bosnia and Herzegovina 'suddenly became our bosses', in the words of a former Serb employee.[9] This led to a widespread shutdown of intelligence activities; incriminating archives were destroyed and what little intelligence was produced was forwarded to party channels, not to state institutions.[10]

The roughly 600 SDB employees in BiH at the time went through a traumatic period in the aftermath of the 1990 elections.[11] Their identity had been tied to the preservation of the SFRY, which was collapsing. Various ethno-nationalist outfits started to organize and arm themselves; this was done with the acquiescence and on the orders of the new political masters,

---

[5]*Sluzba Državne Bezbednosti* (SDB). SDB was also called the *Uprava Državne Bezbednosti* (UDB).

[6]Interview 7 April 2011 with Drago Férs, a former UDB/SDB employee since 1964, Director of the Slovenian Intelligence Service (SOVA) from 1993–2000. SDB changed character at several points after WWII. From 1946 to 1973, the federal level held significant authority over the SDB branches in the republics. In line with overall constitutional changes in 1974, the republics gained more autonomous powers over public security and the accompanying intelligence. The level of independence from the federal level in Belgrade also varied from republic to republic. SDB in Slovenia operated most autonomously, the branch in Bosnia less so. The SDB was part of the Ministry of Interior but reported directly to the Secretary-General of the Central Committee of the Yugoslav Communist Party, and the SDB in each republic also reported to the Central Committee in each of the republics. Thus there was a complex system of reporting mechanisms, political control and 'customers' for the intelligence that SDB produced. The SDB system changed and reflected the various phases of political transformation within the SFRY.

[7]Lučić, 'Security and Intelligence Services in Bosnia and Herzegovina', pp.75–104.

[8]These parties were the Croatian Democratic Union (HDZ), the Party of Democratic Action (SDA) and the Serbian Democratic Party (SDS).

[9]Interview with former employee of SDB, 8 April 2011.

[10]Lučić, 'Security and Intelligence Services in Bosnia and Herzegovina', pp.75–104.

[11]In 1986 the SDB in BiH had 589 employees, with a reserve force of 646 who could be activated in case of war. In 1990 it had 631 employees. Ibid., pp.75–104.

who were formally also the elected political masters of the State Security Service in Bosnia and Herzegovina.[12] Strains appeared in relations between SDB employees of different ethnic origins, and those from the minorities in any given area started to fear for their physical safety. Serbs felt bitter that Croats and Bosniak employees started to align with ethno-national causes – in effect joining the SDB's previous 'enemies' – rather than working for the preservation of the SFRY.[13]

SDB employees received their salaries from the budget of the Republic of BiH up until the outbreak of hostilities in April 1992, but the SDB had effectively ceased to function as a coherent producer of intelligence many months earlier. The institution was not trusted by any of the three main ethno-nationalist parties that clashed politically and later militarily on the territory of BiH.[14] This distance many SDB employees felt towards the ethno-nationalist causes might have made (re)unification in 2004 somewhat easier to achieve. Nevertheless, the SDB employees parted ways before full-scale civil war broke out in April 1992. SDB BiH continued to exist, but with mostly Bosniak employees. Croat intelligence officers parted from their Bosniak colleagues later than did Serbs, but as Croat-Bosniak fighting increased in late 1992 the split among Croat and Bosniak intelligence personnel also commenced.

There were several institutions that produced intelligence during the 1992–5 war. Much of this activity was tied to the three military command structures that fought each other in a partly three-way and partly two-way civil war that also drew in neighbouring Croatia and Serbia. But all three ethnic groups also retained institutions with some continuity from the SDB BiH. Most of the Serb employees of SDB formed the State Security Service (SNS) of the Ministry of Internal Affairs of the Serb Republic in Bosnia and Herzegovina. In 1998 this service was renamed the Intelligence-Security Service (OBS – *Obavestajno-bezbednosne sluzbe*). Croats eventually formed the National Security Service (SNS – *Sluzba nacionalne sigurnosti*) based out of Mostar. In 1996 the Bosniaks established the Agency for Research and Documentation (AID – *Agencija za istràivanje i dokumentaciju*) from what was left of SDB BiH.

The war in Bosnia from 1992–5 had huge human costs. Around 100,000 people died and half of the pre-war population of four million people were displaced. Compared to these horrors, the suppression experienced during the preceding communist period seemed minor. The public was thus largely apathetic to the presence of unreformed intelligence structures from 1996 onwards. They had more pressing worries like refugee return, return of property, and jobs. In general too, there was a democratic deficit and a resulting passivity of the electorate since the international High Representative effectively held executive and legislative powers and annulled many

---

[12]Marko Attila Hoare, *How Bosnia Armed* (London: Saqi Books 2004).

[13]Interview with former employee of SDB, 8 April 2011. On 10 June 1991 the mostly Muslim SDA established the Council of National Defence with a military wing attached. A significant number of SDB employees of Bosniak (Muslim) identity participated.

[14]Interview with former employee of SDB, 8 April 2011.

domestic political initiatives or in fact pressed forward with reforms out of impatience with the slow workings of the domestic 'democratic' system. It was therefore quite parallel to the reform drives overall in Bosnia that a process of intelligence and security sector reform, including the sector's formal 'democratization', was driven by international agents/organizations rather than domestic political forces.

At various points from 1995 onwards, talks were held between HDZ and SDA officials, the main Croat and Bosniak political parties respectively, about a unification of the (Croat) SNS and the (Bosniak) AID intelligence services to reflect the Washington Agreement that established the Federation in 1994.[15] However, the two services remained wholly separate until 2002, when, due largely to international pressure, a combined Bosniak-Croat civilian intelligence service – FOSS – was formed in the Federation.[16] From 1996 onwards some NATO countries established influence over the domestic intelligence structures. Their offices were frequently raided by SFOR troops, and international pressure was applied to create new, more modern, organizations fully equipped with laws and oversight mechanisms but with separate ethno-national organizations. However, major Western intelligence agencies also facilitated talks between SNS and AID as well as with OBS in the early 2000s.[17] In addition to the international pressures and initiatives, certain elements from within the domestic intelligence structures themselves pushed for reform lest they become obsolete and subject to budgetary slashing.[18]

Starting in the late 1990s the OHR employed a wide array of means to overcome Serb and some Croat political resistance to increased centralization of security sector functions. Intelligence reform[19] attracted less attention from the Bosnian public, its politicians, international bodies, foreign diplomats and experts than the defence and police reforms but no less striking transformations took place. The sector in effect went from three ethnically divided services in 2001 to one unified, state-level intelligence-security agency in 2004. From the OHR, the reform was less driven by a vision to 'democratize' the intelligence and security sector than to affect a political *coup de grâce* to the sub-state political ambitions of Republika Srpska. However, once a political agreement was within reach on the centralization of the sector, work on the legal framework proceeded according to 'best practices' for external control and oversight.[20] The draft laws were

---

[15] Lučić, 'Security and Intelligence Services in Bosnia and Herzegovina', pp.75–104.

[16] FOSS – *Obavjestajno-sigurnosna sluzba Federacije BiH* (Intelligence-Security Service of the FBIH).

[17] Interview with former head of OBS, October 2006.

[18] Interview with former employee of SDB, 8 April 2011.

[19] 'Intelligence reform' in Bosnia relates to both internal security and external intelligence collection, with the external and internal aspects as of 1 June 2004 combined in one agency, the BiH Intelligence and Security Agency (*Obavestajna-Sigurnosna Agencia*, OSA).

[20] Kalman Kocsis, 'Bosnia and Herzegovina' in Stuart Farson, Peter Gill, Mark Phythian and Shlomo Shpiro (eds.) *PSI Handbook of Global Security and Intelligence: National Approaches Volume 2* (London: Praeger Security International 2008).

distributed for comments by various international bodies and corresponded well with high standards for parliamentary oversight and political control. In fact, OHR often wrapped its political objectives into requirements for better democratic standards.

To some extent 'piggybacking' on the political legwork necessary to the formation of the Defence Reform Commission, which was tasked with providing a new and more centralized and 'democratic' defence structure, a similar Expert Commission on Intelligence Reform (ECIR), was set up by the High Representative in May 2003.[21] It consisted of an international chair, a former Hungarian intelligence chief, Ambassador Kálmán Kocsis, and six professionals appointed by the directors of the two entity intelligence-security services. The ECIR was tasked with drafting a state-level law, which it tabled in September 2003.

Tainted Past: Unifying the Ethno-Nationalist Secret Services

A wide range of processes had to be coordinated with the drafting and passing of the state-level intelligence law. A handful of international experts were put to work to manage the various aspects of the reform. Most of these worked for the Office of the High Representative, but a few were hosted by the OSCE Mission to BiH in the Intelligence Reform Implementation Section (IRIS). Former head of the Slovenian Intelligence Service, Drago Férs, was in charge of IRIS, working together with experts from the entity intelligence services to prepare more than 20 rulebooks to guide the future work of the BiH Intelligence and Security Agency (OSA). This ranged from issues of internal control, vetting and security clearances, internal organization, handling of classified information, operational methods, registration and remuneration of informants, to the use of firearms, transfer of archives, etc.

Unlike the case with defence and police reforms, Bosnian politicians took little interest in what the assigned experts on intelligence reform hammered out. There was a professional atmosphere free from direct political interference.[22] This state of affairs might appear surprising, as it would seem logical to assume that control of intelligence matters had top priority for the established, ethnically based polities of BiH. But since the intelligence agencies were not heavily armed institutions, they were considered less strategically important than police and defence structures, which could provide protection of last resort should the country slip into civil war once again.

There were probably additional reasons for this lack of hands-on interest (and obstruction) from the politicians. The Bosniak and Croat services, the AID and the SNS, had been involved in various public controversies prior to unification into FOSS in 2002.[23] Public rows continued after the unification

---

[21]OHR, Decision Establishing the Expert Commission on Intelligence Reform <http://www.ohr.int/decisions/statemattersdec/default.asp?content_id=29988>.

[22]Interview with Drago Férs, 7 April 2011.

[23]Some AID personnel had allegedly been involved with Iranian intelligence agents in training militants near the small town of Fojnica in 1996. Press rumours linked intelligence agents to

of the AID and the SNS into the Federation Service, FOSS. All things considered, few politicians in the Federation saw much benefit in being associated with these tainted institutions. They also knew that most voters harboured deep-rooted suspicions about these services, suspicions that dated back to the suppressive days of the SFRY. Not many politicians would get associated with a reform that essentially legitimized the continuation of secret services in BiH.

As regards the Serb service of the OBS, the lack of political interest, and interference, seems to have stemmed from a kind of general political exhaustion after years of sanctions and international pressure, but also from mistrust or indifference among key politicians as regards their own Serb intelligence personnel. International pressure on Serb politicians was overwhelming and a concerted attack on the governing Serb Democratic Party (SDS) was under way. Furthermore, the SNS (the Republika Srpska intelligence service, renamed OBS in 1998) had been internally at odds during the political upheaval in the RS in 1997, when the ruling Serb Democratic Party (SDS) split into two parts, with the Serb President Biljana Plavsic on the one side, and what was considered the pro-Karadzic wing on the other. With the eventual defeat and marginalization of Ms Plavsic, the SNS (OBS) was left with few resources and little trust. However, the electoral victory of the Alliance of Independent Social Democrats (SNSD) over the SDS in 1998 facilitated some reform of the Serb entity's intelligence service under the new name of the OBS.[24] With heavy inputs from the US government, the Parliamentary Assembly of the RS adopted a law in 1998 stripping the OBS of its police powers. Some of the more hard-line, pro-nationalist elements within OBS were then gradually purged.[25]

The Expert Commission on Intelligence Reform (ECIR) tabled a draft law on a state-level intelligence service in September 2003. The BiH Parliamentary Assembly almost unanimously adopted the Law on the Intelligence and Security Agency of Bosnia and Herzegovina (OSA) on 22 March 2004.[26] From 1 June 2004 the entity intelligence services formally ceased to exist, and the state-level Intelligence and Security Agency (OSA) was established.

Establishing the State-Level Intelligence and Security Agency (OSA)

While the law on OSA was discussed in the Parliamentary Assembly during the winter of 2004, the OHR also involved the political parties in the selection procedure for the leadership of the soon-to-be-established agency. The Law on OSA specifies that not more than one of the positions of Director-General, Deputy Director-General and Inspector General may be

---

some high-profile assassinations, and parts of the Croat SNS were alleged to have had a hand in the anti-SFOR and anti-OHR riots in Mostar in April 2001.
[24]Interview with former employee of OBS, 8 April 2011.
[25]Interview with former employee of OBS, 8 April 2011.
[26]Kocsis, 'Bosnia and Herzegovina'.

filled by a representative of any one constituent people (ethnic group).[27] Agreement was reached that the Director-General would be a Bosniak, the Deputy Director-General a Serb and the Inspector General a Croat. Various international stakeholders from the intelligence community, diplomatic circles and the ICTY were involved in opposing and lobbying for candidates to all three positions. The process had its share of attempted foul play, but compromise and agreement gradually emerged.[28] The formal decision was taken by the BiH Council of Ministers after consultations with the three-member state-level Presidency.

The Director-General, upon assuming his post in June 2004, reined in most potential for rough, unauthorized activity and leaks within the agency by instilling a fairly hierarchical and authoritative leadership style from the very start. Furthermore, together with his Deputy Director-General and the Inspector General, the young and dynamic Director-General was able to present a unified front both internally and externally. Although some of the media continued to post stories from within the intelligence sphere well into 2005, it became apparent that the sources were old hands no longer employed in OSA.[29]

From its formal establishment in June 2004, OSA was given a transition period to complete the unification of FOSS and OBS. All 961 registered employees in the two entity services at the time of unification underwent a vetting procedure and new criteria for professional qualifications were established. Court archives and intelligence in Bosnia and archives at the ICTY were consulted. Informally, some foreign organizations gave inputs on specific names. In all, 69 employees failed at least one of the criteria but the remaining 892 employees still exceeded the 702 posts established in the new organization. Dismissed personnel were eligible for up to a year of severance payment. When the decisions about future employment and dismissals were announced in January 2005, the leadership troika spent a further two months deliberating on appointments to mid-level management positions. Formally, the Director-General took all those decisions on his own; informally he consulted extensively with his two nearest colleagues and also allowed some international scrutiny but no veto powers before decisions were announced.[30]

During the formal period of transition to a state-level agency, which lasted for some nine months until at least March 2005, some of the foreign intelligence services requested that ongoing operational cooperation should continue as uninterrupted as possible. This in fact proved favourable also to the long-term institution-building efforts that were aided by OHR and OSCE. Ongoing operations with major Western intelligence agencies and the ICTY gave the Bosnian intelligence personnel a sense of purpose in the early phase of OSA's establishment. The other Bosnian security institutions, like the

---

[27]Law on the Intelligence and Security Agency of Bosnia and Herzegovina, IV, Article 36 <http://www.osa-oba.gov.ba/zakoneng.htm>.
[28]Interview with Drago Férs, 7 April 2011.
[29]Author's observation 2004 and 2005.
[30]Author's observation 2005.

prosecutors or the police, did not request much intelligence initially, nor were there any requests for raw data or analyses from the responsible executive organ in the Council of Ministers. This situation, with OSA operating in a sort of national vacuum, reflected the dysfunctional nature of the Bosnian state. Foreign requests gave some much needed sense of purpose and pride to the operatives. The lack of directives from the Bosnian executive to OSA also translated into or reflected a lack of political control by any elected institutions.

Tasks and Organization of OSA

The Law on OSA is detailed, comprehensive and in line with Western 'democratic standards' as they existed at the time (2003). It specifies duties and tasks of the agency, external and internal direction and oversight, methods that can legally be employed, as well as rights and duties of the employees. Most Western intelligence and security services had (and still have) far briefer and less inclusive laws, if indeed there are any laws governing their activities at all. The law states that OSA 'shall be responsible for gathering intelligence both within and outside Bosnia and Herzegovina regarding threats to the security of Bosnia and Herzegovina'. Threats to the security are 'understood to mean threats to the sovereignty, territorial integrity, constitutional order, and fundamental economic stability (...) as well as threats to global security'.[31] In addition to threats common to similar agencies like terrorism, espionage, organized crime, trafficking and WMD proliferation, the law also mentions 'acts punishable under humanitarian law' and 'organized acts of violence and intimidation against ethnic and religious groups' as tasks of OSA.[32]

The internal organization of the agency is specified in a confidential rulebook adopted by the Council of Ministers. The details are classified, but OSA resembles other similar organizations in having directorates for administration, operations, analyses and technical support and collection. Each directorate is composed of departments. There are four field offices – in Sarajevo, Mostar, Banja Luka and Brcko – as well as a few minor detachments in smaller towns around the country. The Deputy Director-General is also the head of the Directorate of Operations. Internal oversight is carried out by the Inspector General. The Director-General, the Deputy Director-General and the Inspector General are directly appointed and dismissed by the Council of Ministers.

External Direction: In Charge – But In Name Only

After the Cold War, the newly democratizing countries of Central and Eastern Europe all harboured deep popular resentment and distrust of the secret

---

[31] Law on the Intelligence and Security Agency of Bosnia and Herzegovina, II, Article 5 < http://www.osa-oba.gov.ba/zakoneng.htm >.

[32] Law on the Intelligence and Security Agency of Bosnia and Herzegovina, II, Article 5 (h) and (i) < http://www.osa-oba.gov.ba/zakoneng.htm >.

police and intelligence agencies that had been instrumental in upholding the power of the now ousted regimes. A growing international consensus emerged during the 1990s and early 2000s on the issue of democratic oversight of intelligence services. According to the Chairman of the ECIR, Ambassador Kálmán Kocsis, the principles expressed in recommendation 1402 (1999) of the Council of Europe[33] were, from the side of the so-called international community, non-negotiable when the Law on OSA was drafted and passed.[34] And although the driving forces behind the intelligence reform from the international agents were hard *realpolitik* in so far as it sought to create a more centralized state, a not negligible side effect was that a comprehensive 'democratization' of intelligence, at least formally, was introduced. This democratization process adopted the same standards and took as its example transitions already in motion in other parts of Europe. The experiences of Hungary and Slovenia were especially prominent as two of the key international staff in Bosnia came from these two former communist states but also other countries experiences became part of the knowledge base through the work of institutions such as the Centre of the Democratic Control of Armed Forces (DCAF) in Geneva.

Executive control of OSA is placed under the Chair of the Council of Ministers (CoM), who 'shall supervise, and be politically responsible for, the work of the Agency'.[35] This arrangement was strongly favoured by the then High Representative Paddy Ashdown as part of a larger political project to strengthen the role of the Chair relative to other bodies within the state system.[36] In order to deal with the widely established practice and demand of equal influence of all constituent peoples in BiH, other executive bodies besides the Chair have been allocated certain responsibilities in the Law on OSA. The tripartite Presidency is to direct the Inspector General on internal investigative matters; the Presidency is entitled to receive intelligence, and approve, *inter alia*, international intelligence cooperation undertaken by OSA. The Council of Ministers in plenum is responsible for the Intelligence-Security Policy Platform, the annual Activity Programme, and for defining principles for coordination and assistance between OSA and other bodies and institutions. The Chair is further tasked with establishing an Executive Intelligence Committee (EIC) to 'advise the Chair on his tasks'.[37] The members of the EIC shall be ministers in the Council of Ministers, and the composition of this advisory body must reflect 'representation of all three constituent peoples'.[38]

---

[33] <http://assembly.coe.int/Mainf.asp?link=/Documents/AdoptedText/ta99/EREC1402.htm>.

[34] Presentation by Ambassador Kálmán Kocsis at DCAF, Geneva 4 November 2005. Remarks available at <www.dcaf.ch>.

[35] Law on the Intelligence and Security Agency of Bosnia and Herzegovina, III, Article 9 <http://www.osa-oba.gov.ba/zakoneng.htm>.

[36] Paddy Ashdown, *Swords and Ploughshares: Bringing Peace to the 21st Century* (London: Weidenfeld & Nicolson 2007) p.244.

[37] Law on the Intelligence and Security Agency of Bosnia and Herzegovina, III, Article 12 <http://www.osa-oba.gov.ba/zakoneng.htm>.

[38] Ibid.

This structure of executive control over OSA might appear cumbersome and impractical. The Director-General primarily serves the Chair but needs to consider the influence and opinions of persons holding other key political posts in the presidency and in the CoM. That OSA would be thus hamstrung is one way of interpreting the system of executive control. But the peculiar dynamic of institutional and political life in BiH since 2004 has caused quite a different kind of problem. For long periods, the agency has been without much executive control and direction whatsoever.

Four factors stand out. First, the three politicians who held the post of Chair of the CoM between 2004 and 2013 had a range of profound political challenges to cope with. Thus, to be proactive towards OSA did not become a priority. They dealt, at best, with the intelligence issues that circumstances forced upon them. Second, they did not have a dedicated staff to carry out executive responsibility.[39] Third, involvement in intelligence affairs appears to be no vote-winner. There is in Bosnia, as in many former socialist republics, no love lost between intelligence-security structures and the people. In addition, in a deeply fractured society like Bosnia there would be instant suspicion from other politicians and parties if the Chair, or anyone else, even within their legal rights, were seen to have a close hand in the affairs of intelligence agencies. Fourth, the general political influence of international bodies in BiH, and the fact that some of those bodies had a keen interest in the priorities of OSA and were also very satisfied with the work, priorities and autonomy of the Director-General, meant that any Chair would have had to establish his authority over OSA at some political peril to himself. None chose to take that risk. As long as public scandals and profound ethnic bias could not be associated with OSA, and as long as key foreign partners expressed their satisfaction with the agency, the Chairs were basically content with the status quo and their own diminished role compared to the responsibilities defined in the law.

Parliamentary Oversight: Not What It Seems But Still Standing

Parliamentary oversight is grounded in the Law on OSA. The two chambers of the parliamentary assembly each appoint six members to a joint Intelligence-Security Committee. The Chairman must be from a party that 'is not part of the governing coalition'.[40] The committee shall hold sessions at least biannually. The committee may call hearings and conduct inquiries as to the legality of the agency's work. It also provides opinions on appointments to the top three positions and reviews budgets and expenditures.

---

[39]According to the Law on OSA, the Chair shall establish an Intelligence-Security Advisory Service (OSSS) within the Council of Ministers 'for the sole purpose of providing support to the Chair'. Since 2006 there have been no staff employed in the OSSS.

[40]Law on the Intelligence and Security Agency of Bosnia and Herzegovina, III, Article 18 <http://www.osa-oba.gov.ba/zakoneng.htm>.

The function of oversight is clearly separate from but also affected by the function of executive control. The first oversight committee was appointed mid-term in the parliament that sat from 2002 to 2006. After the elections in 2006, all 12 members of the original committee were replaced by a new set of delegates, although the administrative secretary remained. Eleven out of 12 members were again shifted after the elections in 2010. The parliamentary oversight committee has generally tended to its responsibilities more approximating the intentions of the law than appears be the case for the function of executive control. The committee has been quite active and sessions have been held more frequently than strictly required by law. Especially the committee that sat from 2006 to 2010 initiated activities like inspections to OSA locations, visits to counterparts in other European countries, organizing a regional forum for oversight bodies, and arranging public outreach session to inform on the status of the intelligence-security reform. Most of these were truly domestically-initiated activities although funding assistance and some administrative support was provided from international partners.[41] The establishment in 2006 of the post of a subject-matter adviser to the committee was instrumental in organizing, structuring and spurring its oversight activities. The committee formed after the elections in 2010 has been less proactive although the reasons are a bit unclear but is probably down to the new personalities in the committee and their priorities rather than any deeper and concerted political agenda to backtrack from effective oversight.

The profundity and clout of oversight functions in general can often be doubted. Members of oversight bodies are not necessarily familiar with intelligence and security affairs, and may often not know what to ask or inquire about. If they are rebuffed by the agencies or the executive, it is difficult for them to move ahead. One could say that the establishment of oversight bodies can give a sense of false security about independent oversight and that this indeed is the purpose from the outset. Such bodies serve to reassure the public that there is independent and democratic control, whereas reality might fall somewhat or massively short of this. In other words, if the intelligence agencies fail to report on their real activities, or if they lie when probed, few tools are available to oversight bodies unless they happen to be exceptionally zealous and backed up by an interested media. Whatever formal redress these oversight bodies might have will often be obstructed by informal political and practical barriers. The same criticism might be levelled against the joint Intelligence-Security Committee of the BiH parliamentary assembly. Even if the level of activity has at times been high, the Committee has been dependent on OSA actually volunteering to report as it should according to the law. Up until 2013, this symbiosis seems to have worked rather well with the leadership of OSA seeing it as a form of protection (from political pressure and media criticism) to have the parliamentary oversight committee involved and informed of their activity. OSA seems to have

---

[41] Main donors were the Norwegian government, the OSCE and the Geneva Centre for the Democratic Control of Armed Forces (DCAF).

operated largely according to the law and therefore had little to fear from inviting close oversight

The law on OSA attempted to reduce the risk of a too-pliant oversight committee by requiring the chair to be from the opposition. The downside of this could be that the chairperson uses the position to score political points or gain public attention to his/her political profile by voicing criticisms against the agency that might or might not be fair. A certain degree of overzealousness might have appeared from time to time during the term of the first committee that sat from 2004 until 2006. The next chairman also tried to gain some personal public attention through the position but significantly more by publicly explaining the role of OSA and in fact defending it against (perhaps) undue allegations and suspicions. The two chairmen chose different tactics although both were from the opposition. The relationship between OSA and the second chairman was, unsurprisingly, far more harmonious than with the first.

Effectiveness and Efficiency of Intelligence Reform

As of this writing, nine years have passed since the BiH Intelligence-Security Agency (OSA) was established in 2004. The transition from ethnically exclusive services to a unified state agency was no small step after the civil war of the early 1990s. Prior to the actual unification, many considered the attempt to merge FOSS and OBS into OSA to be a 'mission impossible'.[42] It was assumed that entities aspiring to secession and/or statehood would be loath to relinquish capabilities like intelligence collection and covert action. Even in a long-established alliance like NATO, intelligence has remained under the firm control of each member state.

There is little doubt that OSA made some real steps towards integration and modernization during the first few years of its existence. Leaks more or less stopped, personnel were re-organized into the new structure largely according to the adopted rulebooks, contacts with foreign intelligence representatives were centralized and generally made to adhere to an authorized character, and a new set of mid-level management personnel was appointed. Requests from foreign intelligence services, especially on counter-terrorism issues, kept many OSA employees professionally preoccupied throughout the period of transition. This contributed to a sense of pride and purpose that also facilitated organizational strengthening, and the introduction of new more sophisticated and less oppressive methods and operations. The near-consensus attitude in political circles on the importance of counter-terrorism activities and cooperation with foreign intelligence services served to position OSA outside the most intense ethno-nationalist politicking in Bosnia.

International support and engagement with the intelligence operatives in Bosnia also increased after OSA was established. Some cooperation and support from foreign intelligence services had existed since before the war

---

[42]Kocsis, 'Bosnia and Herzegovina'.

ended in 1995, but training, specialized courses and material assistance expanded drastically after 2004. A couple of foreign governments, like the UK and Norway, even started to provide OSA with support over their regular and more transparent donor budgets. The OHR and OSCE helped to fund and arrange team-building workshops and other activities for intelligence personnel. On the whole, however, intelligence reform involved less publicity, material support and fewer foreign personnel than other security sector reforms in Bosnia. This hands-off approach created greater space for local leadership.

Still, the Director-General of OSA spent some considerable energy during the first months after his appointment in 2004 in carving out autonomy from the many organizations of the so called international community.[43] Many different circumstances and factors were involved in determining the steady evolution of intelligence reform in Bosnia, but the role played by the leadership of OSA stands out as particularly important. The relatively multi-ethnic and non-partisan attitude of the leadership troika provided a solid basis for overall unity in the lower ranks. The Serb and Croat representatives in the leadership did not encourage the development of ethnic blocs within the agency – nor did the Director General, a Bosniak, give them much room to do so. There probably existed perceptions in the agency that Bosniaks had been accorded a slightly more favoured and trusted status, but this never became a real bone of contention or a disturbing rallying cry for internal dissent.

Deliberate decisions were also made within OSA to shield it from political pressures that might otherwise tear at its internal fabric. Taken at face value, the duties and tasks listed in article 5 of the Law on OSA would have landed the agency in the midst of the most intense ethno-political disputes in the country: OSA is, after all, tasked with preventing threats to the 'sovereignty, territorial integrity, constitutional order' of Bosnia and Herzegovina.[44] Not surprisingly, the gravest threats to the security of Bosnia and Herzegovina came, and continue to come, from the rhetoric and practice of key politicians and religious leaders in the country. In addition, secessionist sympathies continue to abound among the average Serbs and Croats. OSA found ways to manoeuvre in this difficult landscape, rather than interpreting the law to the exact letter which would have made half the population potentially 'suspicious'.

Assessing Democratization of Intelligence in BiH

The three top positions in OSA have not changed hands between 2004 and 2013. The leadership has established and maintained significant distance and

---

[43]Helge Lurås, 'The Danger of Optimism: Building States From Incoherent Fragments' in Harry i Yarger (ed.) *Transitions: Issues, Challenges and Solutions in International Assistance* (Pennsylvania: PKSOI 2011) pp.27–41.

[44]Law on the Intelligence and Security Agency of Bosnia and Herzegovina, II, Article 5 <http://www.osa-oba.gov.ba/zakoneng.htm>.

autonomy from executive (political) control. Parliamentary oversight has at times been frequent but its effectiveness remains somewhat in doubt, especially since 2010. Does this mean that the democratization of intelligence in BiH remains unachieved?

The lack of executive control – or indeed the lack of a proactive interest on the part of the political parties to conduct this control effectively – should imply such a lack of democratization but the full picture is complicated by the ethnic divide and its institutional implications. In fact, the entities are still strong politically and the 'Bosnian state' hardly exists at all even in 2013 and after years of efforts by international bodies to move responsibilities and institutions from the entity to the state level. Most state institutions are hamstrung by parallel ethnic reporting channels and/or inefficiencies due to oversensitivity to ethnic balance at all levels. Nor do we have a unified society in Bosnia were the population at large perceives a common interest versus the state and elite. What we still find in Bosnia are at least three ethno-national power structures and patronage networks that compete for the resources allocated to the (nominal) state. And the state of BiH is still fundamentally contested as a political concept by at least two of the three 'constituent peoples'. The Bosnian society is highly divided based on religion and ethnicity. State institutions therefore are weak in their internal fabric and lack legitimacy among significant portions of the electorate.

Bosnia is still formally under international supervision by the Peace Implementation Council and the OHR although their direct role in political developments is much diminished since approximately 2006. Political influence in BiH is highly fragmented with no single political party or ethnic group dominating. The country is still torn internally and influenced from abroad. There is no 'polity' or society with a common set of values and visions. This fragmented situation naturally reflects on the intelligence and security agency as well. The circumstances are well aligned for the director of OSA to manipulate these external circumstances to control the agency on quite autonomous terms. There is no single power centre strong enough to replace easily the leadership outside the normal rotations. But alternatively, this structural situation could also be conducive to a very weakly led and managed agency because the leadership would not have any powerful (and democratically elected) political patron backing its activity and being able to shield it if it became embroiled in controversy.

In Bosnia from 2004 to 2013 there has been strong leadership of the intelligence agency due to the proactive position, personality and political strength of the OSA Director General and the cooperative and flexible attitude of his two (Serb and Croat) 'deputies'. OSA has to a large extent been the Director-General's personal 'fief'. Such independence from political control is hardly in accordance with democratic standards or the wording of the law on OSA. But the Director-General has not used his powers without some accountability and supervision. Nor does lack of control necessarily mean abuse of powers, only that much then hinges on the moral character (and personal circumstances) of the leadership. To a large extent, the absence of domestic political control and effective or at least sustained parliamentary oversight, has also been somewhat compensated for by an informal supervision conducted by international agents like the OHR, the OSCE and a handful of foreign intelligence agencies. Thus, the Director-General of OSA has been far from free to do as he pleases. He has kept his position for these many years not least because he has steered a middle course within the legal framework for operations. For instance, actual investigations carried out by the parliamentary oversight committee have not resulted in finding any systematic unlawful use of covert surveillance. In one case in 2011, all of the phone numbers that OSA had tapped were leaked and published (in an essentially Serb newspaper – the *Nezavisne Novine* – that was hostile to OSA), and so the parliamentary oversight committee could easily check if there were prior judicial authorizations for the communication control. One could also suggest that it is precisely because OSA has been free from political (democratic) control that it has stayed on the right side of the law. Bosnia is a very contested country and some of the Chairs of the CoM who have been in nominal political control of OSA have likely harboured intentions to eventually break up the very constitution that OSA is set to preserve.[45]

'Democratization' of intelligence in Bosnia and Herzegovina has followed its own unique path because the country and its history and demographics are unusual. Unlike in Bosnia, where the old political structures completely collapsed, most other transition countries went step by step from a situation with strong authoritarian states to more democratic politics and relatively free and fair elections. With good reason one suspected the intelligence services and other security institutions might possibly drag their feet and potentially undermine the new emerging political rulers and their (at least nominal) adherence to liberal freedoms and human rights. Democratization of intelligence therefore meant giving democratically elected politicians de facto control of the intelligence services under the assumption that these politicians really reflected the society and its post-authoritarian aspirations for protection of individual rights, legality, efficiency and effectiveness. Bosnia, on the other hand, was plunged into a civil war which did not end or peter out but stopped in 1995 primarily because of foreign intervention. The end of the civil war did not leave a unified society under a winning party that looked to reform the state security institutions which were in general deemed too strong and authoritarian. In Bosnia, the challenge rather was to establish something qualifying as a state at all on the ashes of three mutually hostile ethnic groups and their war-torn autonomous fiefdoms. The challenge from 1996 onwards was to create a state from almost nothing, not to dismantle/weaken a strong and authoritarian one.

It must be recognized that the Intelligence and Security Agency (OSA) in BiH has the technical means to carry out covert interception and surveillance and that more than nine years after its establishment the system of political control and parliamentary oversight is far from functioning according to the

---

[45]From 2006–10 the Chairman of the CoM came from the Party of Independent Social Democrats (SNSD) with a leader, Milorad Dodik, that has frequently threatened to take Republika Srpska to a referendum on independence from BiH.

letter of the law or being institutionalized such that it will be robust if rocked by events and personalities. The divided nature of politics in the country makes it possible for adept intelligence officials to carve out significant autonomy. But as long as there is multi-ethnic employment in OSA there are small chances for a truly oppressive intelligence regime to surface, as the only mobilizing factor for such a regime would be ethnicity/religion. And employees from the other sides would forewarn should such developments towards hijacking the agency for narrow ethnic interests get entrenched. Support for a 'strong state' in BiH is so confined to only about half the population – the Bosniaks – that a systematically pro-state and anti-liberal intelligence service is unlike to establish itself, at least not until the country itself is on the verge of another (unlikely) collapse into civil war. Institutionalized democratization of intelligence has thus not happened yet in BiH, but there would likely be forewarnings to any radical reversal of a rather benign although informal practice of check and balances since 2004. However, in the coming years, when the international presence is further weakened, the relative autonomy of the agency from domestic political control, and bickering, might also be affected. In short, attempts may be launched to rein in OSA from its somewhat autonomous existence – although this is no foregone conclusion. Whether such 'reining in' of OSA would be characterized as increased democratization of intelligence or not is hard to judge, given the fragmented nature of politics in BiH.

Concluding Remarks

OSA will obviously not be able to outlast the existence of Bosnia and Herzegovina should the state crumble and society again turn on itself in an ethno-nationalist spiral of tension. The SFRY had relatively strong and professionally competent institutions, like the State Security Service (SDB) but, all the same, the federal state disintegrated in the early 1990s. The same could still befall Bosnia and Herzegovina, which has much less competent institutions and even less cross-ethnic legitimacy than did the SFRY. In his 38th biannual report to the UN Security Council, the High Representative in 8 November 2010 warned of the 'marked increase in divisive anti-Dayton rhetoric disputing the sovereignty and constitutional order of BiH'.[46] During the ensuing years political problems continued. All this is bound to strain the further progress towards unification, also in the various state-level institutions that have been established – including the BiH Intelligence and Security Agency. As long as this inherent political weakness remains, and it will, 'democratization' of intelligence will not have the highest priority in BiH but will be overshadowed by the danger that there will be little of an institution to oversee at all. For there to be oversight, there needs (first) to be something to oversee.

---

[46]'Thirty-Eighth Report of the High Representative for the Implementation of the Peace Agreement for Bosnia and Herzegovina to the Secretary-General of the United Nations' <http://www.ohr.int/ohr-info/pdf/38th_report.pdf>.

Balancing Democratic Civilian Control with Effectiveness of Intelligence in Romania: Lessons Learned and Best/Worst Practices Before and After NATO and EU Integration

FLORINA CRISTIANA (CRIS) MATEI

ABSTRACT This article reviews Romania's intelligence reform after 1989. Specifically, it looks at intelligence reform before and after Romania's accession to the North Atlantic Treaty Organization (NATO) in 2004, and the European Union (EU) in 2007. It finds that Romania has made considerable progress in intelligence reform. That is because Romania, which expressed its desire and commitment to join NATO/EU after 1989, has worked hard to comply with these organizations' membership demands (including intelligence reform). After NATO/EU integration (when demands on balancing control and effectiveness virtually vanished), despite continued openness efforts made by agencies, control/oversight diluted. Thus, post-NATO/EU, while effectiveness is being strengthened, democratic control lessens.

Introduction

This article reviews Romania's efforts to reform its intelligence agencies after the transition to democracy in December 1989, before and after integration into the North Atlantic Treaty Organization (NATO) and European Union (EU) in 2004 and 2007, respectively. First, it briefly depicts the role of intelligence during the non-democratic regime. Then, it provides a description of Romania's endeavors to balance democratic civilian control of its postcommunist intelligence apparatus with effectiveness, before and after accession to NATO and EU. The paper continues with an analysis of the status of reform, which utilizes a conceptual framework proposed by Thomas

C. Bruneau and Florina Cristiana Matei for the study of Civil–Military Relations (CMR), followed by conclusions.[1]

Romania is a relatively new democracy, which transitioned violently from one of the most oppressive communist dictatorships in Central and Eastern Europe to a democratic society.[2] It is now a full member of the Organization for Security and Cooperation in Europe (OSCE), NATO, and EU, as well as a security partner to many other countries and organizations. Its path to a free society has been protracted and burdensome but, despite a series of limitations and even temporary failures in democratic institution building, Romania has developed basic democratic institutions from scratch. Institutionalizing democratic reform of intelligence has been a key component of the overall democratic reform process. Toward this end, Romania has been undergoing a major review and reform of the central institutions involved in national security, defense, and intelligence, seeking to achieve democratic civilian control/transparency and effectiveness of the intelligence agencies created after the end of communist dictatorship. Specifically, Romania has strived to institutionalize and develop the following requirements for democratic reform of intelligence: establish standards and procedures for democratic civilian control and oversight of the intelligence agencies; consolidate the democratic nature of this control through explicit mechanisms; and, develop relevant expertise and capacities to support intelligence activities (to include organizational reform, openness to new roles and missions, and removing the 'systemic impurities' from the authoritarian past).[3]

Two decades after the end of the Cold War, Romania has made considerable progress in intelligence reform. After the 1989 Revolution, Romania worked hard to comply with the membership demands of the

---

[1] For a thorough discussion on the reasons why intelligence reform can be considered an element of civil–military relations, see Bruneau and Tollefson, *Who Guards the Guardians* (Austin: University of Texas Press 2006); Thomas C. Bruneau and Steven C. Boraz (eds.) *Reforming Intelligence: Obstacles to Democratic Control and Effectiveness* (Austin: University of Texas Press 2007). The conceptual framework, which consists of a trinity of democratic civilian control, effectiveness, and efficiency (fulfilling the assigned roles and missions at a minimum cost) of the armed forces, police, and intelligence agencies, will be described in detail later in this paper. Thomas C. Bruneau and Florina Cristiana (Cris) Matei, 'Towards a New Conceptualization of Democratization and Civil-Military Relations', *Democratization* 15/5 (2008) pp.909–29; and Thomas C. Bruneau and Florina Cristiana Matei (eds.) *The Routledge Handbook of Civil Military Relations* (London: Routledge 2012).
[2] Freedom House score for Romania in 2011 was 3.36, on a scale of 1 to 7, with 1 representing the highest level of democratic progress and 7 the lowest. See <http://www.freedomhouse.org/report/nations-transit/2012/romania>. Nevertheless, due to the political crises occurred in 2012, including the fall of the Boc and Ungureanu cabinets in winter and spring, respectively, and the impeachment of the President in the summer, as well as continuous political infighting, it is to be seen if the score changes in the following years, thus whether or not Romania's democracy is in danger.
[3] Timothy Edmunds, 'Intelligence Agencies and Democratisation: Continuity and Change in Serbia after Milošević', *Europe-Asia Studies* 60/1 (2008) pp.25–48.

European and Euro-Atlantic collective security organizations. Under these circumstances, a glance at Romania's intelligence reform today should capture a more or less 'poised' balance between transparency, accountability, and democratic control, on the one hand, and effectiveness, on the other hand. Yet, the balance is more inclined toward effectiveness, and less toward accountability and democratic control. Admittedly, before NATO/EU integration, despite decision/policy makers' limited expertise and knowledge in intelligence and intelligence reform, there had been more (outside driven) interest, willingness, and focus on democratic control and oversight, in order to secure Romania's full membership in the two organizations. And when/if Romania stumbled, did not undertake rigorous reforms, or when wrongdoing happened in the intelligence realm, civil society and the media stepped in to expose these problems to both national and international public (including NATO/EU), ultimately coercing the government to continue reform. However, after NATO/EU integration (when demands on balancing control and effectiveness virtually vanished) and despite continued efforts toward transparency and openness by several intelligence agencies (which will be addressed later in this article), Romania still lacks improved accountability and better functioning control/oversight mechanisms of intelligence. Interest and political will are scarce, although expertise and knowledge are increasing among outsiders, including policy makers.

Background on the Communist Dictatorship and Transition to Democracy

Between 1947 and 1989, Romania was a highly repressive communist dictatorship; the intelligence apparatus[4] was enshrouded by virtually total secrecy, concealing law breaking and abuses against Romanian citizens, living both in the country and abroad, in order to defend the regime in power. The hardship and cruelties of the communist-era intelligence apparatus had become even more prominent after dictator Nicolae Ceausescu took power in 1965; by 1989, when the regime ended, Ceausescu's political police, the Securitate, had become so powerful that it successfully installed an omnipresent state of fear in Romania.[5]

---

[4]Consisting of the General Directorate of State Security (DGSS), established in 1951, which was transformed by Ceausescu in the late 1960s into the Department of State Security (DSS), also known as the Securitate. It should be noted that within the DSS functioned the Department of External Information (DIE), which was Romania's main foreign intelligence and counterintelligence organization. See <http://www.sie.ro/En/index_e.html> and <http://www.ceausescu.org/ceausescu_texts/revolution/die.htm>.

[5]For detailed information on the Securitate's role in defending Ceausescu and his regime, see the following: Kieran Williams and Dennis Deletant, *Security Intelligence Services in New Democracies: The Czech Republic, Slovakia and Romania* (London: Palgrave 2001); Cristiana Matei, 'Romania's Transition to Democracy and the Role of the Press in Intelligence Reform', in Bruneau and Boraz (eds.) *Reforming Intelligence*; Florina Cristiana (Cris) Matei, 'Romania's Intelligence Community: From an Instrument of Dictatorship to Serving Democracy', *International Journal of Intelligence and Counterintelligence* 20/4 (2007)

In December 1989, Romania transitioned to democracy by abolishing the communist regime, killing Ceausescu, and dismantling the Securitate.[6] Since then, Romania has been able to craft a new intelligence system (which initially consisted of at least nine agencies) within a legal framework including defined mandates, and democratic civilian control/oversight, as well as being tailored to the current security environment with its risks, challenges, and threats. Today there are six intelligence agencies:[7] four independent – the Romanian Intelligence Service (SRI); the Foreign Intelligence Service (SIE); the Guard and Protection Service (SPP); the Special Telecommunication Service (STS) – and two ministerial – Directorate for Intelligence and Internal Protection (DIPI); the Directorate for General Information of the Armed Forces (DGIA). Reforming intelligence in Romania has followed two directions: one required by democratization – the need for accountability, openness, transparency, and democratic civilian control; and the other drawn by security trends – the need to utilize effective intelligence to counter current security challenges such as terrorism, organized crime, and cyber threats.

Democratic Reform of Romania's Intelligence Agencies

This comprehensive institutional and organizational democratic reform, driven by both an initial need for intelligence transparency and a subsequent need for effectiveness, has essentially known two main phases (pre- and post-NATO/EU integration), with several (overlapping) stages.

Phase 1: Pre-NATO/EU Integration

The first phase, the pre-NATO/EU accession, included roughly three stages, and aimed at establishing democratic intelligence institutions, hence a particular interest in democratic control and oversight, as well as openness, to ensure a move away from the dictatorial past, and secure full NATO and EU membership.

The first stage was a 'wake up' period lasting from December 1989 to 1991, which was mostly dominated by *ad hoc* and often perfunctory measures involving intelligence, such as the dismantling of the Securitate, creation of the SIE and SRI (February and March 1990, respectively), the SPP (May 1990), as well as the creation of the Intelligence Agency of the Ministry

---

pp.629–60; Larry Watts, 'Control and Oversight of Security Intelligence in Romania', Geneva Centre for Democratic Control of Armed Forces (DCAF) Working Papers, 2003.

[6]The Securitate was placed under the Armed Forces in December 1989. Romania reportedly functioned without an intelligence organization for at least three months after the end of dictatorship. A new intelligence system was created in March 1990, however on the ruins of the Securitate.

[7]It should be noted that the CSAT created a National Intelligence Community in November 2005, and the Prime Minister created a Center for Situations in his chancellery, which will be discussed later in this article.

of Interior (February 1990). This stage was characterized by several controversies including the establishment of intelligence and security institutions without a proper legal framework, or the reactivation and appointment of the former Securitate officers in several agencies (but most importantly in the Ministry of Interior).[8] Interestingly, during this stage, two committees for defense, public order and national security were created within both chambers of Parliament and quickly (May 1990) empowered with a host of prerogatives including: adoption of laws pertaining to intelligence; the control, review of the budget, and assessment of the draft budgetary allocations; investigations to be conducted through either permanent committees or special committees of investigations, interpellations, and questions; simple motions and censorship motions.[9] Nevertheless, legislative control/oversight of the committees was derelict during this stage.[10]

The second stage was an 'institution building' period, lasting from February/March 1991 to 1996/1997 during which Romania established several institutions aimed at developing democratically accountable intelligence agencies. Examples include the following: establishing the National Defense Supreme Council (CSAT) (1991) as the main executive control mechanism, as well as national security and defense coordinator; creating the National Defense College (NDC) (1992) to provide defense education for military personnel as well as civilians within the military system and outsiders; and shaping and improving the legal basis for security and intelligence by drafting and adopting several laws and government resolutions on defense and security matters, including a new Constitution (1991), National Security Law (1991), and statutory laws for several agencies (e.g. STS 1996). This stage is also marked by the first attempts to professionalize intelligence agencies: hiring young generations of personnel, mostly graduates from universities or representatives of civil society, with

---

[8] For more information, see the following: Matei, 'Romania's Transition to Democracy and the Role of the Press in Intelligence Reform' in Bruneau and Boraz (eds.) *Reforming Intelligence*; Matei, 'Romania's Intelligence Community', pp.629–60; Liviu Muresan, 'Security Sector Reform – A Chance for the Euro-Atlantic Integration of Romania', paper prepared for a Workshop on Security Sector Reform in Central and Eastern Europe: Criteria for Success and Failure sponsored by the Geneva Centre for the Democratic Control of Armed Forces (DCAF), Geneva, Switzerland, 22–23 November 2001, pp.2–3; Williams and Deletant, *Security Intelligence Services in New Democracies*; Watts, 'Control and Oversight of Security Intelligence in Romania'.

[9] Razvan Ionescu and Liviu Muresan, 'The Monitoring Exercise of Instruments and Mechanisms for Parliamentary Oversight of the Security Sector in Romania' (pilot project) of the EURISC Foundation, the Commission for Defense, Public Order and National Security of the House of Deputies, Parliament of Romania, and with the support of Geneva Centre for the Democratic Control of Armed Forces (DCAF), Bucharest, Romania, 2004, p.23; Constantin Monac, 'Parlamentul si Securitatea Nationala', Bucharest, Monitorul Oficial, 2006, pp.191–3; Williams and Deletant, *Security Intelligence Services in New Democracies*.

[10] Even if, due to the public fear for a Securitate comeback, SRI reported to Parliament in November 1990; Watts, 'Control and Oversight of Security Intelligence in Romania'.

pro-Western attitudes and generally flawless conduct;[11] improving personnel management policies, and providing intelligence professionals with a career path based on motivation and a promotion system based more on merit and performance.[12] There was investment in intelligence education and professional training through the creation of the Romanian National Intelligence Academy (ANI)[13] (1992), as well as other education and training institutions, which educate future intelligence agents in specific intelligence issues, foreign languages/cultures, legal matters, as well as technical skills.[14] Relevant to civilian control/oversight of the military intelligence was the appointment (1993) of the first two civilians in command positions within the military system (a deputy director of the National Defense College and a deputy Minister of Defense), as well as the appointment of the first civilian as Minister of Defense (1994). In addition, through the adoption of the National Security Law in 1991, judicial oversight was established.

All of these developments were possible due to NATO/EU pressure to bring about institutions and mechanisms of democratic civilian control of intelligence. NATO's Partnership for Peace (PfP) and the EU's *Acquis Communautaire* served as guides to intelligence reform. Their requirements included: establishing democratic control, achieving interoperability and compatibility with the Atlantic Alliance's members, and harmonization of domestic legislation with the Western countries. Nevertheless, Romania's then lackadaisical pace of intelligence reform halted (together with other reform challenges) Romania's accession in the first wave of enlargement of the Atlantic Alliance in 1997. For instance, the continued employment of former Securitate employees – in particular those who were corrupted, did political policing roles, and violated human rights – because of the desire to maintain expertise[15] was a drawback for the reform,[16] and hence for Romania's chances of NATO and EU membership.[17] In addition, democratic

---

[11] There were situations, however, when conduct was far from flawless: intelligence personnel were engaged in numerous acts of corruption and bad behavior.

[12] Interview by Ion Petrescu with General Lieutenant dr Sergiu Medar, *Observatorul Militar*, no. 45, 9–15 November 2005.

[13] Initially known as the 'Superior Intelligence Institute'; Florina Cristiana Matei, 'Shaping Intelligence as a Profession in Romania: Reforming Intelligence Education after 1989', Research Institute for European and American Studies (RIEAS) Research Paper 110, p.20 <http://rieas.gr/images/rieas110.pdf>

[14] For detailed information on intelligence education and training, see ibid.

[15] The need for continuity in specific intelligence fields and areas of expertise, or lack of expertise of the newly hired agents; 'Rolul Serviciilor de Informaţii intr-o Societate Democratică si in Procesul de Aderare a Romaniei la NATO', Special Edition broadcast by Romanian Television, 23 March 2002 <http://www.sie.ro/Arhiva/es2.html>.

[16] Early retirement of the former Securitate employees was also problematic. Without a legal basis on the statute of intelligence officers, many of them became the first generation of Romanian (corrupt) businessmen, while others created parallel private intelligence agencies (competing with the government institutions); these personnel helped expand corruption and organized crime.

[17] With regard to protection of classified information.

civilian control was also less than perfect. With regard to legislative control/oversight, for instance, despite the relatively great authority granted to the parliamentary committees, actual parliamentary oversight has been challenged by deficient parliamentary expertise in intelligence matters, poor cooperation and coordination among parliamentary committees as well as between former and current members of the oversight committees, and the unhelpful stance of the intelligence agencies when requested to forward information and data to committees.

The third stage, lasting from 1996/1997 to 2004, the moment of NATO integration, involved more sustained and comprehensive reforms, to secure accession in the second wave of enlargement, encompassing the following: institutionalizing security policies; improving recruitment and human resource management of the agencies so as to include a vetting process and granting security clearances; consolidating the professionalization of intelligence; demilitarization of Police (including DIPI); developing legislation and a system for protecting classified information;[18] and modernization of equipment, especially regarding military and technical intelligence. Interagency coordination and cooperation, as well as international cooperation was fostered, especially in the aftermath of the terrorist attacks of Washington, DC, and New York in 2001.[19] Legislation on transparency and access to Government information, for example, the Freedom of Information Act (FOIA) was adopted in 2001, as well as legislation enabling the opening of Securitate files (a Law on access to Securitate files was adopted in 1999). More effective openness and transparency endeavors included creating websites to reach out to civil society and the public; press

---

[18]Especially to alleviate NATO concerns. NATO expressed it unwillingness to share information with former Securitate personnel; Florina Cristiana (Cris) Matei, 'The Challenges of Intelligence Sharing in Romania', *Intelligence and National Security*, 24/4 (2009) pp.574–85; Florina Cristiana (Cris) Matei, 'The Legal Framework for Intelligence in Post-Communist Romania', *International Journal of Intelligence and CounterIntelligence* 22 (2009) pp.667–98; Florina Cristiana Matei and Thomas Bruneau, 'Intelligence Reform in New Democracies: Factors Supporting or Arresting Progress', *Democratization* 18/3 (2011) pp.602–30; Thomas C. Bruneau and Florina Cristiana (Cris) Matei, 'Intelligence in the Developing Democracies: The Quest for Transparency and Effectiveness', in Loch K. Johnson (ed.) *The Oxford Handbook of National Security Intelligence* (Oxford: Oxford University Press 2010).

[19]Although executive control, guidance, and coordination of the intelligence existed through CSAT, in 2001 CSAT strengthened executive control by empowered the Prime Minister to exercise control over all the intelligence services during crises; until that time, the Prime Minister would normally only have jurisdiction over the ministerial services, while only the President would coordinate all other agencies. See Radu Tudor, 'Romanian Government to Revamp Intelligence Services Structures', *Ziua*, 16 November 2001. This was a very interesting development. In Romania, which is a semi-parliamentary system, there have always been political struggles between the President and the Prime Minister, with regard to the allocation of intelligence and security. The empowering of the Prime Minister showed mutual consent to set aside divergences and dissent toward a bigger goal: NATO/EU integration.

conferences, news briefings, as well as regular interviews in the media were given by intelligence officials, not only from SIE and SRI, but also from the military intelligence, SPP, STS all contributed to consolidating institutions of democratic civilian control and oversight. During this period, an important stimulus for reform was the 1999-adopted NATO Membership Action Plans (MAP). Another catalyst for transparency was the European Court for Human Rights (ECHR), which was established in 1959 in Strasbourg to handle alleged violations of the 1950 European Convention on Human Rights.[20] Relevant examples of the ECHR's contribution to the oversight of the Romanian intelligence agencies include the Court's resolution on the Aurel Rotaru versus Romania case in 2000, and on Nicolae Haralambie versus Romania case in 2009. In both cases, the Court voted in favor of the plaintiffs: in Rotaru's case, the Court voted the Romanian government violated Articles 13 (the right to an effective remedy), 6 (the right to a fair trial), and 8 (the right to respect for private life) of the Convention; in Haralambie's case, the Court ruled Haralambie was a victim of a breach in Article 8 of the Convention, namely obstruction and delay to access the file created on him by the Securitate.[21]

All of this, but most importantly Romania's support to the United States' security endeavors, as well as its involvement in the war in Afghanistan, enabled it to receive an invitation to join NATO in 2002, at the Prague Summit, and full accession in 2004, at the Washington Summit. Nevertheless, despite the fact that the new legal framework stipulates political neutrality, politicization of some intelligence agencies (and abuses of agencies' exceptional powers, which have, from time to time, been used for vendettas and personal reasons, rather than national security) still happened throughout this stage.

Phase 2: Post-NATO/EU Integration

The second phase (2004–present) has involved the transformation of Romania's military to full NATO and EU (in 2007) membership, in terms of continued transparency and openness,[22] and increased effectiveness.

---

[20] Any state or individual claiming to be a victim of a violation of the Convention has the right to forward an application to the ECHR alleging an infringement by one of the Convention states of any of the Convention's rights; Matei, 'Romania's Intelligence Community', pp.629–60; Ian Leigh, 'Intelligence and the Law in the United Kingdom' in Loch K. Johnson (ed.) *The Oxford Handbook of National Security Intelligence* (Oxford: Oxford University Press 2010).
[21] Both Rotaru and Haralambie were awarded considerable amounts of money for pecuniary and non-pecuniary damages. In the Rotaru case, ECHR recommended changes in the legislation on intelligence. For detailed information on the two cases, see Matei, 'Romania's Intelligence Community', pp.629–60; <http://sim.law.uu.nl/sim/caselaw/Hof.nsf/233813e697620022c1256864005232b7/4f263165e3595d32c125765b003237da?OpenDocument>.
[22] Democratic control, in particular legislative, appears to have lessened after 2007.

With regard to transparency, the completion of the transfer of Securitate files' to the Council for Studying Securitate Archives (CNSAS),[23] between 2004–7 (the year of accession into EU), has led to opening and making public on request of thousands of files, whereby various politicians, academics, intellectuals, sports men and women, clergy members, and journalists have been exposed as Securitate collaborators. Again, EU's pressure toward openness and transparency should be credited for this accomplishment. In addition, almost all intelligence agencies have continued to improve their outreach to civil society and the citizenry, from making their websites more user friendly, to participating in talk shows, interviews, and round tables, alongside NGOs, think tanks, and press representatives. They have contributed to the minimal intelligence culture and literature in Romania with books on security threats, intelligence roles and missions in a democracy, and journals like DGIA's *Infosfera* or SRI's *Intelligence*. In this context, in 2010, the author chaired a panel entitled 'Intelligence Reform and Outreach in Romania' at the International Studies Association (ISA) Convention, in Montreal, Canada, which brought together intelligence practitioners from two Romanian intelligence agencies (SRI and DGIA), including the SRI deputy director, and Romanian academia. They familiarized the participants with current intelligence reform issues in Romania, such as improving analysis, interagency and international cooperation and sharing, and openness/transparency to society, while also seeking out input from these developed democracies on how to tackle these issues. In addition, the ISA papers written by Romanian intelligence professionals were published by intelligence journals in the United States.

Moreover, the Romanian government strove to improve the agencies' effectiveness. A National Doctrine on Security Intelligence was adopted in 2004, a White Book on Security and Defense was developed in 2004, a new National Security Strategy in 2005, a Defense Strategy in 2008, which established new priorities and stipulated additional roles and missions for intelligence, in particular with regard to combating terrorism. Romania's National Intelligence Community (CNI), was created in 2005 to serve as the coordination body of the activity of all current intelligence agencies and to provide centralized processing of intelligence gathered by all its components, and dissemination to relevant consumers.[24] Despite criticism and concern vis-à-vis transparency and

---

[23]CNSAS is a lawful authority set up by a law adopted in 1999 on access to former Securitate, to apprehend the Securitate files from agencies, facilitate Romanians' access to personal records and, most importantly, to examine the past Securitate connections of prominent public authorities.

[24]'Romania: Secret Services to Solve the Problems of Integration in EU', *Axis*, 23 January 2006; Miruna Munteanu and Razvan Ionescu, 'Reforma serviciilor secrete romanesti, capcane si jaloane, CNI – o noua viziune asupra informatiilor (2)', *Ziua*, 14 January 2006; Dan Badea, 'Comunitatea Nationala de Informatii infiintata de Traian Basescu este in afara legii', *Gardianul*, 24 November 2005.

accountability issues,[25] CNI seems to serve its purpose to a certain extent:[26] it increases intelligence agencies' effectiveness and professionalism by eliminating parallelisms and waste of human and material resources, and generates a functional intelligence partnership with the agencies preserving their specific roles and missions while enjoying better coordination of their strategic activities based on professional rather than unfair competition. In 2007, SRI started, with CSAT's approval, a comprehensive reform entitled SRI 'Strategic Vision 2007–2010', which comprised de-bureaucratization, improved flexibility, and better horizontal cooperation among SRI structures, strengthened analysis capabilities, and the like. The Strategic Vision was in line with EU security strategy and NATO's new strategic concept. Reform is still going on within SRI. 'Strategic Vision 2007–2011' is currently followed by 'Strategic Vision 2011–2015. SRI in the Information Age', which attempts to better link the Romanian intelligence agency with the current technological, informational, and cyber security actors. In addition, intelligence agencies have continued to receive increased budget funds, a most recent increase happened in stages, in March 2011 for SIE and STS and May for SRI.[27]

To better suit the current security landscape and the new NATO/EU membership statute, the executive drafted a new security law package in 2005, including a law on the status of intelligence officers, a law on the organization and functioning of the SIE, a law on the organization and functioning of the SRI, a law on national security, and a law on activity of intelligence, counterintelligence, and protection of information. Unfortunately, despite the real need for updated legislation on security, since the drafting of these laws, despite debates, adjustments, and changes of the respective draft laws, Parliament failed to approve the package, and does not seem to have any immediate intent to do so. For instance, the refusal in early 2011 of the European Union to allow Romania's accession to the Schengen Agreement, which pressures Romania to strengthen institutions dealing with border security, as well as to eradicate and counter corruption within security institutions and throughout the Government, requires upgrading and strengthening the legal framework for national security. Yet, the legislators do not seem to show any interest in it.

Controversial during this phase have been the repeated accusations that Romania hosted secret CIA prisons (also known as 'black sites') at the beginning of the Iraq war (2003 to 2005).[28] In the fall of 2005, after

---

[25]Matei, 'The Challenges of Intelligence Sharing in Romania', pp.574–85.

[26]There are still problems and rivalries with regard to cooperation and sharing in a multilateral format; the bilateral format is still highly preferred. Source: discussions with Romanian intelligence officers, 2009–10.

[27]'Bugetul SRI, SIE, STS a fost suplimentat pt personal' <http://www.ziare.com/stiri/sri/bugetul-sri-a-fost-suplimentat-pentru-cheltuieli-de-personal-1098667>.

[28]Some media reports indicated the United States convinced Romania to cooperate in return for NATO membership. Others suggested all NATO allies and partners signed an agreement that allowed CIA operations to run everywhere in Europe. Scott Horton, 'Inside the CIA's

numerous 'Human Rights Watch' allegations, as well as media 'fire alarms', the Parliamentary Assembly of the Council of Europe appointed Senator Dick Marty to investigate 'alleged secret detentions and unlawful inter-state transfers of detainees' involving member states of the Council of Europe, including Romania.[29] Senator Marty issued two reports to the Council of Europe, in 2006 and 2007, respectively, which contained accounts of numerous illegal US detentions and transfers in Europe, including allegations of involvement of Romania and other countries.[30] In response to the allegations, in 2006, Romania's Parliament set up an Inquiry Committee, which, after investigating all the flights between various airports in Romania, concluded that no CIA secret prisons functioned in Romania during 2003–5.[31] In the fall of 2011, Dick Marty issued yet another report criticizing the parliamentary inquiries launched after his initial reports.[32] And, in the winter of the same year, former CIA operatives identified the location of the alleged CIA's secret prison in Romania (the Romanian National Registry Office for Classified Information [ORNISS]). Both President Traian Basescu and ORNISSS representatives denied this while

---

Black Site in Bucharest', *Harper's Magazine*, 8 December 2011; Stephen Grey, 'Secret CIA Prisons Confirmed by Polish and Romanian Officials', *The Guardian*, 7 June 2007; 'Break the Silence on CIA Renditions, Urge MEPs', European Parliament News, Human rights/External relations, 11 September 2012 <http://www.europarl.europa.eu/news/en/headlines/content/20120910STO50933/html/Break-the-silence-on-CIA-renditions-urge-MEPs>; Matt Apuzzo and Adam Goldman, 'AP Exclusive: CIA Flight Carried Secret from Gitmo', Associated Press Writers, 7 August 2010.

[29]'The Council of Europe's Investigation into Illegal Transfers and Secret Detentions in Europe: A Chronology' <http://assembly.coe.int/ASP/APFeaturesManager/defaultArtSiteView.asp?ID=362>; 'Council of Europe: Secret CIA Prisons Confirmed', 7 June 2007 <http://www.hrw.org/en/news/2007/06/07/council-europe-secret-cia-prisons-confirmed>.

[30]The Marty reports contained testimonies of several active duty and former members of intelligence services in the US and Europe, as well as analyses of computer 'data strings' from the international flight planning system. The second report contained allegations that US 'high-value detainees' (HVD), such as Khalid Sheikh Mohammed (the alleged 9/11 mastermind), were detained in secret CIA prisons in Poland and Romania, 2003–5, and that former President Ion Iliescu authorized the secret detentions. In September 2006, President Bush acknowledged the existence of 'black sites' with no indication regarding specific venues. In addition, in 2007 a report of the European Union (i.e. the European Parliament) shared the same conclusion vis-à-vis renditions. For detailed information on the reports, see the following: 'The Council of Europe's Investigation into Illegal Transfers and Secret Detentions in Europe: A Chronology'; '"High-Value" Detainees Were Held in Secret CIA Detention Centres in Poland and Romania, Says PACE Committee' <http://assembly.coe.int/ASP/Press/StopPressView.asp?ID=1924>; 'Council of Europe: Secret CIA Prisons Confirmed'; Carl Ek, 'Romania: Background and Current Issues', Congressional Research Service (CRS) Report, Number RS2257, 23 January 2007, pp.1–6.

[31]'Romanian MPs' Committee Finds No Evidence of CIA Prisoner', Rompres News Agency, Bucharest, 16 June 2006.

[32]'The Council of Europe's Investigation into Illegal Transfers and Secret Detentions in Europe: A Chronology'; 'Council of Europe: Secret CIA Prisons Confirmed'.

the CIA has refused to comment.[33] On the other hand, surprisingly, during all this time, while the international media and Human Rights groups were very vocal about the existence of 'black sites' in Romania and other European countries, and called for thorough investigations of any human rights violations, the Romanian media seemed to be less aggressive vis-à-vis the secret prison concern. In the aftermath of all these revelations, it would be interesting to see whether or not the Romanian parliament will conduct another investigation, as urged by a Resolution adopted by the European Parliament on 11 September 2012,[34] and whether or not the media will have any influence in this particular matter.

Analysis of Intelligence Reform in Romania Before and After NATO/EU Accession

A Framework for Analysis

As previously mentioned, in analyzing the status of intelligence reform in Romania before and after integration in NATO and EU, this paper will utilize the civil–military relations framework proposed by Bruneau and Matei, which advances a 'tradeoff' between democratic control, effectiveness, and efficiency, of security institutions, including intelligence.[35]

In this conceptual framework, Democratic Civilian Control involves a wide spectrum of mechanisms including authority over the institutional control mechanisms that provide direction and guidance for the security forces, exercised through institutions that range from legal bases that empower the civilian leadership, to civilian-led organizations such as a ministry of defense or a civilian-led intelligence agency, parliamentary committees, and a well-defined chain of authority for civilians to determine roles and missions. Oversight must be exercised by the civilian leadership to

---

[33] Crofton Black, 'Romania's CIA Prison Illuminates Failure of European Accountability' <http://www.huffingtonpost.com/crofton-black/romanias-cia-prison-illum_b_1138961.html>; 'CIA "Secret Prison" Found in Romania – Media Reports', 9 December 2011 <http://www.bbc.co.uk/news/world-europe-16093106>; Dick Marty, 'Secret Detentions and Illegal Transfers of Detainees Involving Council of Europe Member States: Second Report', Report of the Committee on Legal Affairs and Human Rights, Doc. 11302 rev. 11 June 2007, pp.1–70 <http://assembly.coe.int/Documents/WorkingDocs/Doc07/edoc11302.pdf>.

[34] 'The Council of Europe's Investigation into Illegal Transfers and Secret Detentions in Europe: A Chronology'; '"High-Value" Detainees Were Held in Secret CIA Detention Centres in Poland and Romania, Says PACE Committee'.

[35] For detailed information on the CMR framework see Bruneau and Matei, 'Towards a New Conceptualization of Democratization and Civil-Military Relations', pp.909–29; Thomas C. Bruneau, Florina Cristiana Matei and Sak Sakoda, 'National Security Councils: Their Potential Functions in Democratic Civil-Military Relations', *Defense & Security Analysis* 25/3 (2009) pp.255–69. Nevertheless, even if efficiency is a necessary dimension of the CMR framework, due to methodological challenges inherent in measuring efficiency of the overall security sector including intelligence, in this paper I will only consider the control and effectiveness elements of the CMR; Bruneau and Matei (eds.) *The Routledge Handbook of Civil Military Relations*.

keep track of what the security forces do and to ensure they are in fact following the direction and guidance exercised by formal agencies within the executive, legislative, and judicial branches. Informal oversight by domestic and international civil society organizations is also important, as is the inculcation of professional norms, which contribute to effectiveness and must be institutionalized through policies for recruitment, education, training, and promotion, in accordance with the goals of the democratically elected civilian leadership.[36]

Effectiveness in Fulfilling Roles and Missions involves at least the following three basic requirements: the existence of a plan, such as a strategy or even a doctrine; the institutionalizing of specific structures and processes to both formulate the plans and implement them, such as ministries of defense, national security councils, or other means that facilitate jointness and/or inter-agency coordination, as well as international cooperation; and allocation of resources, including political capital, money, and personnel.

Civilian Control and Effectiveness of Intelligence Before and After NATO/EU Accession

The preceding discussion indicates that, during the first phase, democratic control/transparency was the main goal for intelligence reform as compared to effectiveness, to ensure irreversibility from the past and to ensure Romania joined NATO and EU. Throughout this phase, despite lack of expertise, Romanian policy makers, due to pressure by NATO/EU and media scandals, were more inclined to set aside differences, learn about defense, security, and intelligence, and undertake reform, especially with regard to control and oversight. Throughout the second phase, while openness and outreach initiated by the agencies continued, and effectiveness strengthened (especially after 9/11), control and oversight was weakened by the legislature.

A summary of findings, in terms of Requirements for Transparency and Accountability and Requirements for Effectiveness during the two phases, is presented in Table 1. All six intelligence agencies operating in Romania are taken into account, based on available information and access. Values are assigned ranging from low to high for each requirement in order to highlight some of the similarities and variations between the two phases.

Requirements for Democratic Control

Romania scores 'Medium-High' in the Institutional Control Mechanisms category during both pre- and post-NATO/EU integration period. Control Mechanisms have been institutionalized through a relatively rich legal framework, varying from organic laws to rules and regulations on national security and intelligence, as well as institutions, to include civilian-led agencies such as SRI, SIE and CSAT, and CNI, seeking to achieve

---

[36] See Bruneau and Tollefson, *Who Guards the Guardians*; Bruneau and Boraz (eds.) *Reforming Intelligence*; Bruneau et al., 'National Security Councils', pp.255–69.

Table 1. Institutional Base for Control and and Effectiveness in Romania.

Romania	Transparency/Accountability				Effectiveness		
	Institutional control mechanisms	Oversight	Professional norms	Plan or strategy	Institutions	Resources	
Pre-NATO/EU	Medium-High	Medium-High	High	Low-Medium	Medium	Medium-High
Post-NATO/EU	Medium-High	Low	High	Medium-High	Medium-High	Medium-High

accountability and transparency of the agencies, along with effectiveness and better coordination and sharing. Of great importance has been the increased understanding of the intelligence agencies' managers of the need to balance secrecy with openness, and the importance of informing outsiders of the need for intelligence in a democracy, a difficult task considering that the post-communist Romanian intelligence started with total secrecy, and people's mistrust due to the legacy of the past.[37] Nevertheless, in the long run, openness and outreach were not impossible. Some agencies became more open than others. SRI was the first to open, as it had no option other than to show people it was not the Securitate (which people associated and occasionally still associate it with). Although almost all SRI and SIE directors had encouraged transparency via websites and declassification of information, gave interviews, and even started partnerships with civil society, for example, the partnership between SRI and civil society launched in 2003, and even more openness was noticed after Maior and Ungureanu took office respectively at SRI and SIE after NATO/EU integration. This openness led to more awareness of the public on intelligence and even support, starting with support in the media, for intelligence activity.[38] Foreign/military intelligence remain more secluded than the SRI, yet are now more transparent and open than during the first phase, for example, DGIA is issuing a journal on intelligence and while representatives of DGIA contributed papers and presented at the 2011 ISA. Romania however scores 'Medium-High' due to the previously-mentioned irregularities within the legal framework and the need for improving transparency, especially regarding outreach to academia.[39]

In the 'oversight' category Romania scores 'Medium-High' during the first period and 'Low' during the second. To begin with, legislative oversight was, admittedly, more rigorous and effective before 2004, when Romania's membership into NATO and EU as well as NATO/EU accession requirements became the 'only game in town' for the Romanians. During that time any political divergences were put aside for the sake of NATO/EU integration, and lawmakers attached greater importance to both transparency and the effectiveness of Romanian intelligence. Now the politicians manifest a 'hands-off' attitude toward intelligence as we saw with the National Security Law package. The judiciary has been weak throughout both phases, due to corruption and limited understanding and knowledge of intelligence and

---

[37]In addition, even when some agencies have showed interest and took action to open to the civil society and the public, occasional 'deterrence' actions undertaken by other agencies' leadership toward the press in order to halt investigative journalism or publication of inconvenient materials, has been a hindrance to intelligence transparency, garnering of popular support, as well as improving the outsiders' intelligence culture.
[38]Support for intelligence may also indirectly stem from citizens' support for Romania's participation in international military operations.
[39]Valentin Fernand Filip and Remus Ioan Stefureac, 'The Dilemmas of Linking Romanian Intelligence, Universities, and Think Tanks', *International Journal of Intelligence and Counterintelligence* 24/4 (2011–2012) pp.711–32.

security issues, but also the faulty legal framework. The current diminutive political will to consolidate and strengthen democratic control and oversight of intelligence agencies is largely due to the disappearance of EU/NATO 'carrots' and to a certain extent 'sticks'. Schengen could be a stick but political unsteadiness and the economic crisis which affected Romania badly and elicited budgetary cuts to Government salaries hinder progress. With no interest or incentive for reform on the one hand, and no 'veto' from the EU or NATO on the other, it is rather difficult to predict whether or not oversight of intelligence by the legislature and even judiciary will become more robust in the foreseeable future. Hopefully, now that the NATO/EU incentives have virtually vanished, the media will continue to watch the intelligence agencies to ensure a balance between security and transparency is maintained in Romania. This leads us to the 'informal' dimension of control and oversight. Informal oversight by the media has been high since 1989, although, arguably, it may have had more power to sway policy and reform prior NATO/EU integration than after. Nevertheless, it needs to remain alert and reveal corruption and wrongdoing related to intelligence.

Professional norms, too, improved since 1989 and Romania scores 'High' in this category in both phases. Intelligence agencies have become professional institutions, based on expertise, responsibility, and corporateness. There are still issues that affect improving professionalism; again, due to limited interest of legislators. For example, notwithstanding the remarkable progress of the SRI reform in certain areas, for example, planning, management, and restructuring, which basically happened as SRI and CSAT bypassed the outdated 1991 Security Law, the reform of additional SRI levels such as demilitarization, which calls for a separate law on the status of intelligence officers and a career guide for the intelligence practitioners, requires further regulations.

Requirements for Effectiveness

Effectiveness of intelligence equated with Romania's desire to be seen as reliable security partner, especially after 9/11, and also due to NATO membership. For instance, Romania scores 'Low-Medium' during Phase 1 and 'Medium-High' during Phase 2 in the 'plan' category. More strategic documents have been issued after 2004 as compared to the 1989–2004 timeframe, aimed at strengthening Romania's intelligence capabilities to fight against terrorism, organized crime, and other security challenges, as well as increasing effectiveness when participating in international military and peace support operations.

In the 'institution' category, Romania scores 'Medium' during the first phase and 'Medium-High' during the second. Perhaps the most plausible explanation for the shift from 'Medium' to 'Medium-High' would be the creation of the CNI in 2005, aimed at improving intelligence sharing and analysis across the intelligence community.

In the 'resources' category, Romania scores 'Medium' during the first phase and 'Medium-High' during the second. Since Romania's participation in the international efforts to counter terrorism and integration into NATO, allocating more resources in terms of budget, personnel, and equipment, has become a priority, at least for the executive. With regard to budget, for example, of all EU member states, Romania allocates one of the highest funding to the intelligence agencies,[40] even in the current conditions of economic crisis. Likewise, the Romanian intelligence agencies have continuously sought to recruit qualified personnel and modern equipment to augment agencies' capabilities. Romania's IC effective contribution to both national and global security has been acknowledged on numerous occasions by foreign counterparts. In recognition of Romania's excellent military intelligence Humint capabilities, for example, NATO established in 2009 a NATO Humint Center of Excellence in Oradea, Romania. Currently, the presence of US rotating military training bases in Romania, as well as US plans to deploy a missile shield in Romania as part of the US anti-missile defense system in Europe, project START, will probably require and actually contribute to strengthening the effectiveness of Romania's security forces, including intelligence.

Conclusions: Lessons Learned from Romania's Intelligence Reform

This article looks at Romania's endeavors to reform intelligence after the fall of the communist regime in December 1989, from the perspective of pre- and post-NATO/EU accession. It finds that reforming intelligence – finding a proper balance between democratic civilian control and effectiveness – has been long and difficult in Romania, but progress was not impossible. Admittedly, the former Securitate 'stigma' has faded away. It is replaced by an intelligence system with redefined democratic roles and missions, more transparent, less politicized, and engaged in international cooperation; thus better serving Romania's citizens and national security.

Nevertheless, Romania is, at the same time, both a 'best' and 'worst' example of democratic reform of intelligence. On the one hand, as was the case for many other Central and Eastern European countries, NATO and the EU were the major drivers of intelligence reform. The pre-NATO/EU integration phase is the period when despite limited knowledge and expertise vis-à-vis intelligence and security on the part of both policy makers and even intelligence professionals, there was almost unanimous willingness to undertake reform, in order to secure membership in these two organizations. And, if reforming intelligence stopped for one reason or another, it was the media that stepped in and brought reform back. During the pre-NATO/EU integration period, transparency dominated the reform, while effectiveness became increasingly relevant after 2001. During the post-NATO/EU integration period, however, effectiveness became the main focus of the reform and has followed a more or less constant trajectory after 2004; control, especially oversight, has plummeted, due precisely to the lack of 'carrots and sticks' of NATO/EU, which has led to decreased willingness/

---

[40]For detailed information of the SRI, SIE, SPP, STS budgets, see the following newspaper compilation: < http://www.ziare.com/articole/buget+sri >.

interest[41] on the part of responsible policy and decision makers within the legislature to continue intelligence reform after accession. As *The Economist* contends: 'in promoting democracy, the EU has less influence on members than on applicants. As one diplomat says: "To join the EU you have to smell of roses. But if you are a member and you start to reek, there is nobody to make you take a bath".[42]

Thus, 20 years after the end of communism, the 'effectiveness/democratic control' balance is heavily towards 'effectiveness' in Romania. One could sensibly argue this is a natural trend of old and new democracies alike, considering the complex and unpredictable security environment which calls for effective intelligence agencies. Nevertheless, bearing in mind Romania's non-democratic experience with intelligence, democratic civilian control should not remain a low priority. Old democracies continue to strengthen control and oversee institutions to keep intelligence accountable and so should Romania. Yet, the lack of political will after NATO/EU integration could not only diminish Romania's credibility among NATO and EU if it fails to maintain transparent and accountable state institutions, as pledged before accession, but could also negatively impact democratic consolidation.[43] All of this could be a 'warning' for civilian elites in all democracies (both old and new) that political will and interest should remain cardinal in maintaining a continuum of democratic civilian control and effectiveness of the intelligence. Hopefully, things will get better in Romania, if/when the Government changes and if the new civilian elites will attach greater interest to intelligence reform.

Acknowledgements

The author would like to thank the Center for Civil--Military Relations, US Embassy, the Romanian intelligence agencies, in particular the Domestic Intelligence Service (SRI) and the Military Intelligence, as well as the International Studies Association (ISA) Section of Intelligence, for facilitating invaluable discussions and insight in support to this research. The views expressed in this article are those of the author and do not reflect the official policy or position of the Department of Defense or the US Government.

---

[41] Although limited knowledge and expertise in intelligence and intelligence reform still exists among policy makers.

[42] 'Hungary's Other Deficit. The European Union Has Few Legal Means to Stop Hungary's Leaders from Eroding Democracy', *The Economist*, 6 January 2011, p.53.

[43] Juan J. Linz and Alfred Stepan indirectly address CMR and intelligence reform as prerequisite for democratic consolidation (*via* institutionalizing five arenas and the existence of state). See Juan J. Linz and Alfred Stepan, *Problems of Democratic Transition and Consolidation: Southern Europe, South America, and Post-Communist Europe* (Baltimore, MD: John Hopkins University Press 1996).

Index

abuses, human rights 51, 81, 142
accession, European Union (EU) 14, 28, 33, 131–48
accountability mechanisms 24–6
Acquis Communautaire, European Union (EU) 14, 29, 33, 136
Acton, Lord 6
African National Congress (ANC) 55
agency 6
Albania 15, 16
Albania, Hoxha 18, 20
Albania, politicization of intelligence 22
Albania, secret police 17
Alfonsín, President Raul 86
Alves, S. 109
Ambros, C. 2, 4, 6, 8–9, 36–64
AMIA bomb (Jewish Community Center Argentina 1994) 88
Amnesty International 27
Andregg, M.M., and Gill, P. 1–10
Anglo-American sphere 2
Angostura case (Ecuador 2009) 81–2
Argentina 5
Argentina, AMIA bomb (Jewish Community Center 1994) 88; De Santibañes 88; Decree No 815 (2005) 88; dirty war 71, 86; disappeared 71, 86; drug trafficking scandal 89; early history 85–6; Fernández de Kirchner 89–90; gradual changes after legislation 85–91; ideological surveillance 87; intelligence bill (1993) 87; intelligence scandals 88; Internal Security Law (1992) 87; Israeli Embassy bomb (1992) 88; Kirchner administration (2003–7) 89; layering 85; legal framework 90; Malvinas 71; Menem's administration 87; Military Junta (1976–83) 71; National Defence Law (1988) 86; National Intelligence Law (2001) 85, 90; National Reorganization Process 71; Nunca Más report 86; outcome 90–1; peculation 87;

secrecy policy 89; spy law 89; tribulations and improvements 86–90
Ariza, E. 52
armed conflict, lingering effects 31–2
Arrow Cross Party (Hungary) 25
Ashdown, P. 123
authoritarian enclave 8
authoritarian regimes 3
authoritarianism, legacy 5
authoritarianism, soft 17

Balkans, heroin route 32
Balkans, intelligence reform compared with East Central Europe 11–35
Barabási, A.-L. 41, 42
Barabási, A.-L., *Burst* 42n
Barrios Altos massacre (Peru, 1991) 74
Basescu, T. 141
Batho Pele process, South Africa 55
Baumgartner, F.R. 41n, 43n, 44
Belarus 14
Berisha, S. 22, 27
Bermúdez, General F. Morales 70–1
Betts, R. 38
biological evolution 40n
BIS (Security Information Service – Czech Republic) 21–2
black sites 140–2
Bonn Powers, Bosnia and Herzegovina 115
Boraz, S., and Bruneau, T. 1, 4
Bosnia and Herzegovina 7, 8, 15, 113–30; anti-Dayton rhetoric 130; assessing democratization of intelligence 127–30; background 115; Bonn Powers 115; Bosniak Agency for Research and Documentation (AID) 117–20; Bosniak-Croat intelligence service (FOSS) 118, 119, 120, 121, 126; civil war (1992–5) 115; Croat National Security Service (SNS) 117–20; Dayton Accords (1995) 115; Defence Reform Committee 119;

INDEX

effectiveness and efficiency of intelligence reform 126–7; elections and SDB (1990) 116; Expert Commission on Intelligence Reform (ECIR) 119, 120; external direction 122–4; Intelligence Reform Implementation Section (IRIS) 119; intelligence reform in the making 115–19; Intelligence and Security Agency (OSA) 114, 119–30; Office of the High Representative 113, 118, 119; parliamentary oversight 124–6; Peace Implementation Council (PIC) 115; Serb Intelligence-Security Service (OBS) 117, 118, 120, 121, 126; State Security Service (SDB) of SFR Yugoslavia 114–17, 130; state structures before Dayton 114; unifying Ethno-Nationalist Secret Services 119–20; war (1992–5) 117; Washington Agreement (1994) 118

Brazil: Cardoso Administration 99; Chamber of Foreign Affairs and Defense (CREDEN) 104; Charter (1988) 105; Constitution (1988) 98, 105; crisis of 2008 and winds of reform 107–11; FIFA Confederations Cup (2013) 111; history of intelligence 95–7; homicides 51; institutional crises and PE 36–64; Institutional Security Cabinet (GSI) 100–1, 110; Intelligence Agency (ABIN) 47–51, 97, 100–4, 107, 108; intelligence community and congress 106–7; intelligence community and transition towards democracy 98–100; intelligence community in twenty-first century 100–4; intelligence control and accountability 104–6; Intelligence PECs 109–11; intelligence sector developments (1999–2008) 47–8; intelligence services and democracy 94–112; Intelligence System (SISBIN) 47–51, 63, 100–3, 101, 102, 106; Intelligence System (SISBIN) crisis (2008) 47–51; intercept of communications 111; intercept telephone calls 49; international events 51; Joint Committee for the Control of Intelligence Activities (CCAI) 107, 109, 110; Law no 9, 883 (1999) 100, 106–7; National Intelligence Policy (PNI) 108–9; National Intelligence School (ESNI) 97; National Intelligence Service (SNI) 95, 96, 97, 98, 103, 106; National Intelligence System (SISNI) 96, 102, 103; Operation Satiagraha 49, 108; oversight and control of intelligence 48; Public Prosecutor 105–6; revolution (1964) 95; Snowden, NSA and Rouseff 111, 112; telephone tapping 108; towards effective transparency 111–12; wiretapping 49

Brazilian Court of Audit (CTCU) 48
Bruneau, T. 67, 132, 142
Bruneau, T., and Boraz, S. 1, 4
Bulgaria 15
Bulgaria, economic reforms and organized crime 19
Bulgaria, secret police 17
Burst (Barabási) 42n
burstiness 42, 44
burstiness, Colombia 53

Canada, Intelligence Review Committee (SIRC) 110
Cantuta University case (Peru 1992) 74
Caparini, M. 2, 4–7, 9, 11–35
Cardoso, Alberto Mendes 99
Cardoso, Fernando Henrique 99
Cardoso, General Fernando 99
Ceausescu, N. 17, 18, 23, 133–4
Centre of the Democratic Control of Armed Forces (DCAF), Geneva 123
Cepik, M. 2, 4, 6, 8, 9, 36–64
change 5–7, 45, 67
change, significant 68
Chavez, H. 53n
Chidambaram, C. 60–1, 63
chuzadas, Colombia 52
CIA: covert actions 3; extraordinary rendition 29–30; rendition 27; secret prisons in Romania 140–2
civil society organizations 26–7
cladogenesis 41n
Colombia 2; bursting effect 53; Central Intelligence Agency (ACI) 53; *chuzadas* scandal (2009) 52–3; DAS elimination 54; DAS related scandals (2005–9) 52; Executive Decree 3, 600 (2009) 53; General Intelligence Directory (DAS) 51–2; human rights abuses 51; institutional crises and PE 36–64; Intelligence Directory (DIPOL) 51; intelligence system crisis 51–4; interception of communications (*chuzadas*) 52; National Congress as Law Project 1288 (2009) 53; National Intelligence System (SINAI) 51; *parapolítica* 52; Revolutionary Armed Forces (FARC) 52, 53n; seven intelligence agencies 51; US intelligence support 53
communist legacies 16–18
communist states, internal security institutions 13
comparison, importance of 11–16
conditionality 32–3
control by scandal 21

INDEX

conversion 68, 68n
Copenhagen Criteria (EU) 29, 33, 34
corporate security 9
Correa, President L. (Ecuador) 78, 81, 82
corruption 6
corruption, threat 8–9
covert skills 3
crime, organized 19, 32
crime, rise after communist fall 19
crisis 9; defined 41; inevitability 8, 37n, 41, 44, 62; transformation 45
critical junctures 68
Croatia 15
Croatia, Euro-Atlantic standards 33
Croatia, European Union 20
Croatia, politicization of intelligence 22
Croatia, war and democracy delays 31
Cwele, S. 57
Czech Republic 14
Czech Republic, control over BIS 21
Czechoslovakia, scandal 23
Czechoslovakia, secret police 17

Dantas, D. 49
Dayton Accords (1995), Bosnia and Herzegovina 115
Dayton Agreement (1995) 31–2
decision making, costs 43
defamation laws 26
definitions 2–4
delayed democratic consolidation 31–2
democratization, literature 8
democratization of intelligence, comparing 1–10; concepts and methods 67–9; studying the process 68–9
developing democracies 37n
dictatorships 69
dictatorships, military 5
Dindic, Z., assassination 32
dirty war, Argentina 71
disappeared, Argentina 71
Dunagate (Hungary 1990) 22–3

East Central Europe, intelligence reform compared with Balkans 11–35
Eastern bloc 14
Eastern bloc, intelligence services 13
Ecuador 5
Ecuador, Angostura case (2009) 81–2; before Correa 78; border conflicts with Peru 80; circumstances of change of course 81–3; Commission to Investigate Intelligence Services (2008) 82; Commission on Transparency and Truth Case Angostura (2009) 82; Correa's tenure (2007–) 78, 81, 82; crisis to crisis 78–85; democracy and military (1979–) 70; early history 79; FARC 80; Integral Plan (1973–7) 70; military regime (1972–9) 70; new legal framework 83; Operaci¢n Montecristi 82; political crises and military influence 79–81; radical praetorianism 70; reform outcome 84; SENAIN 83; Truth Commission (2007–10) 81–2; uprising (1975) 70
enhanced interrogation 3, 27
equilibrium 45
equilibrium, definition 41
Estévez, E. 2, 4–6, 8–9, 65–93
ethical dilemmas 37n
ethics 7
ethics, spies 6
Euro-Atlantic integration 14
Euro-Atlantic standards, Croatia 33
European Court for Human Rights (ECHR), Romania 138
European Union (EU), accession 14, 16; *Acquis Communautaire* 14, 29, 33, 136; anti-organized crime agenda 33; Copenhagen Criteria 29, 33, 34; Croatia 20; intelligence reform 29; membership requirements 7, 29, 32–3; SSR 28
evolution 40n
evolving institutions 41n
external actors and assistance 27–31
extraordinary rendition 27
extraordinary rendition, CIA 29–30

Fair, C.C. 60
FARC (Revolutionary Armed Forces of Colombia) 52, 53n, 80, 81
Farson, S. 2
fat tailed distribution 41n
Fernández de Kirchner, C. 89–90
Férs, D. 119
Fujimori, President A. (Peru) 71–3

Gandhi, Indira 58
General Directorate for Protection and Anti-Corruption (GDPAC) 29
German Democratic Republic (GDR), secret police 17
Gill, P. 67, 104
Gill, P., and Andregg, M.M. 1–10
Gonçalves, J. 1, 7, 94–112
Goulart, President J. (Jango) 95–6
Grupo Colina (Peru) 74

Haralambie, N. 138
Hauly, L.C. 109
Helsinki Committee 27
heroin, Balkan route 32

INDEX

Hizbollah, Argentina 88
Hoxha, E. 18, 20
human rights abuses: Colombia 51; Ecuador 81; Romania 142
Human Rights Watch 27
Humint Center of Excellence (NATO), Romania 147
Hungary 14; Arrow Cross Party 25; Constitutional Court 25; crushed revolution (1956) 17; Dunagate (1990) 22–3; liberalized society 19; lustration act 25; re-politicization 20; scandals 21; secret police 17; soft authoritarianism 17; stalling democracy 14
Hurtardo, M. del Pilar 53

Iliescu, I. 23, 29
Iliescu, I., journalist intimidation 27
Iliescu, I., Romania 20
incrementalism 42
India 2
India: All India Radio Monitoring Service (AIRMS) 58; Aviation Research Center (ARC) 58; Crime and Criminal Tracking Network and Systems (CCTNS) 61; Defence Intelligence Agency (DIA) 58, 59; Indian Unlawful Activities (Prevention) Act (1979) 60–1; institutional crises and PE 36–64; intelligence system (before 2008) 58, 63; intelligence system crisis 58–62; Joint Intelligence Committee (JIC) 58; Kargil Review Committee 59; military intelligence services 59; Multi-Agency Centre (MAC) 61; Mumbai terrorist attacks (2008) 59–60; National Counter-Terrorism Center (NCTC) 61, 62, 63; National Intelligence Grid (NATGRID) 61, 63; National Investigation Agency (NIA) 61; Naxolite-Maoist insurgency 62; post-Mumbai reforms 60; RAND Corporation 59; Research and Analysis Wing (RAW) 58, 61
institutional changes 67; intelligence crises 62–4, 63
institutional crises, Brazil, Colombia, South Africa and India 36–64
institutional friction 44, 45
institutional reform 47n
institutionalism, new 67
institutions, evolving 41n
integration, Euro-Atlantic 14
intelligence agencies, actors and products, politicization 20–2
intelligence crisis 45–7; institutional changes 62–4, 63
intelligence cycle, stages 43–4

intelligence failures 38
Intelligence Studies 38
Intelligence Studies Conference (Canada, 2011), International Studies Association 1
intelligence systems: Punctuated Equilibrium Theory 39–45; varieties and evolution 40
interception of communications: Brazil 49, 111; Colombia 52
International Monetary Fund (IMF) 33
International Political Science Association and European Consortium of Political Research Conference (Brazil, 2011) 1
International Studies Association (ISA), Intelligence Studies Conference (Canada, 2011) 1
Internet surveillance 4
interrogation, enhanced 3
Israeli Embassy bomb (Argentina, 1992) 88

Jervis, R. 13
jihadist threat 8–9
Jiu Valley 23, 29
Jobim, N. 49
Jones, B.D., Sulkin, D. and Larsen, H.A. 43
journalist intimidation, Iliescu 27

K d r, J. 17
Kasrils, R. 55, 56
Kasrils, R., 5 principles of intelligence service professionalism 56n
Kirchner, President Nestor (Argentina) 88, 89
Kocsis, K. 119
Kosovo 7
Kosovo, war and democracy delays 31
Krushchev, N. 17

Lacerda, P. 49, 50, 108
Laplante, L. 74
Lashkar-e-Taiba 59
Latin America: 2; comparing intelligence democratization 65–93; military dictatorships 5; political police 65; roots and common legacies 69–71
layering 68, 68n
layering, Argentina 85
legacy, authoritarianism 5
Leigh, I. 40
libel 26
Lithuania, CIA 29–30
Lula da Silva, Luis Inacio 49, 109
Lurås, H. 1, 5, 7, 8, 113–30
lustration: act 25; defined 24; trust 23–4

Macedonia 15
McSweeny, B. 69

INDEX

Malvinas (Argentina) 71
Maqetuba, M. 57
Marty, D. 30, 141
Masetlha, B. 55
Matei, C. 1, 4, 5, 7, 67, 131–48
Mbeki, President T. 56
media, muzzling of 27
media, organizations 26–7
Mello, Fernando Collor de 98
Mendes, Justice G. 49
Menem, President Carlos (Argentina) 86, 87
method 2–4
military dictatorships, Latin America 5
military regimes, US support 7
Milosevic, S. 16, 22, 31
Moldova 14
Montenegro 15
Montesinos, V. 71–3
Mumbai terrorist attacks (India, 2008) 59–60

National Intelligence Law (Argentina, 2001) 85, 90
National Reorganization Process (Argentina) 71
National Security Agency (NSA), leaks 3–4
national security sector, crises 47
new institutionalism 67
Nezavisne Novine 129
Noguera, J. 52
North Atlantic Treaty Organization (NATO): Article 5 – collective defence 30; entry into 7, 35; Partnership for Peace (PfP) 136; SSR 28
Norway, Institute of International Affairs (NUPI) 114
Norway, Ministry of Foreign Affairs 113

Open Society Foundation 27
Opportunity Group 49
Orbán, V. 14
Organization for Security and Cooperation in Europe (OSCE) 33, 132
organized crime: Bulgaria 19; problem 32
OSA (Intelligence and Security Agency BiH) 114; assessing democratization 127–30; effectiveness and efficiency 126–7; establishment 120–2; executive control 123–4; mission impossible 126; parliamentary oversight 124–6; rulebooks 119; tasks and organization 122
oversight, mechanisms 3–4
oversight, value of multiple 24–6

Paniagua, V. 74
parapolítica (Colombia) 52

Partnership for Peace (PfP) (NATO) 136
path dependency 4; Ecuador 81; theory 67
Patil, Shivraj 60
Peñate, A. 52–3
Perón, President Juan Domingo 86
Peru 5; Alvarado regime 70–1; Barrios Altos massacre (1991) 74; Bermúdez regime 70–1; Cantuta University case (1992) 74; Commission on Truth and Reconciliation 74, 76; crisis to change 71–8; early history 72; *Grupo Colina* 74; humanist revolution 70; Law no 28, 664 (2005) 76–7; legacy of Fujimori-Montensinos era 72–3; military reformism 70; military regime (1968–80) 70; new democratic administration's prioritization of intelligence 73–6; new legal framework 76–7; Paniagua government 74; reform outcome 77–8; restructuring of police 75; Toledo 74–5
Plavsic, B. 120
Poison process 42
Poland 14; CIA 29–31; political victim 27; rendition 27
policialization 66n
policymaking cycle 43
political macro-system 44
political police 69
political police, Latin America 65
politicization, intelligence agencies, actors and products 20–2
Portugal, Intelligence System Supervision Council 110
power functions 41n
power-law relations 41
priorities 42
private security 9
probability theory 42
process tracing 67, 68
professionalism, South Africa 56n
Punctuated Equilibrium Theory 4, 38n
Punctuated Equilibrium Theory, intelligence systems 38–45, 62, 64

radical praetorianism, Ecuador 70
Rákosi, M. 17
RAND Corporation (India) 59
regimes 7–9; authoritarian 3; military 7
rendition, CIA 27; Poland 27
resistance, suppression 17
Revesz, B. 21
Reyes, R. 53n, 81
Romania 4, 5, 15, 16, 131–48; adoption of NATO MAP 138; Ceausescu 17, 18, 23, 133–4; CIA 29–30, 140–2; civilian control and effectiveness of intelligence

INDEX

143–7; communist dictatorship and transition to democracy 133–4; Council for Studying Securitate Archives (CNSAS) 139; defence and security strategy 139; democracy score 132n; democratic control 143–6; democratic reform of intelligence agencies 134–42; effectiveness requirements 146–7; and EU 28–9; European Court for Human Rights (ECHR) 138; Freedom of Information Act (FOIA) 137; human rights abuses 142; Humint Center of Excellence (NATO) 147; Iliescu 20; institutional base for control and effectiveness 144; intelligence reform analysis framework 142–3; intelligence reform before and after NATO/EU integration 131–48; Intelligence Service (SRI) 134, 138–40; lessons learned from reform 147–8; National Defence College (NDC) 135; National Defence Supreme Council (CSAT) 135, 137n; National Doctrine on Security Intelligence 139; National Intelligence Academy (ANI) 136; National Intelligence Community (CNI) 139; National Security Law (1991) 135, 136; neo-totalitarianism 19–20; path to democracy 132; political police 133; project START 147; reform post-NATO/EU integration 138–42; reform pre-NATO/EU integration 134–8; Revolution (1989) 18, 132; scandals 23; secret CIA prisons 140–1; secret police 17–18; six intelligence agencies 134; SRI Strategic Vision 140; support for US 138; transparency 143
Rospigliosi, F. 74–5
Rotaru, A. 138
Rousseff, D. 50n, 95n, 109

Samper, E. 51
De Santibañes, F. 88
Santos, President J.M. (Colombia) 53, 54
Satiagraha operation, Brazil 49
scandals 9; control by 21; Czechoslovakia 23; Hungary 21; Romania 23; varying impact 22–3
secrecy 3; Lord Acton 6
secret police: Albania 17; Bulgaria 17; Czechoslovakia 17; former personnel 19; GDR 17; Hungary 17; protection of socialist state 16–17; Romania 17
security sector reform (SSR) 28
September 11th terrorist attacks (2001) 137
Serbia 15; Committee for Defence and Security (CDS) 25; politicization of intelligence 22; war and democracy delays 31
Singh, M. 60
Slovakia, stalling democracy 14
smuggling 32
Snowden, E. 111, 112
social phenomena 42
socialist state, protection from secret police 16–17
Sólyom, L. 25
South Africa 2; agencies and controls 54; *Batho Pele* process 55; centralizing reform (2010–11) 57–8; commission to review intelligence legislation (2006) 56; Constitution (1996) 54; illegal surveillance 55; institutional crises and PE 36–64; intelligence crisis (2005) 55; intelligence system crisis 54–8; National Intelligence Agency (NIA) 54–5; National Strategic Intelligence Act (1994) 54; post-Apartheid national intelligence system 54; Proclamation 59 (2009) 57; Project Avani 55; State Security Agency (SSA) 57
South America, dilemmas of intelligence services 66
Soviet Union, collapse (1989–91) 2; domination of state security system 18; KGB 5
spies, ethics 6
Stabilization and Association Process (SAP) 33
Stalinist-era leaders 13
START project (Romania) 147
starting points 68
stasis 40n
state 7–9; building 16; power 4; socialism 5
state security system, Soviet domination 18
Stb (Czechoslovakia State Security) 23
Stepan, A. 97
Streeck, W. 68
structure 6
surveillance 17

Techint 112
terrorism, Indian Unlawful Activities Act (1979) 60–1
Thelen, K. 41n, 68
Toledo, President A. (Peru) 74–5
torture 27
transition 5
transition, triple 18–20
Trezza, W.R. 49–50, 108
triple transition 18–20
trust, lustration 23–4
Tudjman, F. 16, 31

INDEX

Turkey 12
Tusk, D. 27

United Nations Development Programme (UNDP) 32
United States of America (USA), oversight structure 3–4
Uribe, President A. 51–3
Uzbekistan 14

Vaca, E. 87
Velaco Alvarado, General Juan 70, 71
Velit, J. 74–5
vetting 23–4

Warsaw Pact, collapse (1989–91) 2
Western Balkan states 15
whistleblowers 27
wiretapping, Brazil 49
wiretapping, Colombia 52
World Bank 32

Yugoslavia 5, 114, 115
Yugoslavia, assassination 18
Yugoslavia, State Security Service (SDB) 17–18, 114–16, 130
Yugoslavia, war and organized crime 32

Zuma, Jacob 55–6, 62